BYZANTINE EAST AND LATIN WEST

Archangel of the Ascension. Detail from early 15th century fresco in Pantanassa Convent, Mistra, Greece (exemplifying art of the Palaeologan Renaissance).

BYZANTINE EAST
AND LATIN WEST:
TWO WORLDS OF CHRISTENDOM
IN MIDDLE AGES
AND RENAISSANCE

*Studies in Ecclesiastical
and Cultural History*

DENO J. GEANAKOPLOS

HARPER TORCHBOOKS ❦ *The Academy Library*
Harper & Row, Publishers
New York and Evanston

To Father Francis Dvornik,
Alexander Turyn and George H. Williams.

BYZANTINE EAST AND LATIN WEST

Copyright © 1966 by Deno J. Geanakoplos.

Printed in the United States of America.

First published in 1966 by Basil Blackwell, Ltd., Oxford, England, and HARPER TORCHBOOKS, New York.

Library of Congress Catalog Card Number: 66-29030.

PREFACE

In something of the same manner that the world is today split into eastern and western camps, so medieval Christendom became increasingly divided into two worlds, that of the Byzantine East and the Latin West. The main purpose of this book, or series of related essays, is to examine certain key points or themes in the interaction of these two worlds during the medieval and Renaissance period with particular emphasis on the ecclesiastical and cultural influences of the Byzantine and post-Byzantine East on the West—influences which, as is not generally realized, continued even after the fall of Constantinople to the Turks in 1453 and as late as 1600. It is hoped that this work, or sections thereof, will be of interest not only to students of medieval history, western as well as Byzantine, but to those interested in the Renaissance, especially in the humanistic revival of Greek letters, and perhaps to Renaissance art historians. And not least, in view of the present Vatican Council and the current movement toward ecclesiastical rapprochement, it is the author's hope that the book, by providing some account of earlier efforts for union of the Greek and Roman churches, will, by analogy, shed light on some of the problems involved in modern efforts at 'ecumenism'.

While this book was in press Pope Paul VI of Rome and Patriarch Athenagoras of Constantinople, on December 7, 1965, in a remarkable act of ecclesiastical statesmanship, lifted the now historic excommunications launched in 1054 by the legates of Pope Leo IX and Patriarch Michael Cerularius. This act, annulling excommunications originally involving essentially only Cerularius and the legates, cannot of course at one stroke erase the religious schism of a thousand years. But it is the first positive step in the right direction of healing a breach between eastern and western Christians which, as is the underlying theme of this book, developed not only as a result of ecclesiastical differences, but, in a much broader context, of political, cultural, and psychological considerations as well.

CONTENTS

List of Plates and Maps   vii

Acknowledgments   ix

Prologue: The Two Worlds of Christendom   1

PART I
EAST AND WEST IN THE MIDDLE AGES

CHAPTER

1. The Influences of Byzantine Culture on the Medieval Western World   11

2. Church and State in the Byzantine Empire: A Reconsideration of the Problem of Caesaropapism   ...   55

3. The Council of Florence (1438–39) and the Problem of Union between the Byzantine and Latin Churches   84

PART II
BYZANTIUM AND THE RENAISSANCE

4. The Greco-Byzantine Colony in Venice and its Significance in the Renaissance   112

5. The Cretan Role in the Transmission of Greco-Byzantine Culture to Western Europe via Venice...   139

6. An Overlooked post-Byzantine Plan for Religious Union with Rome: Maximos Margounios the Cretan Humanist-Bishop and his Latin Library Bequeathed to Mt. Athos   165

Appendix: Bibliographical Note   194

Index   201

LIST OF PLATES

Facing
Page

Frontispiece   Archangel of the Ascension. Detail from early 15th century fresco
in Pantanassa Convent, Mistra, Greece (exemplifying art of the
Palaeologan Renaissance). [Photo in G. Tarsouli, *Mystras*, Athens,
M. Pechlivanides.]

Plate 1 (above) Justinian and his court. Mosaic of San Vitale, Ravenna (mid-6th
century). [From A. Grabar, *Byzantine Painting*, Geneva, Skira,
1953.]

(below)   Silk from the grave of Charlemagne at Aachen. It was preserved
in the Kunstgewerbe Museum, Berlin, but now no longer exists·   38

Plate 2 (left)   Byzantine-inspired bronze doors at Charlemagne's palace chapel at
Aachen. [From F. J. Tschan, *Saint Bernward of Hildesheim*, III, in
Publications in Medieval Studies, 13, University of Notre Dame, 1952.]

(right)   Bronze doors of Cathedral of Trani, Italy.   39

Plate 3 (left)   King Roger II of Norman of Norman Sicily crowned by Christ.
Mosaic in the Martorana of Palmero (mid-12th century). [Photo in
Otto Demus, *The Mosaics of Norman Sicily*, London, Routledge and
Kegan Paul, 1949.]

(right)   Byzantine Emperor Manuel II Palaeologus (early 15th century).
[Portrait in Ms. of Bibliothèque Nationale, Paris, suppl. no. 309.]   54

Plate 4 (left)   Emperor John VIII Palaeologus entering Florence on his way to
the Council. Detail from fresco 'The Procession of the Magi' by
Benozzo Gozzoli in Capella Medicea (c. 1459).

(right)   Emperor Michael VIII Palaeologus. Miniature in Greek Ms. VII,
22, of Marciana, by George Klontzas (1590).   55

Plate 5   Christ Pantocrator. Byzantine mosaic in dome of Norman palatine
chapel in Palermo (mid-12th century). [Photo in Otto Demus,
The Mosaics of Norman Sicily, London, Routledge and Kegan Paul,
1949.]   70

Plate 6 (left)   Christ Pantocrator. Byzantine mosaic in dome of church at Daphni
near Athens (11th century). From A. Grabar, *Byzantine Painting*,
Geneva, Skira, 1953.]

(right)   Christ Pantocrator. Byzantine mosaic in dome of St. Sophia, Kiev
(11th century). [Photo in V. Lazarev, *Mosaics of the Sophia Church*,
Moscow, 1960.]   71

Plate 7   The Lamentation of the Virgin. Byzantine fresco in church of
Nerezi, Yugoslavia (mid-12th century). [From A. Grabar, *Byzantine
Painting*, Geneva, Skira, 1953.]   86

Plate 8 (left)   The Lamentation. Detail from fresco by Giotto in Arena Chapel,
Padua (1303–05). [Photo in *Horizon*, Summer 1965, VII, no. 3.]

(right)   Descent from the Cross. Detail from fresco by Theophanes the
Cretan in Catholikon of Laura Monastery on Mt. Athos (1535).
[Photo in M. Chatzidakes, 'The Painter Theophanes Strelitzas',
in *Nea Hestia*, Athens, Christmas 1963.]   87

Plate 9(above)   Venice in 1492. [From *Supplementum Chronicarum*, Venice, 1492.]
(below)   Interior of St. Mark's, Venice.   134

Plate 10 (left) Interior of St. Sophia, Constantinople. Lithograph by Fossati.
(right)   Greek church of San Giorgio as it was in the late 18th or early 19th
century; from Venice.   135

Plate 11 (left)   Christ in Benediction. Icon, Lavra, Mt. Athos (14th century). [Reprinted with permission of The Macmillan Company from *El Greco Revisited* by Pal Kelemen. © Pal Kelemen (1961.]

(right)   Christ in Benediction. Mural in church at Kritsa, Crete (14th century?). [Reprinted with permission of The Macmillan Company from *El Greco Revisited* by Pal Kelemen. © Pal Kelemen 1961.]   150

Plate 12 (left)   Christ in Benediction. Painting by El Greco in Greco Museum, Toledo, Spain, reproduced by permission.

(right)   Christ in Benediction. Icon by Michael Damaskinos (?), 16th century Cretan. [Reprinted with permission of The Macmillan Company from *El Greco Revisited* by Pal Kelemen. © Pal Kelemen 1961.]   151

Plate 13 (left)   St. Catherine of Alexandria. Icon in Heraklion, Crete. [Reprinted with permission of The Macmillan Company from *El Greco Revisited* by Pal Kelemen. © Pal Kelemen 1961.]

(right)   St. Catherine of Alexandria. Painting by El Greco in Metropolitan Museum of Art, New York, reproduced by permission.   166

Plate 14 (left)   John the Baptist. Painting by El Greco in M. H. de Young Memorial Museum, San Francisco, reproduced by permission.

(right)   John the Baptist. Painting by Titian, Venice E.N.T.E. [Reprinted with permission of The Macmillan Company from *El Greco Revisited* by Pal Kelemen. © Pal Kelemen 1961.]   167

Plate 15 (left)   The Cretan Pope Alexander V (d. 1410). Sketch from mosaic in church of St. Paul, Rome, published in *Chronologia Romanorum Pontificum superstes in pariete australi Basilicae Sancti Pauli Apostoli*, Rome, 1752.

(right)   Cardinal Bessarion (d. 1472). From engraving by Tobias Stimmer in Paolo Giovio, *Elogia virorum literis illustrium*, Basle, 1577. [Reproduced by permission of the Vatican.]   182

Plate 16 (left)   Marcus Musurus (d. 1517). From engraving by Tobias Stimmer in Paolo Giovio, *Elogia virorum literis illustrium*, Basle, 1577.

(right)   Metropolitan Gabriel Severus (d. 1616). After oil painting conserved in Greek Colony in Venice.   183

LIST OF MAPS

THE BYZANTINE (ROMAN) EMPIRE IN 565 UNDER JUSTINIAN.   Page 14

THE BYZANTINE EMPIRE AND THE EARLY CRUSADES.   Between pp. 15-16

VENETIAN COLONIES IN THE GREEK EAST FROM THE FOURTH CRUSADE (1204) TO THE RENAISSANCE.   Page 138

DIAGRAM

Greek and Latin views of the Trinity, to illustrate the *filioque* question.   Page 101

ACKNOWLEDGMENTS

In a book containing essays which cover such a wide span of time and subject matter and are the fruit of a decade or so of intermittent effort, the author must inevitably be indebted to many institutions and individuals. I am grateful to the Guggenheim Foundation, American Philosophical Society, American Council of Learned Societies, and the University of Illinois Center for Advanced Study, all of which provided generous grants enabling me at one time or another to carry on research in the libraries and archives of Western Europe, Greece and Russia. Among the many individuals to whom I am deeply indebted for scholarly advice on specific aspects of these studies, I should include Professors Alexander Turyn, Henry and Rene Kahane, and Antonio Továr of the University of Illinois, Professors P. Kristeller of Columbia, M. Anastos of UCLA and J. Gill, of the Pontifical Oriental Institute in Rome, Professor Giuseppe Schirò of the University of Rome, Professors Talbot Rice of Edinburgh University and Dimitri Tsellos of Minnesota University; also Professor Victor Lazarev of the University of Moscow, Mme. Alice Bank and Professor M. Goukovski of the University of Leningrad, and my young friend Boris Fonkich and Mme E. Granström of the Gorky University and public library of Moscow and Leningrad respectively. In Athens I was able to draw on the knowledge of Professors Manolis Chatzidakes, Nicholas Tomadakes, Hamilcar Alivizatos, and Mr. Panagiotes Nikolopoulos, and in Thessalonika to consult with Professors M. Pelekanides, Manoussos Manousakas, and Basil Laourdas. Here too I want to acknowledge the help of the former Greek consul in Venice, Mr. Constantine Mertzios, and of Father Georgio Fedalto of the same city, in addition to that of the librarian-monk Father Athanasios who, on my visit to Mount Athos in 1962, permitted me to catalogue certain Latin books preserved in the monastery of Iviron. In Heraklion, Crete, Mr. N. Stavrinides of the Vikelaia Library and Dr. S. Alexiou of the Heraklion Museum offered welcome assistance, as did Professor Sebastian Cirac of the University of Barcelona, Father Gregório Andrés of the Escorial library, and F. Fernández-Pomar of the National Library in Madrid. Later, in America Professor Sydney Ahlstrom of Yale was helpful with suggestions, as was Mr. Pal Kelemen, the art critic. I do not wish to forget the assistance of Cardinal Cushing of Boston and of the Rt. Rev. J. Willebrands of the Vatican's Secretariat for promoting Christian Unity, through whose efforts I was enabled in 1963 to attend the opening sessions of the Vatican Council in Rome. Lastly, I must make mention of the aid during recent years of my assistants at the University of Illinois, James Forse, Christ Patrinelis, now of Athens, and George Demetrakopoulos, as well as of the encouragement of Mr. George Vournas and William G. Helis, Jr. To Professors Francis Dvornik, Alexander Turyn, and George H. Williams, each of whom in his own way has had an intimate connection with these essays, the dedication is a token of my appreciation and esteem.

PROLOGUE: THE TWO WORLDS OF CHRISTENDOM

One of the great tragedies of the medieval period, some of the effects of which are still with us, was the increasingly sharp division of Christendom into two disparate and ultimately hostile worlds, the Byzantine East and the Latin West. The Christian community, of course, was originally united, constituting one political organism, the Roman Empire, and one undivided church. But already in the first centuries of the Byzantine era, even before the foundation of Constantinople as the 'new Rome' in 330, certain differences—linguistic, cultural, and to a lesser extent religious—can be discerned between the Greek and Latin halves of Christendom. To these nascent but gradually developing differences the foundation of the Germanic kingdoms in the West added the element of political disunity. And when in 800, the pope crowned the German Charlemagne Roman Emperor in denial of Byzantine claims, a veritable political schism between East and West was created.

Two centuries later, in 1054, at the Great Church of St. Sophia in Constantinople, occurred the mutual excommunications of papal legates and Patriarch Cerularius, a celebrated episode which has traditionally been taken to mark the definitive breach between the Greek and Roman branches of the Christian church. But even this ecclesiastical schism (of which most people in East and West were then hardly aware) and the mutual distrust subsequently engendered by the first crusades, did not, it would seem, irreparably damage Greco-Latin relations. For earlier religious schisms between Rome and Constantinople (notably that of Photius over papal claims to intervene in internal affairs of the Greek church) had been successfully healed, though to be sure leaving scars. And after 1054 and even the initial crusades, most western travellers or pilgrims on their way to Jerusalem continued to be amicably received in the Greek East.

It was only after 1204, when a Latin army under the guise of a holy crusade sacked Constantinople itself, carved up the Byzantine Empire, and forcibly imposed 'Roman Catholicism' on the Greek people, that the growing animosity of the Greeks for the Latins

was transformed into a mass revulsion, a permanent hostility that
permeated every level of society and was to poison all subsequent
relations between the two peoples.[1] It is at this point, when the
ecclesiastical schism became ethnic and political as well as
religious in scope, that the break between the two churches may
be said to have been truly consummated.

Even after the Greek recovery of Constantinople in 1261[2] the
Byzantines, on the defensive in the face of continuing Latin
aggressiveness and fearing a repetition of the notorious Fourth
Crusade, came increasingly to view the Latins as predatory, semi-
ignorant 'barbarians', and out-and-out heretics.

The Latins were hardly less antagonistic toward the Greeks.
Accusing the latter of treachery in the crusades and irritated by
the Greek rejection of the religious union pronounced at Lyons
in 1274, the Westerners became more and more contemptuous of
what their chroniclers termed the 'perfidious, cowardly, schismatic
Greeks'. Ambitious Latin statesmen and covetous Italian
merchants refused to give up the idea of a restoration of Latin
domination in the Greek East. Indeed some western propagand-
ists of the fourteenth century, in order to achieve their aim of a
united Christendom to combat the Muslims, openly advocated
another crusade against Constantinople in the aim of reducing the
Greek East to obedience to the pope. A prime factor in this
process, according to one leading theoretician, was to be the
Latinization of key members of each 'schismatic' Greek family so
that as a result Orthodoxy would be completely stamped out.[3]

---

[1] The problem of Byzantine-Latin relations as a continuous development during
Middle Ages and Renaissance has not yet been dealt with in any synthesis, though
episodes such as the ecclesiastical schism and the 'two emperors question' have
received much attention. For bibl. see below, Appendix A and passim. On 1054
and 1204 see works of Runciman, Congar, Michel, etc., listed in Appendix B and C,
and Chapter 3.

[2] See Chap. 5, D. Geanakoplos, *Emperor Michael Palaeologus and the West*, 1258–82
(Cambridge, Mass., 1959).

[3] The crusader propagandist who particularly advocated 'Latinizing' (we might
say 'brainwashing') the East by sending one child from each Greek family to the
West to be reared in the Latin faith, was the Dominican Brocardus: *Directorium ad
passagium faciendum*, in *Recueil des historiens des croisades, Documents Arméniens*, II (1906)
367ff. Some years earlier the French publicist Pierre Dubois, *De Recuperatione terre
sancte*, ed. V. Langlois, in *Coll. de textes pour servir à l'étude . . . de l'histoire* (Paris,
1891) Ch. 61, pp. 51–52, had suggested the sending of educated, noble Latin girls to
the East (to both the Greeks and Saracens) to do charity work in hospitals, the
more comely to marry important Greek personages (especially clerics!) in the
ultimate aim of converting the East to the Latin faith.

But not all Greeks or Latins of the thirteenth and fourteenth centuries shared these inimical sentiments. There were a few men of good will, of an ecumenical spirit so to say. And here and there a rare idealist, such as Pope Gregory X, the French theorist Humbert of Romans, the Greek monk John Parastron, or the famous Greco-Italian scholar Barlaam,[4] was of the enlightened view that through a greater understanding of the customs and religious beliefs and practices of their estranged brethren—what a modern authority would perhaps term the 'psychology' of each people—a peaceful solution to the problem of mutual antagonism could be achieved, to the benefit of Christendom as a whole.

Most Greeks, however, recalling their bitter experience as a dominated people during the Latin occupation, and especially the forced conversion of the Greek clergy and people to Catholicism with the installation of a Latin patriarch in Constantinople, remained fanatically anti-Latin. But with the advance of the Ottoman Turks in the later fourteenth and fifteenth centuries, a small but increasingly articulate minority of Greek *politiques* and intellectuals, including as we shall see important refugee scholars to the West, became less intolerant of the Latins. For in the face of the Turkish threat to the very existence of Byzantium, they began to look to the West as the sole source of military aid and, as a result of expediency or conviction, even to favor ecclesiastical reunion with Rome as a means of salvation for the state.

On the Latin side some evidence can be found of sympathy for the plight of the Byzantines, especially on the part of Italian humanists, a few of whom went to Constantinople itself to study Greek. But on the whole, the Latin world, despite its growing passion for the *ancient* Greek classics, retained virtually undiminished its traditional animosity toward the *medieval* Greeks. Even the great fourteenth century Italian humanist Petrarch, whose love for ancient Greek literature is well known, could make an unfavorable comparison between 'the enemy Turks and the schismatic Greeks who are worse than enemies and hate and fear us with all their

[4] On Pope Gregory X who pronounced religious union (it proved ephemeral) at the Council of Lyons in 1274 see Geanakoplos, *op. cit.*, 237–45ff. On Humbert of Romans, see his remarkably objective treatise, *Opus Tripartitum* (in Mansi, *Concilia*, XXIV, cols. 109–36) about the problem of union with the Greeks before the Council of Lyons. On Parastron see Geanakoplos, *op. cit.*, 267–69, and on Barlaam see below Chap. 3, text and notes 25–29.

souls'. The result was that in the fifteenth century most western statesmen, disturbed over the abortive religious union pronounced at Florence in 1439 or engrossed in the Hundred Years' War and internecine Italian politics, seemed almost indifferent to the fate of the Byzantine world, when, in 1453, Constantinople finally succumbed to the Turks.

The brief sketch provided above is intended of course only to mark some of the more important points in the complex, centuries-long development of East-West estrangement—those events which seem most to have inflamed Greco-Latin antipathy. We must be wary of making generalizations about the emotional or mental attitudes of entire blocs of peoples, since, as noted, exceptions on the part of certain groups or individuals can almost always be cited, and the intensity of feeling engendered was not always parallel on each side. Keeping these qualifications in mind, however, it may be said that the process of alienation between East and West seems to have been cumulative, reaching its peak of intensity in the thirteenth and perhaps early fourteenth century, after which, through force of circumstance, a certain slackening of tension may be observed with regard to some of the upper classes—a few intellectuals, politicians, or an occasional high-minded cleric. Nevertheless, for the great mass of the population, the average Greek more than the Latin, mutual almost unreasoning hostility toward the other people continued to remain deeply rooted in its psychology. And the medieval image projected on either side of the 'perfidious schismatic Greek' and the 'aggressive heretical Catholic', though of course mitigated and blurred by the passing of time, has persisted to the present day in the substratum of each people's mentality as an unhappy legacy of the medieval world.

Despite the growing ideological separation of the medieval Byzantine and Latin worlds—by the twelfth or certainly the thirteenth century a citizen of Paris aware of the East looked upon his contemporary in Constantinople as completely alien[5]—

[5]Already in the ninth century Hincmar, Archbishop of Reims, could look upon the East as alien in character (see *Opuscula et Epistolae Hincmari*, in MPL, vol. 126, cols. 345–50); and Bishop Liudprand in his famous embassy to Constantinople for the German Emperor in 969 branded the Greeks as liars, weaklings, and non-Romans (*Relatio de legatione constantinopolitana*, ed. J. Becker in *Scriptores rerum*

East and West in many respects were gradually being brought into closer contact with one another. The vast outpouring of men of all classes to the East during the early crusades, the concomitant Latin economic penetration of Byzantium and Islam, the desire of certain western and a few eastern scholars and theologians to acquire each other's learning—not to overlook the actual occupation of Byzantine and Muslim territories by the crusaders—brought the two segments of Christendom into direct physical contact on a scale greater than ever before. The result was not only a sharpening of mutual antipathies, but, at the same time, an increasing awareness of each other's culture.[6]

The following studies are concerned with various aspects of the contacts between these two worlds. The main focus of the work is on the role of the Byzantine East, particularly in its interaction with the West in the ecclesiastical and cultural spheres. This is not of course to imply that the West, on its side, exerted no cultural influence on the East during this period, as is clearly apparent from such examples as the Byzantine adoption of certain Latin chivalric practices and feudal terminology in the twelfth century, or, later in the fourteenth, the appearance of a virtual cult of Thomism in the Byzantine court itself.[7] Part One of this work deals with certain developments in the Middle Ages until the fall of Constantinople to the Turks in 1453. Part Two, with

Germanicarum, 3rd ed. [1915,] Chaps. 5, 30, 54 esp.). Ca. 1120 Abbot Peter the Venerable of Cluny wrote to the Byzantine emperor and patriarch of 'our mutual spiritual love'. But cf. his castigation of the Greeks after the failure of the second crusade in 1147, for which the Greeks were blamed (MPL, vol. 189, cols. 260–61). Also see the twelfth century crusader account of the Chaplain of the French king, Odo of Deuil (*MGH, Scriptores*, XXVI, 66), who considered the Greeks as perfidious and inferior to the Latins. For Petrarch's remark see his *Lettere Senili*, below Ch. 3, n. 77.

[6] See E. Barker, *Social and Political Thought in Byzantium* (Oxford, 1957) 18–19.

[7] In the twelfth century Emperor Manuel I Comnenus adopted the western tournament, presenting jousts in the Hippodrome (Ch. Diehl, 'La société Byzantine à l'époque des Comnènes' [1919] 13ff., 23ff.). Previously the Norman Bohemund, in 1108, swore allegiance to Alexius I Comnenus in the Latin manner, the term liege (Greek, *lizios*) being used. Under Michael Palaeologus, later thirteenth century, the term is even more frequent (Geanakoplos, *Michael Palaeologus*, 209–210). Regarding the fourteenth century Greek Thomists who centered around the Grand Logothete and famous scholar-theologian Demetrios Cydones, see esp. M. Jugie, 'Demetrius Cydonès et la théologie latine à Byzance du XIVe et XVe siècles', *Echos d'Orient*, XXXI (1928) 385–402. Other Latin cultural influences on the East can easily be cited. (By the fourteenth century the Gasmules, children of Greco-Latin unions, were to be found everywhere in the East). Nevertheless, the Greek influence on the West was far stronger than the reverse.

the period of the Renaissance from a few years before 1453 to about 1600 when, despite the disappearance of the Byzantine state, the influences of Byzantine civilization on the West continued, sometimes with even more striking effect than before.

It is not the aim of these studies to trace in any systematic fashion the development of East-West connections, but rather, through essays on selected topics, to illustrate some specific yet basic aspects in the relations between the two worlds. The most obvious and dramatic of the issues involved, given the religiously-oriented mentality of medieval man, was of course the ecclesiastical schism, so fateful for medieval Christendom and which still persists until our own day. The intent of this book is not to disparage the significance of the schism, but to make it even more meaningful by placing it in the broader context of East-West relations—a context which included political, cultural, and psychological factors as well as differences in dogma and ecclesiastical organization. As will be noted, the schism was not only sharpened by these non-religious factors, but, by the end of the thirteenth century, had become in the public mind the focal point of the differences between the two peoples. Some of these more basic differences—or in some cases similarities— will be pointed out in the course of the following studies.

The first essay, an enlarged version of an unpublished lecture delivered at the University of Minnesota in 1960 at a symposium on Byzantine civilization, attempts, after a brief historical résumé of the channels of contact, to assess the cultural contribution of Byzantine civilization to the medieval West. Some of the material is of course not new, but to my knowledge no previous attempt has been made to synthesize, in one study of this kind, individual aspects of the Byzantine influences on the West beginning with the fourth century and extending into the period after 1453. It is hoped that in this essay, which covers selected fields of culture (and which because of its scope obviously cannot claim to be exhaustive) the reader will find some new information and fresh points of view, especially regarding the relative importance of the ancient Greek vis-à-vis the more purely Byzantine elements in the process of western acculturation to Byzantine civilization.

The second essay, on church and state in the Byzantine Empire and the question of Caesaropapism, is a much expanded version of a paper given at the American Historical Convention in 1963 (Philadelphia) and is included here in order to give the reader an understanding of what was probably the most basic factor in Byzantine civilization, the church.[8] It is obvious that one can have no clear picture of the many medieval attempts at union of the Roman and Orthodox churches if he lacks an appreciation of Byzantine ecclesiastical polity which was so different from that of the West. The pope in fact often claimed, probably erroneously, that it was the emperor's absolute power over the church that prevented a true union of the churches.[9] Though the subject of Byzantine Caesaropapism is an old and celebrated one, another analysis of the problem, on the basis of a new organization of the material, may be justified in order to define more clearly the degree of actual imperial control over the eastern church.

The next essay, on the Council of Florence in 1438-39 (originally a paper delivered at the 1954 meetings of the American Historical Association and printed in *Church History* for 1955), is the only study in the book to have been published elsewhere.[10] It is reproduced here, in revised form, to provide a picture of the last and greatest confrontation between the eastern and western halves of Christendom. The efforts of popes and emperors to reconcile their churches, intermittent since 1054, reached a dramatic climax at this council—a conclave extremely meaningful for theologians today, as any modern attempt to unite the two churches must perforce take as its point of departure the acts and decisions at Florence. In the proceedings of this council, especially the personal encounters between pope and emperor on the one hand, and pope and patriarch on the other, we can readily observe, symbolically at least, how much the traditions of eastern and western Christendom had grown apart since the one undivided church of the early, patristic period.

Earlier episodes in the history of the schism—the ninth century conflict between Pope Nicholas and Patriarch Photius, the famous episode of 1054 with its mutual papal and patriarchal

[8] Barker, *Social and Political Thought*, 41, playing on Aristotle's expression, terms the Byzantine citizen an 'ecclesiastical animal', who, through religion, found an outlet for the 'spirit of democracy and debate'.

[9] See esp. M. Jugie, *Le schisme byzantin* (Paris, 1941) esp. 10. Cf. below, Ch. 3, note 41.

[10] Thanks to *Church History* for permitssion to print this revision of my article. While this book was in press my 'Church and State', *Church History* (1965) appeared.

excommunications, and the unionist Council of Lyons in 1274—
have been extensively dealt with elsewhere, and it has therefore
not been considered necessary to analyze them again here.

Most scholars, Byzantinists themselves being perhaps the
most guilty, treat the history and influence of Byzantium as if it
suddenly ceased to exist precisely on May 29, 1453, when Emperor
Constantine XI fell before the Turkish besiegers on the ramparts
of Constantinople. These scholars then turn their attention almost
exclusively to the West in order to deal with the increasingly
important problem of the impact of classical Greek learning on
the western Renaissance, forgetting that the Byzantines, as
custodians of this learning for over one thousand years, had
inevitably set something of their own stamp upon their ancient
inheritance. In art, too, the Byzantine tradition was not cut off
in 1453 but continued to live on in the East, especially in Crete
and Mt. Athos.[11] And in the West, through the work of a painter
such as the great El Greco, it was blended with western forms
and techniques so as to create another synthesis.[12]

One modern scholar has aptly named the century or so after
Constantinople's fall *Byzance après Byzance*,[13] signifying a period
when the still viable Byzantine culture continued to exert an
influence on the West, now through large numbers of Greeks
emigrating from their Turkish or Venetian-held homelands.
(Such post-Byzantine influences were at this time also affecting
some of the Slavic areas especially Russia.)[14] No one today of
course can believe that the Greeks of this diaspora, as we may
term this movement of émigrés, began the Renaissance. At its
inception the Renaissance was certainly of Latin inspiration, and
had begun even before refugee Greeks in any great numbers
came to the West. Yet it is not sufficiently realized that much of
what these Greek exiles brought with them from the former
Byzantine areas, now under foreign hegemony, was still molded
to a considerable extent by the thousand year old traditions of
Byzantium.

[11] For bibl. see below, esp. Chs. 5 and 6.
[12] Prof. M. Chatzidakes of the Byzantine Museum in Athens tells me that another
Greek painter who blended Byzantine and western techniques was Antonios
Vasilakes of Melos (called Aliense), pupil of Veronese, who did many paintings in
the Ducal Palace of Venice (see *Great Greek Encyclopaedia* [in Greek], III, 811 ff.). On
the much-debated question of influences on El Greco see below, Chaps. 4–5.
[13] N. Iorga, *Byzance après Byzance* (Bucharest, 1935).
[14] I am preparing a monograph on this question.

Chapter four discusses what came to be looked upon by most Greeks of the diaspora in the West as their substitute homeland, the Greek colony in Venice. The reconstruction of the little-known history of this community not only provides a new dimension for the study of the role of the Greeks in the Renaissance revival of Hellenic letters but helps to destroy the stock, exaggerated image of the post-Byzantine refugee as a lone, friendless individual with no place for himself in the West. Some of the material in the central portion of this essay has appeared in another form in my recent book, *Greek Scholars in Venice*.[15] But the present study has been extended up to 1600, set in a different framework and a lengthy section added on the significance of the colony for the rise of Venice to primacy in Greek studies.[16]

Chapter five concerns certain Cretan intellectuals who were intimately associated with the Greek colony in Venice and who emigrated from there to still more distant areas of northern and western Europe. The considerable contribution of the island of Crete, formerly Byzantine and now ruled by Venice, to western Renaissance culture has been surprisingly little studied, except in connection with a few important but seemingly isolated figures like El Greco in Spain and certain editors or professors of Greek in Italy such as Marcus Musurus at the University of Padua.[17] The present essay attempts to evaluate only one part of this contribution of the Cretans, their role in transmitting Greco-Byzantine culture to the West by way of Venice. Other aspects of the Cretan influence not only on western civilization but on the Slavs of the Balkans and even on Russia during this period of late Byzantine and post-Byzantine influence, I hope to discuss at length in a forthcoming book devoted exclusively to this subject.

The final essay treats of the career of the Cretan Maximos Margounios, probably the leading theologian-scholar of the Orthodox church in the later sixteenth century. Though his name is hardly known to western historians, he had remarkably

---

[15] *Greek Scholars in Venice: Studies in the Dissemination of Greek Learning from Byzantium to Western Europe* (Cambridge, Mass., 1962). Acknowledgement is due to the Harvard University Press for permission to draw on certain materials from this book. *Greek Scholars*, we should note, extends only to 1535, this, to 1600.

[16] This essay and the next one, in much briefer form and in Italian, were read in Venice in September of 1963 at the Fondazione Giorgio Cini's Congress on 'Venice and the East'.

[17] On Musurus see Geanakoplos, *op. cit.*, Chap. 5.

wide contacts with many personalities of the Renaissance and Reformation. The core of the study consists of the publication of a catalogue of his library of Latin books now in the Orthodox monastery of Iviron on Mount Athos and the contents of which have been hitherto unknown.[18] This last essay marks in a sense an appropriate close to our study of East-West relations, since Margounios, at least theoretically, made the last attempt to bring together the western and eastern churches in the context of the medieval Council of Florence and through his own approach to the historic problem of the *filioque*. At this time when the Byzantine state had ceased to exist but the legacy of East-West antagonism remained, the most meaningful attempt at *rapprochement* of the two peoples, as Margounios realized, would be through ecclesiastical union. If El Greco, who was born and spent his early manhood in Crete,[19] can be referred to by some scholars as the last important Greek painter to be influenced by the old Byzantine artistic traditions,[20] Margounios, his contemporary compatriot, may even more appropriately be described as the last significant Byzantine, or rather post-Byzantine, theologian-humanist in the succession of the fourteenth century Demetrios Cydones and the fifteenth century Bessarion.

From 330 to 1453 and even to 1600, despite the considerable inroads of Latin influence and the destruction of the Byzantine state itself by the Turks, there may be traced in the East an unmistakable continuity of the Byzantine cultural tradition. How this Byzantine or, more accurately, Greco-Byzantine tradition, against the backdrop of increasing alienation, interacted with and influenced the western world at various points during the Medieval and Renaissance period is the underlying theme connecting the individual essays in this book.

[18] My thanks to the American Philosophical Society for a grant enabling me to catalogue these books on Athos in the summer of 1962.

[19] For a remarkable new notarial document, recently discovered, indicating that El Greco probably lived in Crete as late as his 25th year, see below, Chaps. 4–5.

[20] See below Ch. 1, n. 80 and Chaps. 4–5.

PART I

EAST AND WEST IN THE MIDDLE AGES

CHAPTER ONE

THE INFLUENCES OF BYZANTINE CULTURE
ON THE MEDIEVAL WESTERN WORLD

I T is frequently asserted that from a cultural point of view the
chief function of Byzantium was to serve for over one thousand
years as the bulwark of Christendom against invading infidel
hordes and in this capacity to preserve for the world the literary
and philosophic heritage of ancient Greece.[1] There is no doubt
of course of the signal service rendered by Byzantium as a pre-
server of Greek learning. After all, the Greek language and
literature had virtually disappeared from the German-dominated
West of the so-called Dark Ages. But Byzantium was certainly
more than a mere passive repository of ancient civilization. On
the contrary, as her culture developed, it reflected a remarkable
amalgamation not only of the philosophy and literature of Greece,
but of the religious ideals of Christianity—which in the East
underwent a development significantly different from that of the
Latin West—and thirdly, of a certain transcendent, mystical
quality that may at least partly be attributed to the diverse influences of Syria, Egypt, the Jews, even Persia. These three
elements, then, Greco-Roman classicism (including the governmental tradition of Rome), the Byzantine brand of Christianity,
and what we may call the oriental component, were blended by
the Byzantines into a unique and viable synthesis that made
Constantinople, at least until 1204, the cultural capital of all
Christendom. It was this many-faceted cultural amalgam, as we
shall attempt to show, that enabled Byzantium to play a far from
insignificant part in the formation of western civilization.[2]

---

[1] For example N. Baynes, *Byzantine Studies and Other Essays* (London, 1955) 71–73.
[2] For bibl. on the Byzantine cultural influence on the West see Appendix,
Bibliographical note A.

Now to analyze the Byzantine cultural influence on the West is a complex problem spanning more than a millenium of history and involving, in one way or another, most of the countries of Europe. One could perhaps make facile generalizations about the natural tendency of the less developed western civilization to draw upon or be influenced by the more complex, sophisticated Byzantine. But one must not forget that as the medieval period progressed, Byzantium and the West were becoming increasingly estranged—indeed by perhaps the ninth century they had become almost two different worlds[3]—and that many westerners, especially those who did not come into direct contact with the East, were not receptive to Byzantine influences. To demonstrate a *definite* cultural impact of the Christian East on the West can accordingly sometimes be a rather difficult, even elusive matter, particularly in regard to those fields which are less tangible in nature or in which the evidence remaining is inadequate. In order therefore to deal with the problem on as firm ground as possible and at the same time to provide a kind of historical frame of reference, we shall consider first the points of actual physical contact between Byzantium and the Latin West during the medieval period—that is, the specific channels through which cultural transmission could and seems to have taken place. Then, having established such a pattern of contacts, we shall move to the main section of the essay and examine, insofar as time permits, selected cultural fields in which it can be asserted that the Byzantines affected western civilization—philosophy, science, law, political theory and diplomacy, music, art, and such lesser known but important aspects as religious piety, commercial practice, and more refinement in the manner of living.

I

Originally constituting two halves of the ancient Roman Empire, the eastern (Byzantine) and the western (Latin) areas in the early centuries of the Christian era had possessed certain

[3] A date picked because of the creation of Charlemagne's revived Roman Empire in 800 (disputing Byzantium's claim), the collapse of the Ravenna exarchate in 751, and the Slavic invasions of the Balkans in this general period, all of which served to cut off Byzantium, though not entirely, from western contacts. F. Dvornik, *The Slavs: Early History and Civilization* (Boston, 1956) emphasizes that the Bulgar invasion of Illyricum cut off this basic bridge between Latins and Greeks.

cultural elements in common, Christianity and the Greco-Roman
tradition. In the East, however, the Greek element continued
from the Hellenistic period onward to predominate, while in the
West the Latin language and culture obtained. Moreover, while
the East technically preserved an unbroken continuity of the
Roman Empire—as late as 1453 the Byzantines continued to call
themselves Romans not Greeks[4]—the western areas early fell to
the German invaders and, with the passing of time, the German
element largely displaced in the West the more refined Greco-
Roman. This emergence of a strong Germanic strain in the
western cultural synthesis is to be contrasted to the Byzantine
synthesis, with its inclusion of an Oriental component, absent in
turn from the West.

In the sixth century, under the Emperor Justinian, Byzantium
recaptured much of Italy and established the so-called exarchate
of Ravenna, a fact which once again brought an important area
of the West into direct dependence upon Byzantium. The
exarchate—and this included the city of Rome—remained in
Byzantine hands until 751 when Ravenna was finally captured by
the Lombards.[5] Before its collapse, however, Ravenna had
become a center for the radiation of Byzantine cultural influence,
especially in connection with Byzantine art and the dissemination
of Byzantine, that is Roman law.

More significant for our study are the areas of Sicily and
southern Italy, which were Byzantine provinces until the ninth
and eleventh centuries respectively. What served to maintain—
some scholars would prefer to say 're-establish'—the Hellenization
of these areas especially in southern Italy after the period of
antiquity, was the successive waves of Greek exiles who emigrated
there from the East. Thus in the seventh century refugees from
Syria, Palestine, and Egypt fled to southern Italy (especially
Calabria) before the attacks of the Arabs. And in the eighth and
ninth centuries, according to certain scholars, as many as 50,000
eastern monks and, to a lesser extent, ecclesiastics arrived in
Calabria in order to escape the persecutions of the Byzantine

---

[4] There are a few earlier traces of a return to the ancient term Hellenes. See
Geanakoplos, *Emperor Michael Palaeologus*, 35, for term in thirteenth century. Also
A. Vakalopoulos, *History of Modern Hellenism* (in Greek) I (Salonika, 1961) 75ff.

[5] Ch. Diehl, *Etudes sur l'administration byzantine dans l'exarchate de Ravenne* (Paris,
1888).

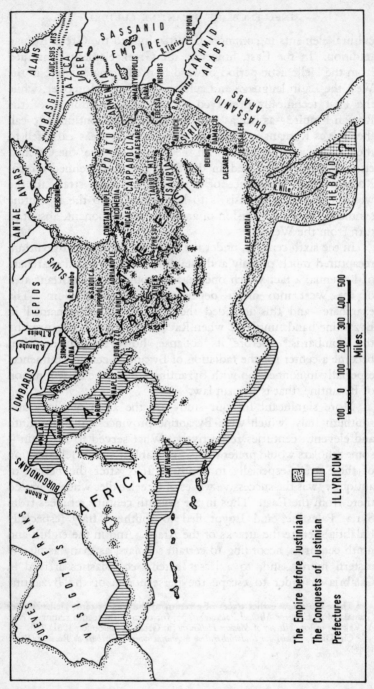

THE BYZANTINE (ROMAN) EMPIRE IN 565 UNDER JUSTINIAN

Map 1

Iconoclast Emperors. Whether the Greek language spoken by the population of southern Italy was derived from the ancient Greek of Magna Graecia or was rather the product of subsequent Byzantine influence we may pass over here. The significant point is that by the eleventh century parts of southern Italy, primarily Calabria, had become almost completely Byzantinized in both culture and religion[6] and that as late as the fifteenth century it would constitute the leading outpost of Byzantine influence in the West.

Even the Arab conquest of Sicily in the ninth century did not put an end to Greek influence on the island. For the Arabs were fascinated by ancient Greek and, to a much lesser degree, Byzantine science and philosophy. Indeed, when subsequently in the late eleventh century, the Norman invaders took the island from the Arabs, Greco-Byzantine culture continued to be a vital element in the island's civilization. Under the Norman King Roger II and his successors, for example, three official languages were employed in the documents of the Sicilian chancery, Latin, Greek, and Arabic. Moreover, the Normans appointed as ministers of state such learned Greeks as Eugene the Emir and the more famous Henry Aristippus, who, at a time when western Europe knew only a fragment of one of Plato's dialogues, the *Timaeus*, translated into Latin two more Platonic works. Though relations between Byzantium and Norman Sicily were generally hostile, we know that gifts were not infrequently exchanged by their rulers, sometimes including valuable Greek manuscripts of philosophic or scientific content such as the famous *Almagest* of Ptolemy.[7]

Among the first Italians to have had active commercial contacts with Constantinople—and the Italians were to have the closest relations economically with the East—were the citizens of

[6] Best work on this question is J. Gay, *L'Italie méridionale et l'empire byzantin* (Paris, 1904). On the 50,000 emigré monks see L. White, *Latin Monasticism in Norman Sicily* (Cambridge, 1938) 15–17. Also K. Setton, 'The Byzantine Background to the Italian Renaissance', *Proceedings of American Philosophical Society*, C 1956) 7 with bibl. cited.

[7] On Eugene see now E. Jamison, *Admiral Eugenius of Sicily* (London, 1957). On Aristippus (who some think may not have been Greek) see Setton, 'Byzantine Background', 19. On the Platonic dialogues see R. Klibansky, *The Continuity of the Platonic Tradition during the Middle Ages* (London, 1939) 27–31, 51. The *Timaeus* had been translated by Chalcidius in the fourth century.

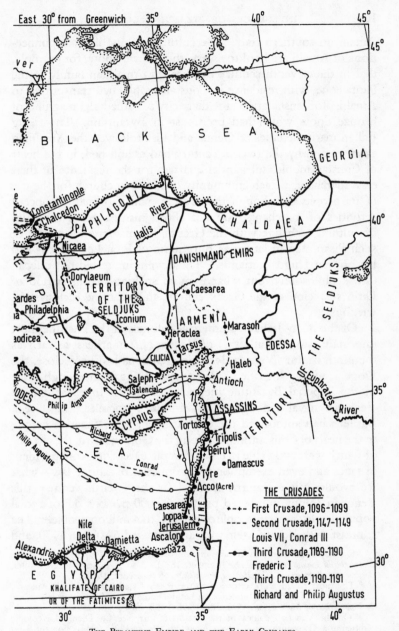

THE BYZANTINE EMPIRE AND THE EARLY CRUSADES
[For the Latin Empire, which replaced the Byzantine Empire after the Fourth Crusade see the map entitled 'The Age of Latin Rule in Constantinople' in Ostrogorsky, *History of the Byzantine State*, New Brunswick, 1957.]

Amalfi, in southern Italy. The cultural results of those connections of Amalfi are hard to assess, though we know, for example,
that in the eleventh century the wealthy Amalfitan family of the
Pantaleone, with residence in Constantinople, had transported to
Amalfi, for installation in that city's cathedral, magnificent
bronze doors which had been cast in Byzantium. The rising
Italian maritime cities of Genoa and Pisa followed the Amalfitan
example and by the twelfth century had established, in the heart
of Constantinople, substantial quarters for the residence of their
own merchants. Each community had a Latin church for the use
of its people and though the sources, which primarily concern
activities of merchants,[8] do not afford many specific examples
of cultural exchange with the Greeks, we may cite the names of
such Pisan men of letters as Burgundio of Pisa, Leo Tuscus and
his brother Hugo Eterianus.[9] These were interested not only in
Greek philosophy, but what is more striking in this period of
Latin suspicion of the Greek church, in Byzantine ecclesiastical
writings.

Of the many Italian commercial colonies in the East the most
important was certainly that of Venice. From at least as early as
the ninth century Veneto-Byzantine relations had been close, the
Doge acquiring the title of *Protosevastos* and a high enough place
in the imperial Byzantine hierarchy of titles. In exchange for
Venetian naval aid against Byzantium's enemies, the Greek
Basileus had authorized the establishment of a Venetian colony
in the heart of Constantinople, along the Golden Horn, the citizens
of which were soon able to enjoy complete freedom from payment
of taxes and even exemption from imperial Byzantine law—what
we would call extraterritoriality. In the twelfth century this
Venetian colony numbered perhaps 20,000 persons out of a total
population in Constantinople of 800,000 to a million people.[10] The
contrast with Venice itself with an estimated 64,000 in 1170, and

[8] On Latin merchants in Byzantium the main work is W. Heyd, *Histoire du
Commerce du Levant au Moyen Âge* (Leipzig, 1885). Also documents in G. Müller,
Documenti sulle relazioni delle città toscane coll'Oriente (Florence, 1879).

[9] The most recent work referring to the Pisans listed here is by M. Anastos,
'Some Aspects of Byzantine Influence on Latin Thought', *Twelfth Century Europe and
the Foundations of Modern Society* (Madison, 1961) 138–49.

[10] On the Venetian colony in the twelfth century see Ch. Diehl, 'La colonie
vénitienne à Constantinople', *Etudes byzantines* (Paris, 1905) 204ff. For the later
period see below Chap. 4; on the number of Venetians in Constantinople see
Geanakoplos, *Greek Scholars in Venice*, 14, n. 3.

with Paris, then the West's largest city with a population of less than 100,000, is remarkable.[11]

To be sure, the Venetian colonists, having the mentality of merchants, were rarely interested in anything but commercial profit. Thus of course they learned to speak enough Greek for their commercial transactions. But this was the colloquial vulgar Greek (the lingua franca of the East) and it was not sufficient as a rule to permit the reading of classical works or the exchange of ideas on a higher intellectual level. (The literary Greek of Byzantine intellectual circles was different from the spoken, every-day Greek.) Exceptions do exist such as the case of the famous James of Venice, who a recent scholar believes was a Greek living in Venice. James translated Aristotle's *Ethics* into Latin and acted as interpreter at ecclesiastical disputations held before the imperial Greek court on questions of difference between the Greek and Latin churches. Such occasions must surely have afforded some opportunity for cultural exchange.[12]

What brought the people of the West and the Byzantines into direct contact on a far greater scale, however, was the vast movement of the Crusades, which began at the end of the eleventh century. Entire western armies now passed through Constantinople on the way to the Holy Land, and pilgrims flocked eastward via Constantinople, all being exposed to the richer and more cosmopolitan manner of living of the medieval Greeks. Inevitably, jealousies and antagonisms between the two peoples now began to develop and with the passing of time to increase. The shattering climax came in 1204 with the notorious Fourth Crusade, when the western armies, led by the Venetians, diverted their crusade from Jerusalem to Constantinople and actually captured the Byzantine capital. After a barbaric sack of three days, a tremendous amount of booty—sacred relics associated with the life of Christ and the saints, precious manuscripts, silver and gold religious treasures, and countless objects of art—was seized in this richest of Christian cities and carried back to adorn

[11] In the eleventh and early twelfth century Rome had probably no more than 50,000 people. On Paris, Venice, and Rome see T. Chandler, *Cities of the World* (New York, 1940) 10, and references in Geanakoplos, *op. cit.*, 14, n. 3.

[12] On James of Venice see Ch. Haskins, *Studies in the History of Medieval Science* (Cambridge, 1924) 144–45, 227–32. Also L. Minio-Paluello, 'Jacobus Veneticus Grecus', *Traditio*, VIII (1952), 265–304.

the churches and palaces of the West. The enumeration of this booty and the recounting of its seizure fill several volumes in the works of a noted French scholar of the history of the Christian East during the Crusades.[13]

As a result of the Fourth Crusade a Latin Empire was established on the ruins of the Byzantine state. Attempts were made by the western conquerors, and especially the pope, to Latinize the Greek people by forcible conversion to the Roman faith. But this unwise policy, as might be expected, provoked the violent opposition of the mass of the Greek population. The Latin Empire existed until 1261, when Constantinople was recaptured by the Greeks.[14] Then the hitherto predominant Venetian influence in Byzantium diminished, to be displaced by that of the Byzantine allies, the Genoese. The Venetians, however, managed to retain control of certain of their Greek colonies in the East—several points in the Peloponnesus, the Aegean isles, and especially the great island of Crete. With the Ottoman Turkish advance on the Byzantine territory of Asia Minor in the fourteenth and fifteenth centuries, the Greek animosity toward the Latins began of necessity to be mollified. And in fact some of the Byzantines, especially of the court circles, came to view the West not only as the sole source of possible aid against the Turk but, still later, even as a place of refuge from Turkish domination.[15]

Before and for at least a century after 1453, then, large numbers of Greeks—a veritable diaspora of intellectuals, merchants, mercenaries, and others—poured into the West, many of whom sought asylum in Venice. By the end of the fifteenth century there was a very substantial Greek colony established in that city. This was in fact the greatest colony of

[13] There is a large bibliography on pilgrimages to the East and on the Fourth Crusade, e.g., A. Atiya, *Crusade in the Later Middle Ages* (London, 1938) and R. Wolff's article in K. Setton ed., *The Crusades*, vol. 2 (Philadelphia, 1962). The French scholar cited above is P. Riant, *Exuviae Sacrae Constantinopolitanae*, 3 vols. (Geneva, 1877–1904).

[14] On the attempt to 'Latinize' the Greek church soon after 1204 see R. Wolff, 'The Organization of the Latin Patriarchate of Constantinople 1204–61. Social and Administrative Consequences of the Latin Conquest', *Traditio*, VI (1948) 33–60. Also Geanakoplos, 'On the Schism of the Greek and Roman Churches: A Confidential Papal Directive for the Implementation of Union (1278)', *Greek Orthodox Theological Review*, I (1954) 16–24. On the Greek reconquest of Constantinople by Michael VIII Palaeologus in 1261 see now Geanakoplos, *Emperor Michael Palaeologus and the West*, Chap. 5. On Brocardus see also above, Prologue, note 3.

[15] Geanakoplos, *Greek Scholars*, 18.

Greeks to be established in the West after 1453. The Greeks of this community were granted the right to build a church and they also possessed a large dockyard, or *scala*, on an important Venetian canal for the loading and shipment of goods abroad. We shall see that, from the cultural viewpoint, these Greek émigrés to the West were to play a significant role in the development of humanistic learning in the Renaissance.[16]

There is time only for brief mention of several other Italian centers affected by or radiating Byzantine influence during the medieval period. Further reference should certainly be made to the papal capital Rome, which, after the fall of Ravenna and throughout the entire Middle Ages, had intimate contact with Byzantines or Byzantine ideas. A large community of Greek monks seems always to have lived in Rome, and up to the third century Greek was even the language of the Roman liturgy. Moreover, during the later seventh and early eighth centuries many of the popes themselves—eleven of thirteen to be precise —were Greek or Syrian in origin and shared the cultural proclivities of the East.[17]

Other western areas further removed from the East were also at one time or another in direct contact with Byzantium. In the early ninth century, the German court of Charlemagne at Aachen was exposed to considerable Byzantine influence, as we know from the architectural evidence of its palace chapel as well as from certain Byzantine art works and textiles that remain. In the tenth century more intensive Byzantine influence was felt at the German court as a result of the marriage of the future Holy Roman Emperor Otto II to the Byzantine princess Theophano. So imbued did their young son, the half-Greek Otto III, become with Byzantine political ideals that he adopted Byzantine titles for his court and envisioned the reunion of both East and West in one Empire in the manner of Justinian.[18]

[16] *Ibid., passim.*

[17] L. White, *Latin Monasticism*, 22, points out that from 678 to 752, 11 of the popes were Orientals, that is Greek or Syrian. Also now see J. McNulty and B. Hamilton, ' "Orientale lumen" et "Magistra Latinitas": Greek Influences on western Monasticism', *Le millénaire du Mont Athos* (Chevtogne, 1963) 181–217, and B. Hamilton, 'The City of Rome and the Eastern Churches', *Orientalia Christiana Periodica*, 27 (1961) 2–26.

[18] J. Bryce, *Holy Roman Empire* (New York, 1913); W. Ohnsorge, *Das Zweikaiserproblem im früheren Mittelalter* (Hildesheim, 1947). Also on art D. Talbot Rice, *English Art 871–1100* (Oxford, 1952) 21 f.

Similarly, we hear that there were at various times communities of Greek merchants or monks in early medieval France—such as at Narbonne.[19]   And in the later medieval period, French crusaders were to bring back from the East Byzantine art objects, new ideas, and different building techniques, the adoption of which helped gradually to make for a more refined mode of life. Because of the distance involved the Byzantine influence on England was perhaps the least penetrating of all. But sporadic traces of such influences do remain such as, for example, in the late Anglo-Saxon and possibly Norman use of the imperial Byzantine title Basileus, to apply to their kings; and in the Northumbrian sculptured stones of the seventh century, so extraordinarily Byzantine in feeling and execution. Inspiration for the latter probably came from the East, however, rather through the mediation of the English connection with Rome.[20]

There is one western area, Spain, where the influence of Greek and to a lesser degree of Byzantine philosophy and science were of capital importance for their effect on western culture as a whole. These influences, however, came through the mediation not of the Byzantines but of another people, the Arabs. In the early years of the Islamic expansion, the Arabs had come into contact with heretic Nestorian and Monophysite refugees from the Byzantine East and from these they acquired an interest in ancient Greek philosophy and science, especially the Aristotelian. These Greek works the Arabs carried with them into Spain, and it was from this region that in the twelfth and thirteenth centuries the bulk of Aristotle and other Greek scientific treaties were brought back to the Christian West, with the results we shall note shortly.[21]

These, then, are the principal foci, direct and indirect, for the reception and diffusion of Byzantine culture in the western world.

[19] Talbot Rice, *Byzantine Art*, new ed. (London, 1962), 247.
[20] See R. S. Lopez, 'Le Problème des Relations Anglo-byzantines du Septième Siècle', *Byzantion*, XVIII (1948), esp. 161–62. On Norman use of the title 'Basileus' but only in the coronation *laudes* see P. Schramm, *A History of the English Coronation* (Oxford, 1937) 30. On art see Talbot Rice, *Byzantine Art*, 250 ff. and his *English Art*, 22, 133, esp. 135, 250.
[21] On early Arab contacts with Nestorians and Monophysites see e.g., Ph. Hitti, *History of the Arabs* (London, 1960) 309 ff. On Spain see C. Haskins, *Medieval Science*, *passim*.

Now that we have pointed out the chief lines of possible transmission and provided in the process a historical background, let us concentrate on certain selected areas of culture in order to show in each case what the Byzantine contribution seems to have been.

II

PHILOSOPHY AND SCIENCE

First let us consider the important realm of philosophic and scientific ideas. According to the famous French scholar Etienne Gilson, western medieval and Renaissance intellectual thought underwent two fundamental crises in the course of their development, both under the impact of the re-introduction of Greek philosophy. First in the twelfth and thirteenth centuries with the reception of Aristotle from Arabic Spain, and, second, in the fifteenth century when an interest in Plato was diffused in the West following the coming to Florence of a Byzantine delegation to negotiate religious union with Rome.[22] Now it cannot of course be said that a knowledge of the Greek language *per se* was indispensable for advance in culture. After all, classical Latin was also a flexible and highly expressive language. But the point is that reception of the ancient Greek philosophic works brought along with them that greatest gift of ancient Greece to the world —the emphasis on natural reason. In the period of the so-called Dark Ages such an attitude contrasted starkly with the unquestioning, superstitious *Weltanschauung* of the West regarding nature and the world. Hence it is clear how traumatic it must have been for the more thoughtful western man suddenly to come upon works of Aristotle with his convincing explanation of the cosmos based solely on reason and entirely without reference to the supernatural elements of Christianity.

But as we have elsewhere observed, the Aristotelian philosophy and science that entered the West in the twelfth century

[22] See an even stronger statement by E. Gilson, in *History of Christian Philosophy in the Middle Ages* (New York, 1955) 541: 'Practically every notable event in the history of Western thought in the Middle Ages is tied up with the presence of a man who had studied in Greece, or who knew Greek and had translated some Greek philosophic writings or had access to such translations.'

did not come directly from Byzantium but via the Arabs of
Spain. The point is that this Aristotelian thought was colored by
Muslim theological interpretation which, aside from being non-
Christian (as on the question of the eternity of matter), sometimes
had even confused Aristotelianism with aspects of Neo-Platonism.[23] It was not until after the Latin conquest of Constantinople
in 1204 that most of the original Greek texts, of Aristotle and
other scientific writers, in more or less unadulterated form, were
made available to western scholars. It is a striking commentary
on the distrust felt by the West for the Greek 'schismatics', as the
Byzantines were referred to, that for a considerable period the
westerners actually preferred the second or even third-hand
Arabic version of Aristotle to the purer version the Byzantines
could provide.

The introduction of the 'Muslim' Aristotle from Spain
provoked such a sensation in western intellectual circles that the
pope, sensing danger for the church, had to forbid the reading of
portions of that author at the University of Paris, then the chief
center of theological study in the West. But as usually happens
with this type of censorship, the prohibition proved impossible
to implement. Latin scholars, dazzled by the wealth of new
material in Aristotle and other Greek authors, simply refused to
obey. And ultimately the great Dominican Thomas Aquinas was
appointed to minimize the danger by attempting to reconcile
Aristotle's cosmology with that of Catholic Christianity—with
the results that are well known.

It is worth noting that fully five hundred years before St.
Thomas, a conciliation of Christian faith—but this time of
Orthodoxy—with Aristotelian reason had already been attempted
in the Byzantine East by the theologian John of Damascus.[24] A
copy of John's famous *Fountain of Wisdom*, which is still perhaps
the basic work for the theology of the Orthodox Church, was
apparently known to and utilized by Aquinas in the composition
of his own great *Summa Theologiae*. It was also Aquinas who
suggested a vast undertaking to William of Moerbeke, the

[23] On Muslim interpretation and the admixture of Aristotelian and Neo-Platonic
thought see T. Arnold and A. Guillaume, *The Legacy of Islam* (Oxford, 1931) 240–41;
and Hitti, *History of the Arabs*, 307. See now R. Walzer, *Greek into Arabic* (Cambridge, Mass., 1962) 60–113.
[24] John died ca. 750. He was in the employ of the Arab Caliph in Damascus.

Latin Archbishop of Corinth—a revised, literal translation made
directly from the Greek of almost all of Aristotle's works,
including the famous political treatise, the *Politics*.[25]

For the most part, medieval western translations of Greek
writings were limited to logical treatises, the sciences, and, to a
much lesser extent, to theology. Significantly, they failed to
include classic Greek poetry, history, and much of philosophy[26]—
that is, the more humanistic writings. And the latter works did
not in general come to the West until the period of the Renaissance. We have no time here to discuss specific works of this
nature. But we should note that the original texts—say of the
Greek tragedies—had in many cases been established in Constantinople by Byzantine scholars at the time of Photius and
Arethas and especially in the thirteenth and fourteenth centuries
and then brought westward mainly by Greek refugees or
exiled scholars who settled in Venice and other Italian centers.
One has only to examine a list of the personnel of the famous
Academy of Aldus Manutius in Venice, which, at the end of the
fifteenth and early sixteenth centuries, printed many first editions
of these influential Greek texts and which counted among its
editors many Greeks, including the famous Cretan Marcus
Musurus and the Constantinopolitan humanist-diplomat Janus
Lascaris.[27]

Of parallel significance to Aristotelianism for the development
of western thought and learning, as we have noted, was the
introduction in the fifteenth century of Platonic philosophy.
This, however, is exclusively to be associated with Byzantium
and was not the result of mediation through the Arabs. To be
sure certain Neo-Platonic works had earlier been known to the
West. Already in the ninth century, during the so-called Carolingian Renaissance, the Irish scholar John Scotus Erigena had

[25] On Moerbeke's translation of the *Politics* see E. Barker, *Social and Political
Thought in Byzantium* (Oxford, 1957) 136. From the end of the twelfth to the end of
the thirteenth century the proportion of translations made from Greek to those from
the Arab, at second hand, gradually increased. It is not usually known that Moerbeke
also translated the *Poetics* of Aristotle (P. Kristeller, *Studies in Renaissance Thought and
Letters* [Rome, 1956] 340–41 and 23.) The *Poetics* was thus known to the thirteenth
century western world. On Aquinas and John of Damascus see Gilson, *History of
Christian Philosophy*, 92. Thomas himself cites John (see *Summa Theologica*, pt. I,
quaestio 36, art. 2 ad tertium). Thomas' knowledge of John of Damascus' work was
probably only rudimentary.

[26] Yet see previous note on the *Poetics* of Aristotle.

[27] Geanakoplos, *Greek Scholars in Venice, passim*, esp. 284–86.

secured from the library of Charles the Bald, the King of the Franks (to whose predecessor Louis the Pious it had been sent by the Byzantine Emperor) a copy of the work of the Byzantine Neo-Platonist Maximos the Confessor.[28] Erigena also had at his disposal in the writing of his famous *On the Division of Nature*, the work of the most highly influential mystic of the entire medieval world, the early Byzantine Dionysius the Areopagite, which Erigena translated into Latin. Dante in his *Paradiso* drew on material from Dionysius' *Celestial Hierarchy* and even the fourteenth century German mystic, Meister Eckhart, owed something to the profound mysticism of Dionysius.[29]

In the Byzantine East, where pure Platonism was usually suspect to the church, the last significant revival of genuinely Platonic thought took place in the fourteenth and fifteenth centuries at Constantinople and especially at Mistra, near ancient Sparta. There the philosopher and social reformer Gemistos Pletho had founded a virtual cult of Platonic studies.[30] In the West, on the other hand, Plato had been practically unknown since antiquity (despite the good intentions of Boethius in the sixth century and the pervasive Neo-Platonic thought reflected in Augustine). And it was not until the coming to Italy of Pletho and other Greeks to attend the famous Council of Florence in 1438–39 that the original Platonic texts once again were brought into direct contact with the mainstream of the western tradition. To save Constantinople, now completely surrounded by the Turks, the Greek Emperor, in a last desperate measure, had assembled a large number of his prelates and officials (many of whom were also scholars) and gone to Florence in the hope of securing military aid through religious union with the West. The papal price for western help against the Turks of course was the submission of the Greek church to Rome. The proceedings of this Council, the greatest medieval confrontation between East and West, lasted one and a half years, during which period opportunity was afforded for the westerners to acquire

[28] On Erigena, M. Cappuyns, *Jean Scot Erigène, sa vie, son oeuvre, sa pensée* (Louvain, 1933).

[29] Dionysius had been first brought to the West in the ninth century through Abbot Hilduin of St. Denis. See M. Viller and K. Rahner, *Askese und Mystik in der Väterzeit* (1939). L. Levillain, *Etudes sur l'abbaye de Saint Denis . . .* (Paris, 1921) and *Etudes Dionysiennes, I: Hilduin* (Paris, 1932).

[30] F. Masai, *Pléthon et le platonisme de Mistra* (Paris, 1956).

from the Greeks a knowledge and and appreciation of Platonic philosophy. Cosimo de' Medici, the ruler of Florence, was in fact so impressed by Pletho that he soon founded his Platonic Academy, whence, ultimately, interest in Plato became diffused throughout the entire West.[31]

On the purely religious side the Florentine Marsilio Ficino achieved a synthesis of Platonic and Christian thought, which had an important impact on the religious outlook of many western humanists.[32] According to some modern scholars the reception of Plato's philosophy did more to widen the intellectual horizon of the West during the Renaissance than any other single factor. Certain other authorities, however, take a narrower view. They believe that the most significant contribution of Platonic philosophy consisted rather in an emphasis on a mathematical type of thinking derived from certain Pythagorean materials incorporated in Plato. It was this mathematical emphasis, in contrast to the medieval western Aristotelian stress on logic that, according to this theory, paved the way for the advent of modern western science, especially acceptance of the Copernican theory.[33]

If the Italian Ficino was responsible for producing the first complete Latin translation of the Platonic dialogues, it was, as is not always realized, a Byzantine or rather a post-Byzantine— Marcus Musurus, the Cretan editor of the Venetian Aldine Press —who made the first printed edition of the original Greek text. To this work Musurus prefixed his famous 'Hymn to Plato', a composition which, at least from the philological point of view, some scholars rank as the finest piece of Greek poetry written since antiquity.[34]

[31] See below, Chap. 3. Also A. della Torre, *Storia dell' Accademia Platonica di Firenze* (Florence, 1902).

[32] Apparently Ficino did not use the works of Pletho.

[33] On this important conflict see esp. E. Burtt, *Metaphysical Foundations of Modern Physical Science* (London, 1925) 40 ff., who emphasizes the importance of the mathematical type of thinking in Plato (via Pythagoras) to be found in Neo-Platonic thought. This, he says, led to the Copernican theory. Burtt is opposed by E. W. Strong, *Procedures and Metaphysics* (Berkeley, 1936) and J. Randall, 'Development of Scientific Method in the School of Padua', *Journal of History of Ideas* (1940) 176–206, who emphasizes rather the method (Aristotelianism) of Padua University for the rise of modern science. See also J. Randall, *The School of Padua and the Emergence of Modern Science* (Padua, 1961); P. Duhem, *La système du monde* (Paris 1954), VII–VIII, stresses the continuity of medieval and early modern science.

[34] See below, Chap. 5, note 59.

Mention must be made, if only briefly, of the most celebrated ancient Greek scientific work that passed to the West—the *Mathematike Syntaxis* of Ptolemy (known better under its Arabic title of *Almagest*), a mathematical explanation for the universe which was to dominate the astronomical thinking of the West up to the time of Copernicus. It is known that in the twelfth century the Byzantine Emperor Manuel I Comnenus sent a copy of this work as a diplomatic gift to the Norman king of Sicily Roger II.[35] And it was from this manuscript that the first Latin version was made. William of Moerbeke, mentioned above, also translated a great part of the corpus of Archimedes. And at the very end of the Byzantine period, the fifteenth century philosopher Gemistos Pletho's introduction of the *Geography* of Strabo to the West influenced Renaissance conceptions of the configuration of the earth and, thus, indirectly, was a contributory factor leading to Columbus' discovery of America.

The Byzantine scientific tradition was essentially unoriginal, being based on ancient Greek, Hellenistic, and Roman achievements. But despite this broad heritage in natural science, the Byzantines, much like their ancient Greek forbears, were unable to develop a technical equipment, technology that is, and thus were usually unable to apply their sometimes not inconsiderable theoretical knowledge to practical use. Nevertheless, we may point out a few instances in which the Byzantines seemed to have anticipated certain modern technological developments. Kallinikos' invention of the famous Greek fire and the Byzantine technique of shooting this fire from copper tubes, constituted, according to several modern authorities, 'the prototype of modern gunpowder . . . , starting the military technicians not merely of Byzantium but of Islam, China, and the West on the trail of ever more combustible mixtures'. Though the watermill for producing power dates from the ancient world, it is quite possible that the overshot water-wheel (in which water runs over the top of, not underneath, the wheel) was an improvement of the early Byzantine period. In the sixth century Anthemius of Tralles (architect of St. Sophia) not only wrote on parabolic

---

[35] See A. Vasiliev, *History of the Byzantine Empire* (Madison, 1952) 491. The Latin version had been translated from the Greek in 1160 in Sicily. In 1175 Gerard of Cremona translated the work from the Arabic at Toledo.

mirrors, but, as a joke, harnessed steam pressure to simulate a small earthquake. In the same century John Philoponus rejected the Aristotelian notion of the impossibility of producing a vacuum and even anticipated Galileo's experiment that two weights dropped from the same height reach the ground at approximately the same time. Finally, the famous mechanical *automata* of the Byzantine court (the rising throne, lions roaring, and birds singing), used to impress foreign visitors such as the tenth century Bishop Liudprand, may indirectly have influenced the development of the western mechanical clocks of the four-teenth century.[36]

LITERATURE

Apart from a certain influence on western historical writing as revealed through such works as the papal librarian Anastasius' ninth century translation of the Byzantine chronicler Theophanes, the Byzantine influence on western medieval literature was small. Creativity in Byzantine literature was relatively rare, except in the sometimes remarkable poetry found in the Byzantine hymnology and the unique eleventh century epic poem, 'Digenes Akritas'.[37] Byzantium never produced a Dante, though probably the most learned scholar of the entire medieval world was the ninth century Patriarch Photius. This deficiency in literary creativeness is usually attributed (perhaps with a certain exaggeration) to the slavish Byzantine imitation of the ancient literary models. The cultured Byzantine felt that ancient Greek literature had reached such a state of perfection that in many respects it was impossible to surpass, a fact which led not only to the close Byzantine imitation of ancient rhetorical style but, more important, to the

[36] L. White, *Medieval Technology and Social Change* (Oxford, 1962) 80, 90, 96 ff., 124 f.; M. Anastos, 'The History of Byzantine Science', *DumbartonOaks Papers*, XVI (1962) 411; his 'Pletho, Strabo and Columbus', *Ann. de l'inst. phil. et d'hist. orient. et slaves*, XII (1952) 1–18; and G. Brett, 'Byzantine Waterwheel', *Antiquity*, XIII (1939) 354 ff.

[37] See in N. Baynes and H. Moss, *Byzantium: An Introduction to East Roman Civilization* (Oxford, 1961) the essay by F. Marshall and J. Mavrogordato, 'Byzantine Literature', 221 ff. Also cf., R. Jenkins 'The Hellenistic Origins of Byzantine Literature', *Dumbarton Oaks Papers*, XVII (1963), esp. 39 and 52, and N. B. Tomadakes, *Introduction to Byzantine Literature* (in Greek) I (Athens, 1958), esp. 16 and ff. The basic work on Byzantine literature is K. Krumbacher, *Geschichte der byzantinischen Literatur* (Munich, 1897).

use by most writers of an artificial form of ancient Greek rather than the living vernacular spoken by the Byzantines themselves. It was this anomalous situation, somewhat analogous to that of an American attempting to write in Chaucerian English, that served in large part to stultify creativity in Byzantine literature.

Since Byzantium was the medieval repository for the ancient Greek literary treasures, it was from there or Byzantine southern Italy that they passed to the West. The medieval Greeks preserved the works of Homer, Aeschylus, Sophocles, Euripides, Aristophanes, and other poets and dramatists when they were unknown to or had been lost to the western world. And it is this work of preservation that some critics have termed Byzantium's most significant cultural contribution to the modern world.

While the classic dramatists were read in the East, they were never apparently performed on the stage, probably because of ecclesiastical objection to their pagan character and occasional immoral themes. As for Homer, he was read by all eastern school boys. But his work did not become familiar to western scholars until the fourteenth century when, at Petrarch's and Boccaccio's commission, Pilatus, a Greek of southern Italy, translated the Iliad and Odyssey into Latin prose. The version was not very successful (he did not know Latin too well), nor was Pilatus very effective in teaching Greek to Petrarch and Boccaccio. (It may not have been entirely his fault since dictionaries and other such aids were then unavailable, nor did the two Italian humanists really like Pilatus.) Nevertheless, Pilatus provided Boccaccio with material for his *Genealogy of the Gods*, the first exposition since antiquity of the Greek myths in their original pagan setting. It was at Boccaccio's initiative, moreover, that Pilatus, in 1361, was appointed at Florence to the first chair of the Greek language to be established in western Europe.[38] A subsequent and more important holder of this post (1396) was the distinguished Byzantine nobleman Manuel Chrysoloras, during whose tenure so many leading Italian statesmen and humanists came to study with him that the formal study of classical Greek letters may be said to have begun in the Renaissance.[39]

[38] A. Pertusi, *Leonzio Pilato fra Petrarca e Boccaccio* (Venice-Rome, 1964), esp. 433 ff. See G. Cammelli, *Manuele Crisolora* (Florence, 1941,) 8, 44, etc.

[39] Cammelli, *op. cit.*, and Geanakoplos, *Greek Scholars* 24.

Researchers differ sharply over the problem of the origin of the so-called Franco-Greek romances, epic poems of the fourteenth and fifteenth centuries about love and adventure which were popular in both the Greek East and the West. Some scholars believe that their genesis is to be traced to the medieval Byzantine East, others to the courtly love poems of France. Still others consider their prototype to be the novel of Greek anitiquity. Certainly, in the late medieval period, Byzantine poets translated into their own language French and Italian narratives of love and combat and also, perhaps to an even greater extent, created their own works of this genre, examples being 'Floire and Blanchfleur', 'Lybistros and Rhodamne' and 'Belthandros and Chrysantza'. Moreover, it is well-known that a number of twelfth century French romances of adventure had their setting in southern Italy, Constantinople, or Rome, and that the names of some of the characters in these works are distortions from the Greek.[40] Thus, whatever the origin of the form of the so-called Franco-Greek romance, it may at least be affirmed that a mutual interaction of Byzantine and western elements in the development of this type of literature is clearly indicated.

MEDICINE

In the early medieval period the only medical knowledge available to western Europe consisted of scattered fragments, in Latin translation, of the ancient Greeks Hippocrates, Galen, Soranus and Dioscorides. The revival of western medicine began in the late tenth or early eleventh century at the medical school of Salerno in southern Italy, where the traditions of Latin, Greco-Byzantine, Arabic, and Jewish medicine met and were blended. Half-legendary tradition has it that the founders of the Salerno school were Salernus who taught in Latin, a certain Pontos who taught in Greek, Adela who instructed in Arabic, and Helinus who taught in Hebrew. Of the several elements represented here it is generally believed that the Byzantine, aside from the ancient Greek proper, was rather negligible. But further research

[40] On the problem of origins and the romance see bibl. in K. Setton, 'The Byzantine Background to the Italian Renaissance', 38–39. Also see *Basic Library* (in Greek) (Athens, 1955), analysis of E. Kriaras. Cf. U. Holmes, *A History of Old French Literature to 1300* (New York, 1937) 146–49.

on the neglected field of Byzantine medicine may reveal that this view may have to be qualified. It is already known for example that a late twelfth century Latin physician at the same medical school, Roger of Salerno, was influenced by the treatises of the Byzantine doctors Aetius and Alexander of Tralles of the sixth century, and Paul of Aegina of the seventh.[41]

Arabic medicine was based largely on the ancient Greek, though in several areas, such as the science of vision, symptomatology and pharmacology the Arabs were able to make a few original contributions. In Byzantium the tradition of the ancients of course also obtained, and though the Byzantines seem to have made few if any important advances (our knowledge of Byzantine medicine is, however, still extremely scanty), they achieved in certain respects a rather high state of practical application. Thus, we know that in the twelfth century the capital city Constantinople had two well organized hospitals staffed by medical specialists (including women doctors), with special wards for various types of diseases and systematic methods of treatment.[42] This situation of course was not typical of the entire Empire, nor of all classes. Yet it is to be contrasted sharply with conditions in the West where, in the early period in general, apart from Salerno, gross superstition was rife.[43]

Arabic, and to a lesser extent, Byzantine medical practice was accordingly far advanced over the contemporary western. Eastern physicians had learned to recognize the decay of tissues

[41] On Salerno's origins see *History of Science Ancient and Medieval*, ed. R. Taton, English transl. (New York, 1963), article by G. Beaujouan, 476. On Roger see A. Crombie, *Medieval and Early Modern Science* (New York, 1959) I, 232–36. Also see P. Kristeller, 'Ancient Philosophy at Salerno in the Twelfth Century' (unpublished paper) where it is shown that in the eleventh century a certain Bartholomaeus knew Greek there. See also his 'Beitrag der Schule von Salerno zur Entwicklung der scholastischen Wissenschaft im 12. Jahrhundert', *Artes Liberales*, ed. J. Koch (Leiden, 1959) 84–90, and his 'Nuove fonti per la medicina salernitana del secolo XII', *Rassegna storica salernitana*, XVIII (1957) 61–75. On early western medicine see L. MacKinney 'Tenth Century Medicine', in 'Symposium in the Tenth Century', *Medievalia et Humanistica*, IX (1955) 10–13. On Soranus (Galen's predecessor) see O. Temkin, *Soranus' Gynecology* (Baltimore, 1956).

[42] Ch. Diehl, *La société byzantine à l'époque des Comnènes* (Paris, 1929) 51–56 and G. Schreiber, 'Byzantinisches und abendländisches Hospital', *Gemeinschaften des Mittelalters*, I (1948), esp. 42 ff. Also G. Sarton, *Introduction to History of Science*, I (Baltimore, 1927) 372 ff.

[43] Exceptions earlier in the West can be seen in medical practice at Theodoric's Ostrogothic court and Charlemagne's court: E. Campbell and J. Cotton, *The Surgery of Theodoric* (New York, 1960) and L. MacKinney, 'An Unpublished Treatise on Medicine and Magic from the Age of Charlemagne', *Speculum* (1943) 494–96.

and in the case of dentistry to treat and fill decayed teeth and do extractions.[44] With the transmission to western Europe in the twelfth and thirteenth centuries of much ancient medical learning from the Arabs of Spain, Sicily, and North Africa, and to some extent also from the medieval Greeks, the body of western medical knowledge began to increase. It was the ancient medical and anatomical texts of Hippocrates and Galen, gradually in more complete form, both in Arabic and Greek versions, that in the fourteenth century were used in the rising medical schools of the West—at Bologna, Padua, Paris and Montpellier. Thus the most influential anatomical textbook in the fourteenth century in the West—indeed it was to remain the most popular until Vesalius in the sixteenth century—was the *Anatomia* of Mondino di Luzzi, a work based largely on Galen, the Byzantine Theophilus, and Arabic authorities.

Much used in the examination of the pulse and the urine, the commonest method of diagnosis in the medieval period, was the treatise of the above-mentioned Theophilus of seventh century Byzantium. But the principal medical work of the Byzantine era was that of the seventh century Paul of Aegina. Emphasizing the practical aspects of medicine, its surgical section was celebrated for its excellence and had considerable influence on the medical science of the West as well as of the Arabs. Another Byzantine treatise, that of the thirteenth century Nicholas Myrepsos, remained the principal pharmaceutical code of the Parisian medical faculty until 1651, while the Byzantine tract of Demetrios Pepagomenos (thirteenth century) on gout was translated and published in Latin by the great post-Byzantine humanist, Marcus Musurus, in Venice in 1517.[45]

INDUSTRY

Before the Latin conquest of Constantinople in 1204 the Byzantines were noted for their industrial techniques—tech-

[44] Crombie, *Medieval and Early Modern Science* I, 234. The work was of course elementary.
[45] See J. Theodorides, 'Byzantine Science', *History of Science Ancient and Medieval*, ed. R. Taton, transl. A. Pomerans (New York, 1957) 440 ff. Crombie, *op. cit.*, I, 220. MacKinney, *loc. cit.*, 12. E. Nordensköld, *History of Biology* (New York, 1942). On, Musurus see D. Geanakoplos, *Greek Scholars in Venice*, 162. Most recent for Byzantine Medicine is O. Temkin, 'Byzantine Medicine: Tradition and Empiricism', *Dumbarton Oaks Papers*, XVI (1962) 96–115.

niques carried over in some cases from the ancient Greco-Roman world, but in others involving processes perfected in Byzantium. Silk manufacture, especially the making of magnificent gold-embroidered brocades and the designing of patterns on rich materials, though partly inspired from the ancient Near East, became a speciality of the medieval Greeks. Remarkable for their longevity are some of the Byzantine textiles still remaining, such as those found in the tomb of Charlemagne dating from the ninth century. The products of Byzantine silk manufacture were so prized by the West that when, early in the twelfth century, the Norman King Roger II attacked Byzantine Greece, he took special care to transport to Palermo the most skilled Theban and Peloponnesian silk workers. The historian of science George Sarton believes that this marked the beginnings of silk production in the West.[46] But it is perhaps more likely that the production of the finer western silk may be dated from this time.

We have already referred to the Byzantine reputation for the casting of bronze doors—examples of which are still to be found in the cathedral of Pisa, the church of St. Paul-outside-the-walls in Rome, at the great monastery of Monte-Cassino, the cathedral of Amalfi[47] and elsewhere. Byzantium until 1204 was also Europe's chief center for the making of glass. After that date the industry began to revive in the West, especially in Venice. There can be little doubt but that the many centuries of Venetian trade with the East and particularly her conquest of the Greek capital in 1204 had a good deal to do with her newly found technological supremacy for which she soon became famous.[48] Interestingly enough, one of the best accounts we have of medieval glass-making, a treatise of the German priest Theophilus, dating from the early twelfth century, prominently mentions the

[46] G. Sarton, *An Introduction to the History of Science* (Baltimore, 1931) 171. F. Chalandon, *Les Comnènes* (Paris, 1912) II, 317 ff. On the Byzantine silk industry see esp. R. Lopez, 'Silk Manufacture in the Byzantine Empire', *Speculum*, XX, 1 ff. Talbot Rice, *Art of the Byzantine Era* (New York, 1963) 106, believes Otto III put Byzantine silks into Charlemagne's tomb in 1000.

[47] H. Bloch, 'Monte Cassino, Byzantium, and the West in the Earlier Middle Age', *Dumbarton Oaks Papers*, III (1946) 163–224. In the tenth century bronze doors were cast at Hildesheim for Bishop Bernward who had them copied from the Byzantine-inspired doors made at Aachen for Charlemagne. See F. Tschan, *St. Bernward of Hildesheim*, II (Notre Dame, 1942) 142, 168–69, and 200, n. 6.

[48] Arabic Egypt had a remarkable glass industry as a heritage from Hellenistic-Roman-Byzantine times. Venice may have been influenced by this too.

Byzantine methods of manufacturing certain types of glassware such as plate glass and drinking vessels decorated with gold leaf.[49]

ADMINISTRATION, POLITICAL THEORY, LAW AND DIPLOMACY

In contrast to the medieval West, where a relatively loose, atomized feudal system obtained, Byzantium, for most of the period, had a highly centralized state organization with a well-developed civil service—a type of government in which virtually all activities were at the command of the emperor. These two elements, the autocracy and the civil service dependent upon it, were basic factors in providing Byzantium with the strength to withstand almost continual foreign invasions and domestic crises.

The autocratic tradition of Byzantium served as an inspiration for the development of a number of medieval western governments. Thus, for example, part of the basis for the Norman ideas of kingship in Sicily, as well as some of the Norman court ceremonial (including the king's own costume), seem to have been borrowed directly from Byzantine usage and from the absolutist concept of the Basileus as vicegerent of God, the ruler of both state and church in the world.[50] (The portrait of Roger II in the Martorana of Palermo is a good example.) This Byzantine concept was opposed to both the earlier western theory of pope and emperor as wielders of the two swords, and the later papal claims to universal spiritual and temporal sovereignty. We know that Roger II of Sicily, when seeking to bolster his claim to control of the Sicilian church *vis-à-vis* the papacy, instructed a Greek monk of his kingdom, Nilos Doxopatres, to draw up a treatise expounding the old Byzantine theory of the

---

[49] See Theophilus Presbyter, *Schedula Diversarum Artium*, ed. H. Hagen (Vienna, 1874), esp. 114–117.

[50] See esp. E. Kitzinger, 'On the Portrait of Roger II in the Martorana in Palermo', *Proporzioni* (1950) no. 3, pp. 30–34, who emphasizes the fact that Roger wears the costume of a Byzantine Emperor (as he does on several coins and seals) and was addressed as Basileus, but also that the German imperial imagery of the Ottonians provides a precedent for Roger's face done in imitation of that of Christ. On the Norman rulers and Byzantine theocracy see also A. Marongiu, 'Lo spirito della monarchia Normanna della Sicilia', *Arch. stor. sic.*, ser. 3, vols. 50–51, pp. 115 ff.; and L. R. Ménager, 'L'institution monarchique dans les états normandes d'Italie', *Cahiers des civilizations médiévales*, II (1959) 303 ff., who opposes such theories.

pentarchy, that is of the equality of all five patriarchs, including the pope, in the governance of the Christian church (though the pope was conceded a primacy of honor). It is probable that the autocratic Byzantine type of government also inspired some of the German Hohenstaufen ideas of royal power and, according to Diehl, helped to shape the subsequent European concept of the divine right of kings.[51]

If the autocracy played a basic role in maintaining the strength of the Byzantine state, it was law which bound together Byzantine society. And it is the Roman law, codified by the Byzantine Emperor Justinian and transmitted via Italy to the West[52] which is perhaps Byzantium's chief practical legacy to the modern world. For while the West was steeped in Germanic, barbaric law with its primitive ordeals and trials by battle, the Greek East was enjoying the benefits of Roman law, which had been leavened by the ideals of Stoicism and other philosophies on the basis of the long experience of the East. It was these concepts of Romano-Byzantine jurisprudence even more than the practical legal enactments themselves that have had the greatest effect on modern western law.

Contrary to common belief, the evolution of Byzantine law did not cease with the reign of Justinian. Because of the great social changes which came about in the Empire the code had to be modified and even expanded by the Macedonian dynasty in the tenth century, at which time all laws were systematically reshaped in Greek. It was the Macedonian code, even more than that of Justinian, which occupied the central position in Byzantine jurisprudence of the tenth century and afterwards.[53]

Previously, in the eighth and ninth centuries, three other codes had been drawn up by the Isaurian dynasty, the rural code

[51] On Nilus Doxopatres see the article of V. Laurent in *Dict. d'histoire et de géog. eccl.*, XIV, cols. 769–71. Also Ch. Diehl, *Byzantium, Greatness and Decline*, 285–87.

[52] See G. Ferrari dalle Spade, 'La legislazione dell'impero d'Oriente in Italia', *Italia e Grecia* (Florence, 1939) 225–53. Cf. Dölger, 'Byzanz und das Abendland vor den Kreuzzügen', 109.

[53] G. Ostrogorsky, *History of the Byzantine State* (New Brunswick, 1957) 216 ff. Also R. Lopez, 'Byzantine Law in the Seventh Century and its Reception by the Germans and Arabs', *Byzantion*, XVI (1942–3) 445 ff. Byzantine law was in force in Byzantine Sicily and southern Italy but had evidently no lasting influence there. Yet Byzantine law was known to and did affect the Franks (Latins) living in the East. The influence of Germanic law was probably responsible for the curious appearance of the ordeal by fire in 1258 at the trial of Michael Palaeologus: see Geanakoplos, *Emperor Michael Palaeologus*, 21–26.

or farmers' law, the military code for soldiers, and an 'admiralty law' based on the old Rhodian sea law. Of the three the latter had a considerable impact on the West. Originally developed in antiquity by the mariners and merchants of the Greek island of Rhodes, the Rhodian sea law had been adopted by the Hellenistic cities and then by Rome as a model of maritime law. In the Byzantine East where it became the official or semi-official sailor's code and 'admiralty law', it offered practical, time-tested regulations for the handling of collision cases between ships and for such 'proto-capitalist' problems as the relation of the owner of a ship to the cargo owner in the event the cargo was lost. As time went on, provisions of the code seem have been transmitted, by custom, to the early Italian maritime cities, which, as we have seen, were in close relation with Constantinople. One of the Italian sea codes, possibly the first, that of Amalfi (enacted ca. 1000 A.D.) seems to have been based upon it. As Byzantine trade declined, however, from the twelfth century onward and Italy secured the primacy in sea power, the Rhodian sea law *per se* fell more and more into disuse. But some of its more important concepts continued to survive and inspired the development of certain of the commercial and maritime practices of Genoa, Pisa, Venice, and even of the famous 'Consolato del Mare', the early Catalan legal code (written down ca. 1300) of more distant Barcelona.

Regarding navigation it appears that as the great western commercial cities of the Mediterranean began to develop their trade, they borrowed a number of nautical and commercial terms from the Greek East. For example the Byzantine (but originally Latin) term *scala* (landing place for merchandise) was used in the Italian documents from the eleventh century onward. The word *gripos* (a Byzantine type of net or fishing boat) also came into common usage in parts of the Mediterranean, especially Italy, as did the Byzantine *palamarion* (a rope or cable), the latter found in Genoese, Venetian, as well as Catalan documents of the thirteenth century and later. Perhaps an even more interesting derivation is that of the old Viking term *dreki*, referring to the larger type of Viking ship, the prow of which was decorated with the head of a dragon or other animal, and which one scholar believes may have been borrowed ultimately from the Byzantine term *drakon* (dragon). (How this term actually came to the North is another question.) It should be pointed out, however, that a recent survey of nautical and maritime terms in use in the Mediterranean would seem to indicate that, especially from the thirteenth century onward, more terms of this type were borrowed by the Byzantines from western usage than vice versa. Examples are the Venetian *cassela*, chest; *marangon*, ship's carpenter; *galion*, warship (which is first mentioned in a Pisan twelfth century document); and the blended Venetian term *arma*, meaning rigging of a ship, which fused with the older Latinism *arma*.[54]

An obvious but important area of cultural transmission, hitherto hardly investigated, is the possible influence of Byzantine statecraft, more precisely diplomatic practice, on the medieval West. Though Byzantine diplomatic methods were originally derived, at least in part, from Rome and the Hellenistic east, Byzantium developed these to a degree of finesse otherwise unknown in the medieval period.[55] Some Byzantine treatises dealing in whole or in part with diplomatic policy and statecraft were composed (Emperor Constantine VII's *On the Administration of the Empire* is perhaps most significant for example), which provided detailed instructions based on theory and experience as to the most expedient ways to handle difficult political situations. Venice, whose relations with Byzantium were always closer than those of other western powers, seems to have profited most from the Byzantine example. Indeed, a comparison of Venetian and Byzantine diplomatic practice in the late medieval and Renaissance period—for instance, the transmission by ambassadors of periodic reports to the home government (*relazioni*) or the organization of an intelligence service—

[54] On Rhodian sea law see esp. W. Ashburner, *Rhodian Sea Law* (Oxford, 1909). Now W. P. Gormley, 'The Development of the Rhodian-Roman Sea Law to 1681', *Inter-American Law Review*, III (1961) esp. 319 ff. On Byzantine navigational terms and the West see H. and R. Kahane and A. Tietze, *The Lingua Franca in the Levant* (Urbana, 1958) esp. 571, 503, 519, 552, etc. For *dreki* see S. A. Anderson, *Viking Enterprise* (New York, 1936) 62 and W. Vogel, 'Nordische Seefahrten im früheren Mittelalter', *Meereskunde*, I, pt. 7, p. 25. But cf. J. De Vries, *Altnordisches Etymologisches Wörterbuch*, who says the German *Drache* (dragon) comes from Latin *draco*, itself from *ancient* Greek. On the influence of Greek shipbuilders in 15th century Venice, F. Lane, *Venetian Ships and Shipbuilders of the Renaissance* (Baltimore, 1934) 56: 'The finest galley builders in early 15th century were still heirs to [Byzantium].'
[55] There is little done on Byzantine diplomacy. See F. Dölger, *Byzantinische Diplomatik* (Ettal, 1956) for documents and analysis, and for general treatment D. Obolensky, 'Principles and Methods of Byzantine Diplomacy', *XIIe Congrès International des études byzantines* (Ochrida, 1961 *Rapports*). There are a number of monographs on the diplomatic relations of individual emperors, the most recent being Geanakoplos, *Emperor Michael Palaeologus and the West*.

would probably reveal no small degree of direct or indirect Byzantine influence. It may be recalled that Venice, from the eleventh and twelfth centuries, had a large colony in the very heart of Constantinople and that early a substantial number of Greeks had settled in Venice.

In view of what has been discussed in this section, we may make an important but little realized assumption: that Byzantium, with its perfected administrative system, offered to the feudal western world, especially in the great city of Constantinople, something lost to the West since antiquity—a living example of a remarkably developed and organized society under the rule of public authority.

GUILDS

Up to perhaps the twelfth century Constantinople was Europe's chief center of commercial activity. And, as such, its gold coin, termed bezant by the West, was for long accepted as the standard of exchange throughout Europe. Given these economic connections between East and West—interrupted to be sure but never wholly destroyed by the Arabic invasions—it is of no little interest that the western guild system closely resembles, in certain respects, the system which for long obtained at Byzantium.

As we know from the tenth century Byzantine Book of the Prefect, all Greek traders and merchants of the capital (and probably of the other cities as well) were organized into corporations or guilds which were under the direct control of the eparch or prefect of Constantinople. Cattle traders, butchers, fishmongers, bakers, spice and silk merchants, the latter of both raw and finished silk, shipwrights, even notaries, money changers and goldsmiths—all had to belong to the guild organization. As in the later western system regulations were carefully prescribed: no man could belong to two guilds, the hours of wages and labor were carefully regulated, attempts to forestall or corner the market were forbidden, along with disclosure of the secrets of manufacture.[56]

[56] E. Freshfield ed., *Roman Law in the Later Roman Empire: Book of the Eparch* (Cambridge, Eng., 1938). A recent article on the guilds is S. Vryonis, 'Byzantine "Demokratia" and the Guilds in the Eleventh Century', *Dumbarton Oaks Papers*, XVII (Washington, 1963) 289–314. See esp. 289–93 and bibl. in notes 5 and 13. Also Lopez, 'Silk Industry in the Byzantine Empire', *Speculum*, XX (1945) 184 ff.

An important distinction is the fact that, unlike the West where the authority of the state had virtually disappeared, the Byzantine system was not primarily intended to serve the interest of the producers and merchants, but mainly to further governmental control of economic life in the interest of the state. What the actual degree of Byzantine influence may have been on the western guilds has not yet been determined. And of course one cannot overlook the fact that guilds, although with a different purpose, existed already in the late Roman world, the Byzantine being an extension of the Roman. More important perhaps is the fact that similar circumstances might well have evoked similar kinds of responses even in areas distant from one another. Yet until a careful and detailed comparison of the medieval guilds of East and West is made, it is hard to believe that the long familiarity of the Italian maritime republics with Byzantine economic life—many Italian cities possessed commercial colonies in Constantinople itself—had nothing to do with the development of western guild organization and practice.

GRACIOUS LIVING

One result of East-West contact that may not immediately come to mind is the impact of the more refined Byzantine way of life on the lower western standard of living. Byzantine cloths, especially silks and silk brocades, as well as Byzantine utensils and other objects were eagerly sought in the West, and their adoption helped to lead to what we might call a more gracious mode of living. The simpler wooden and occasional stone fortresses and residences of the western nobles were gradually replaced during the crusading period by a type of castle with round towers, a construction which permitted a better defense and deployment of forces and which possibly had been inspired by Byzantine usage. The Normans of Sicily undoubtedly learned something of what they know about masonry construction from the Byzantines.[57] Eleanor of Aquitaine, Queen of France in the twelfth

[57] On the round towers see S. Toy, *A History of Fortification* (London, 1955) 86 ff. On the Normans see H. Brown, *The English Castle* (London, 1936) 23. The Arabs learned fortification from the Greeks and the West also learned from Byzantium via the Arabs. A. Choisi, *L'art de bâtir chez les byzantins* (Paris, 1883) is not helpful here. Now cf. A. Tuulse, *Castles of the Western World* (Vienna, 1958), who is more cautious.

Justinian and his court. Mosaic of San Vitale, Ravenna (mid-6th century). (See p. 47.)

Silk from the grave of Charlemagne at Aachen
(perhaps put there by Otto III in 1000).
(See p. 32.)

Plate 1

Bronze doors of Cathedral of Trani, Italy. (See p. 32.)

Plate 2

Byzantine-inspired bronze doors at Charlemagne's palace chapel at Aachen. See pp. 32, 47.

century, who is often credited with introducing more refinement into the lives of the western nobility, especially the women, acquired some of her tastes in the Arabic and Byzantine East while accompanying the French armies of the Second Crusade.[58] Previous to this, in the tenth century when, as we have noted, the Byzantine princess Theophano married the German Emperor Otto II, and brought to what she called 'barbarian Germany' a large Greek entourage, she scandalized the German inhabitants by taking baths (then considered unhealthy by the westerners) and by wearing rich silken garments. One outspoken German nun said she had a dream in which Theophano appeared in hell for these transgressions! And only a few years later Theophano's cousin, Maria Argyra, shocked the good Peter Damiani, an ascetic Italian monk, by introducing the use of forks to the city of Venice.[59]

The many products of exquisite Byzantine craftsmanship brought westward over the centuries—icons, ivory and jewel carvings, illuminated manuscripts, gold and silver chalices, bronze doors, intricate glassware and other luxury goods— would seem to point to a considerable amount of Byzantine influence. But it is not always easy to determine how much of western Europe was actually affected, and to what degree. Another way to show influence of this kind on a more or less permanent basis would be by citing examples of western words— language is after all the most important bearer of ideas—the origin of which has been shown by philologists to be Byzantine. The wide range of terms adduced below will serve to suggest some of the variety of fields in which the East may have influenced the West.

For example, we have from Venice the term gondola (a Venetian boat) which comes from the Byzantine word *kontoura*, a small boat, and which derived originally from the Greek *kontouros*, meaning 'short-tailed'. From the area of Ravenna comes the Italian *anguria*, cucumber, which derives from the Byzantine

[58] A. Kelly, *Eleanor of Aquitaine and the Four Kings* (Cambridge, Mass., 1950).
[59] Runciman, *Byzantine Civilization*, 237, and on Damiani see A. Capecelatro, *Storia di San Pier Damiano* (Florence, 1862). L. Salzman, *English Industries of the Middle Ages* (Oxford, 1923) 171, says that as late as the thirteenth century forks, though known in the West, were seldom provided; the diner used his own knife, and spoons were commonly used.

angurion. In the field of administration, the English word cadaster (register of real estate) is from the Byzantine *katastihon*. In music the French and English *timbre* is from the Byzantine *tympanon* (tambourine), itself from the ancient Greek *tympanon*, a kettle-drum. The Spanish *botica* (pharmacy) comes from the Byzantine *apotheke* meaning storehouse. And, in connection with fabrics, the old French word *samit* (English samite, referring to a heavy silk fabric) comes from the Byzantine *examitos*, 'six threaded'. With respect to furniture the French and English word *tapis* (carpet), Catalonian, *tapit*, is from the Byzantine *tapeti*. In medicine, the Spanish *quemar*, meaning 'to burn', comes from the Byzantine or late Greek *kaema*, meaning a cauterization (a derivative of the ancient Greek *kaio*, to burn).[60] One could go on with many more examples of this kind. But we may observe here only that in the age-old and intricate Mediterranean game of cultural give-and-take, Byzantine material was not always taken over directly by the receiving western culture but was sometimes mediated through a third one, for example the Arabic, just as Byzantium itself on occasion served as a mediator between other cultures.

RELIGIOUS PIETY:
MUSIC AND THE LITURGY

In recent years, with the growth of interest in the Greek church, it has become increasingly realized that that element of Byzantine civilization which was able to weld together the diverse aspects of her culture and provide its greatest distinctiveness was the Orthodox religion. The peculiar ethos of Byzantine piety was expressed most clearly in the eastern liturgy, a vivid ceremonial in which the worshipper, through personal identification with the drama transpiring in the church, was able, even more than in western liturgy, to experience a kind of mystical foretaste of the blessed life of the hereafter. The importance of the liturgy was so central to Byzantine culture in general that we shall devote some space to a discussion of it.

---

[60] For these terms I am grateful to my friends Prof. Henry and Rene Kahane of the University of Illinois. On the Spanish *quemar* specifically, see J. Corominas, *Breve Diccionario Etimológico de la lengua castellana* (Madrid, 1961). For musical instruments see K. Sachs, *History of Musical Instruments* (New York, 1940).

One, if not the chief example, of the artistic creations of Byzantine religious piety is the hymn—those of Romanos the Melodist, for example, or of John of Damascus or the Patriarch Sergius, one of whom wrote the celebrated Akathistos Hymnos.[61] These Byzantine hymns were a combination of metrical poetic text and music, together designed to underline and emphasize the devotional, other wordly character of the liturgy. Since we are as yet not certain exactly how the music of these hymns sounded (much more work remains to be done in this area) we can perhaps best compare their poetry to such thirteenth century western hymn texts as the Dies Irae or to Jacopone da Todi's Stabat Mater—masterpieces which are at least equalled in expressiveness by the Byzantine hymns.[62] (Many scholars acknowledge, incidentally, that the western mass as a whole was probably not nearly so moving as the Byzantine, and it was not until as late as the end of the fifteenth or beginning of the sixteenth century, with the composition of the highly polyphonic liturgical music of the great Palestrina that it may be considered to surpass the Byzantine liturgy.)

For a long time musicologists have been intrigued by certain similarities to be found in Greek and Latin church music, and particularly by the affinity between Byzantine chant and the western Gregorian, as well as by the fact that certain passages of the Catholic liturgy contain isolated Greek words or phrases. One obvious explanation for such similarities is of course the common Syrian-Hebrew background of both the Christian East and West. But significant too are the subsequent influences that flowed westward from Byzantium. We have already mentioned in the first section of this study the existence of Byzantine colonies in many areas of western Europe, especially with respect to the sixth and seventh century Greco-Syrian merchants in southern Gaul. More important, culturally, were the Byzantine monks who brought their ritual with them and who continued, in such

---

[61] On the hymns see esp. E. Wellesz, *A History of Byzantine Music and Hymnography*, 2nd ed. (Oxford, 1961); G. Reese, *Music in the Middle Ages*, 157 ff., 79, and N. Tomadakes, *Introduction to Byzantine Literature* (in Greek) I (Athens, 1958) 171 ff., 187 ff., and now cf. Jenkins, 'Hellenistic Origins of Byzantine Literature', 39, 52.

[62] E. Wellesz, *Eastern Elements in Western Chant* (Oxford, 1947) 13. Also on the authorship of the Akathistos see bibl. in C. del Grande's ed. of *L'Inno Acatisto* (Florence, 1948) 30–31. On the Grottaferrata hymn writing see Wellesz, *History of Byzantine Music*, 130. Also L. Tardo, *L'antica melurgia bizantina* (Grottaferrata, 1938).

places as the Greek monastery of Grottaferrata near Rome, to write original Greek hymns until past the eleventh century. We know that the famous fourth century Gallic monk St. Martin of Tours was in contact with and deeply influenced by the great champion of Nicene orthodoxy, St. Athanasius, and the monastic tradition of the East. In Rome itself, as we have seen, during the first three centuries Greek was the language of the Roman mass and it does not seem at once to have been supplanted by Latin. Still today in the Good Friday service of the Roman Church, according to the noted scholar E. Wellesz, one may hear sung the alternating chant, first of the Greek words 'Hagios athanatos eleison hemas', then of the Latin equivalent, 'Sanctus immortalis, miserere nobis'. Wellesz cites also the interpolation of the Greek trisagion ('Holy, holy, holy') in the western service, which we know came to the West shortly before 529 by way of Burgundy, the rulers of which were then in close rapport with the Byzantine court.[63]

Another consideration of importance is the fact, previously mentioned, that virtually all the popes of the late seventh and eighth centuries were Greeks or Syrians. Thus the western melody of 'Ave [Maria] gratia plena' ('Hail Mary full of grace') has been shown to be connected directly with the Greek Pope Sergius of the seventh century and was originally sung to the Greek text 'chaire keharitomene'. Still another but curious example is the Latin hymn, 'Ave sponsa incorrupta' of Chester (England) which includes a terribly garbled Greek line 'Karikaristo menitra toche partine', the original words of which had come from the Byzantine troparion, 'chaire keharitomene theotoke parthene'.[64] Not all accretions of Greek phrases in Latin service books are of course to be attributed to remnants of a common ecclesiastical heritage. In certain cases, they might rather be ascribed to the influence of Charlemagne and his learned circle (who, according to one scholar, might even have received Byzantine influences in church music via the Muslims of southern Spain, with whom Charlemagne's court had frequent contacts.) Charlemagne, we are told, after hearing members of a Greek embassy to his court chanting their religious hymns, became so

[63] See Wellesz, *Eastern Elements in Western Chant*, 201.
[64] Ibid.

attracted that he ordered the Byzantine hymns to be translated into Latin.[65]

Claims for extensive western borrowings from Byzantine religious music are still a matter of some dispute. It is not yet entirely clear, for example, what influence the Byzantine musical system of *echoi* (a grouping of tones in a kind of scale and constituting a melody type) may have had on the western modal system. On the other hand, there is a reasonable degree of agreement that Pope Gregory the Great, whether or not he should be credited with the reform of the western ecclesiastical chant, was deeply influenced by the eastern hymnody. And this despite the fact that as long-time papal apocrisiarius (ambassador) in Constantinople he had refused to learn Greek on the grounds that the Byzantine clergy were too worldly! But it seems significant that he set about reorganizing his Schola Cantorum, a training school for instruction in the chant, immediately after his return from Byzantium, where we know that he was a frequent observer of the practice of the Byzantine chant at the cathedral of St. Sophia.[66]

Another vestige of Byzantine music that still remains today had to do with the acclamations, or *polychronia*, which were addressed to a newly enthroned emperor. It is worthy of note that at the coronation of Charlemagne in St. Peter's on Christmas day of the year 800, the populace assembled in the Basilica broke forth, at the appropriate moment, into a form of Byzantine *polychronion*—a practice which is today still preserved in the Orthodox salutation to a newly appointed bishop. Though we evidently cannot credit the medieval Greeks with the invention of the organ, Constantinople was the early medieval center for organ building: we know that in 757 Pepin, King of the Franks, requested and received an organ from the Byzantine Emperor.[67]

---

[65] Wellesz, *ibid.*, 168, 201. See John the Deacon's *Life of Gregory the Great* (cited in Reese, *Music in the Middle Ages*, 120). Charlemagne attempted to revise the gospel text with the aid of Byzantine scholars. Wellesz, 201. Also see G. Gray, *The History of Music* (London, 1928) 17. On the Arab influence on Charlemagne's court see H. G. Farmer, *Historical Facts for the Arabian Musical Influence* (London, 1930) 1–39.

[66] On the *echoi* see Reese, *op. cit.*, 90. Also on Gregory see Reese, *op. cit.*, 73, 90 and Wellesz, *op. cit.*

[67] Reese, *op. cit.*, 120. G. Frotscher, *Geschichte des Orgelspiels*, I (Berlin, 1935). The gift was evidently that of a hydraulic organ (which had already been known to the Romans and Egyptians). William of Malmesbury describes a hydraulic organ made by Gerbert (d. 1003), implying that this was still unique in the West as late

Much more evidence of western indebtedness to eastern religious music—and quite possibly a few of the reverse as well—will probably be found by researchers. One hindrance to such a study has been the undue emphasis placed on the schism between the two churches—a fact which has led some too readily to believe that little cultural interaction was possible, at least after 1054, the date commonly taken as marking the complete rupture between the Greek and Latin churches. But this interpretation is probably much exaggerated, because for centuries the two great bodies of Christians had looked upon one another as part of one undivided Christian church.[68] Indeed, the schism did not become truly definitive, it would seem, until as late as 1204, when the Latins captured Constantinople and forced the Greek population to accept Roman Catholicism. On the lower levels in fact the ordinary man of East and West was hardly even aware of any religious rupture until long after 1054 and probably not until well into the twelfth century.[69]

Another subject of significance, the study of which is only now developing, is the influence of Byzantine piety, especially of the Greek 'Basilian' monks, on western monastic life. When during the ninth, tenth and early eleventh centuries many Byzantine monks fled the Arabic invasions of Sicily and southern Italy to move further north, they brought with them the traditional ideals and practices of Byzantine monasticism, especially of the ascetic type. Because of the piety of these monks they were, in this period, almost always well received, and we find examples of Byzantine-Latin symbiosis in certain western monasteries such as at Monte Cassino, where in the late tenth century the famous Greek monk St. Nilus lived with Latin monks and wrote hymns to St. Benedict. (At this time Monte Cassino even had a Greek abbot.) In Rome, at Sts. Boniface and Alexius, Basilian and

as the eleventh century (see *Chronicle of the Kings of England*, transl. J. Giles [London, 1847] 175). On the *polychronion* see H. Tillyard, 'The Acclamation of Emperors in the Byzantine Ritual', *Annual of the British School at Athens*, 18 (1911–12) 239–41.

[68] S. Runciman, *Eastern Schism* (Oxford, 1955) 159 ff. Y. Congar, *After Nine Hundred Years* (New York, 1959).

[69] See discussion and bibl. in D. Geanakoplos, 'On the Schism of the Greek and Roman Churches: A Confidential Papal Directive for the Implementation of Union', *Greek Orthodox Theological Review*, I (1954) 16 ff. Also L. Bréhier, 'Normal Relations between Rome and the Churches of the East before the Schism of the eleventh century', *Constructive Quarterly*, IV (1916) 669 ff.

Benedictine monks lived together, each under its own rule, all under a Greek abbot. The Byzantine traits that most attracted and influenced the West were the high degree of Byzantine spirituality, and the monks' sanctity of life (including their manner of prayer), in a period of general western corruption and ecclesiastical degradation. The severe Basilian ideal of manual labor—at this time western monks usually employed serfs to do their work—and the patristic erudition of some of the Greek monks also seem to have inspired their western counterparts. It is interesting that the monastic houses of the West most connected with the Cluniac reform movement—St. Vannes at Verdun, Cluny under Hugh, and others, had the closest relations with the Greek monks. It is therefore very possible that Byzantine influence may have played a certain role in the western reform movement of the period. This, incidentally, is a consideration which has hitherto been generally overlooked.[70]

Finally, in connection with the development of popular piety in particular, one might profitably investigate the influence of Byzantine ideas on western attitudes regarding veneration of the Virgin—Mariology, that is. After all, when Mariology in the West was still in a rather undeveloped phase, the cult of the Virgin, who was looked upon as the protectress of Constantinople, was second to none in the East. In the late eleventh century a new and influential form of popular literature emerged in the West, the so-called Stories of *Miracles of the Virgin*. These, more imaginative than previous legends of this type, were concerned with the miraculous intervention of the Virgin in the lives of her devotees and, now like the more extravagant stories of the East, came to emphasize her compassion for individuals, not so much her interest in churches or religious corporations as such. Some of the stories of course were taken over from ancient Latin tradition, but it seems certain that a not inconsiderable number now came from the Byzantine East. Thus the famous reformer Peter Damiani, one of the earliest collectors of such stories, tells us that one of his chief

---

[70] I have been for a long time interested in the possible influence of Byzantine ideas and practices on the Cluniac Reform Movement. See for background R. Weiss, 'The Greek Culture of South Italy in the Middle Ages', in *Proceedings of the British Academy* (1951) 23–50 and esp. McNulty and Hamilton, ' "Orientale Lumen" et "Magistra Latinitas" ,' 181–216. Now J. Leclercq, 'Les Relations entre le Monachisme Oriental et Occidental dans le haut Moyen Age, *Millénaire du Mt. Athos* II (Chevtogne, 1965) 76 ff.

sources of information was the Cardinal-priest Stephen, a Burgundian who has served as papal legate to Constantinople in the
mid-eleventh century.

No less important than the newly developing emphasis on
veneration of the Virgin was the influence of the many sacred
relics of the early Christian church which had begun to flow
westwards, already before the twelfth century and especially
after the mass despoiling of the Greek churches by the Latins in
1204. This wealth of relics in certain ways helped to bring about
an alteration even in the appearance of western churches, and
thus, together with the increased emphasis on Mariology,
made a deep impression on the developing western forms of
public and private devotion in this period.[71]

ART

Unlike the Byzantine service to literature which in many
respects may appear to have been mainly a holding operation
from antiquity, the Byzantine contribution to art was essentially
original and attained a degree of expressiveness that has
rarely been equalled. Byzantine art, in particular its painting,
has been much in vogue recently, especially because of its
relatively abstract character as well as richness of color. We shall
have to limit our remarks here to the more important aspects of
Byzantine art, concentrating especially on Italy where its influence was greatest.

It is no exaggeration to say that Italy, from the sixth to the
thirteenth century, was an artistic province of Byzantium. In its
many monuments of painting and mosaics can be seen the dis-
tinctive traits of Byzantine art—its power, mysticism, color and
line—qualities which sought to represent to the viewer something
more than the appearance of nature, rather to evoke emotions
expressing the reality of the other world.

[71] See especially R. Southern, *Making of the Middle Ages* (New Haven, 1953),
246–56. Recent works helpful here are, for the Greek viewpoint, J. Kalogerou,
Mary the Perpetual Virgin Theotokos according to the Orthodox Faith (in Greek) (Salonika)
1957) and J. Anastasiou, *The Presentation of the Theotokos: History, Iconography and
Hymnography* (in Greek) (Salonika, 1959). For the Catholic view, M. Gordillo,
'Mariologia Orientalis', in *Orientalia Christiana Analecta*, 141 (Rome, 1954) and M.
Jugie, *L'Immaculée Conception dans l'Ecriture Sainte et dans la Tradition orientale* (Rome,
1952) 225–40. Also Leclerq, 'Relations', 77 f.

We may begin with the Byzantine mosaics at Ravenna, especially the portraits of the Emperor Justinian, his consort Theodora, and the imperial court. The refulgent cubes (tessera) of colored glass and stone, set at various angles, reflect the light in such a way as to suggest the celestical richness of the court of God's vicar on earth. In these mosaics and also the wall paintings of the Ravenna churches, in some of those of Rome throughout the various medieval centuries (of the artist Cavallini for instance), and in the Norman cathedral of Monreale in Sicily with the imposing figure of the Byzantine Pantocrator in the apse, the tradition of the East is clearly apparent. Further north, in Venice, which was almost a Byzantine city as Diehl puts it (or 'another Byzantium' as Bessarion declared in the fifteenth century),[72] the mosaics of St. Mark's cathedral—the building itself almost an exact replica of the church of the Holy Apostles in Constantinople—also belong to the artistic sphere of Byzantium. Modeled evidently after St. Mark's is the dome structure of the church of Saint-Front in Perigeux, France, while still further to the north, in Charlemagne's capital of Aachen, Germany, Charlemagne's palace chapel was modeled after San Vitale in Ravenna, itself an imitation of the church of Saints Sergius and Bacchus in Constantinople. Also to be found at Aachen are bronze doors and other specimens of Byzantine or Byzantine-inspired workmanship.[73]

While looking with admiration at the great monuments of Byzantine art, the medieval westerner prized even more the smaller but precious works of the Byzantine craftsmen. Some ivory carvings sent as gifts to western princes or prelates still remain, and the French monastery of St. Denis possessed textiles ornamented with figures of eastern type. Along with their creations the Byzantine craftsmen themselves not infrequently moved to the West and they, probably even more than the products of their art, seem to have been responsible for suggesting new ideas and methods to local western artists. Thus in the seventh century when the Greek monk and later Archbishop of Canterbury

[72] Ch. Diehl, *Une République patricienne: Venise* (Paris, 1928). D. Geanakoplos, *Greek Scholars in Venice*, 35. On the Pantocrator see now C. Capizzi, *Pantocrator* (title in Greek, article in Italian) (Rome, 1964) 302–29.

[73] The Byzantine monuments of Torcello, Venice's original settlement, date back to the seventh century, and esp. the twelfth. Also see Tschan, *St. Bernward of Hildesheim*, II, 142, 168–69, and 200, n. 6.

Theodore of Tarsus came to Britain, his entourage may have included easterners expert in the technique of sculpture. Similarly, the painted figures of the Evangelists in the Lindisfarne gospels were modeled basically on Byzantine or Italo-Byzantine originals and we know of the Byzantine style in Northumbria and Mercia, and in the tenth and eleventh centuries in Wessex.[74] At Monte Cassino in southern Italy, in the eleventh century, under the aegis of the Abbot Desiderius, Byzantine art objects—bronze doors among them—were purchased in Constantinople and sent to adorn the great abbey.[75] And later, during the twelfth century, the interior of the great French monastery church of Cluny was decorated by frescoes in so Byzantine a style that they may even have been done by a native Greek.[76]

We must touch, lastly, on the difficult problem of Byzantine influence on the art of the Italian Renaissance. A few scholars believe that even the beginnings of realism in western painting, usually connected with the name of the Italian Giotto (as the Italian sources put it Giotto freed himself from 'la maniera greca', meaning the Byzantine style), should rather be attributed to the inspiration of Byzantine art.[77] Whether this be true or whether it was, as seems more likely, the result of a parallel though independent development of Italian and Byzantine art reverting back in each case to ancient Hellenistic models, there is no doubt that in the late thirteenth and fourteenth centuries a good deal of Byzantine painting was becoming more interested in showing emotion, more personal and individualized—in short more realistic and humanized. We may cite as evidence of these qualities the Byzantine masterpieces at the monastery of the Chora (Kariye Camii) in Constantinople, in the churches of Milesevo, Sopocani,

---

[74] Talbot Rice, *Byzantine Art*, 250–52; Runciman, *Byzantine Civilization*, 238. Also Talbot Rice, *English Art*, 22, 133–35, 250.

[75] Bloch, 'Montecassino, Byzantium and the West', 194. It is believed that the mosaics in the Baptistery of Florence were decorated by Byzantine or Byzantine-trained craftsmen in the thirteenth century. Cf. J. Beckwith's recent *The Art of Constantinople* (London, 1961) 137.

[76] The church of Cluny was begun in 1089 and dedicated in 1131. See J. Gay, 'L'abbaye de Cluny et Byzance au début du XIIe siècle', *Échos d'Orient*, XXX (1931) 84–90. Also J. Leclercq, 'Spiritualité et culture a Cluny', *Spiritualità Cluniacense* (Todi, 1960) 101 ff.

[77] See P. Schweinfurth, 'Die Bedeutung der byzantinischen Kunst für die Stilbildung der Renaissance', in *Die Antike*, IX (1933) 2. Also cf. the old work of R. Byron and T. Rice, *The Birth of Western Painting* (London, 1930) and C. Diehl, *Manuel de l'art byzantin*, 2nd ed. (Paris, 1925–26) 743–44. Also see next notes.

and Gracanica in Yugoslavia, to a lesser extent in the churches of
Mistra (near Sparta), and the very recently uncovered paintings
at St. Nicholas Orfanos and in other churches of Thessalonika.
Certain similar characteristics are to be found in Italy in the
works of the Florentine artist Cimabue, the Sienese Duccio, and
in certain other Italian Trecento painters.

In the view of the critics Charles Diehl and especially the
more recent authority André Grabar, it was Italian painting,
through the Byzantine influence exerted on Duccio and Giotto,
that derived the greater benefit from the renewed contact of the
Byzantines with paintings in the Hellenistic spirit. For despite
their superb creations the Byzantine artists inspired by the realistic
aesthetic of the Hellenistic models remained in the minority.
And during the course of the fourteenth century, when their
Italian contemporaries were advancing to the freer art forms
which were to become characteristic of the Italian Renaissance,
Byzantine painting in general reverted to the more conventional
Byzantine forms. Nevertheless, despite this reversion to the
older, more traditional methods (a phenomenon perhaps attributable, according to Grabar, to Byzantine mistrust of anything
connected with the Latins), some paintings were produced
during this period which equal or surpass in brilliance and
decorativeness the best works of the earlier Byzantine epochs.
What is particularly striking is that scenes in these fourteenth
century paintings display almost a new type of experimental
boldness which, in the elongated, attenuated figures and the
extraordinary coloring used, seems in certain respects to anticipate
the style of El Greco.[78]

These two developments in Byzantine painting, then, both a
part of the remarkable Palaeologan Renaissance of the thirteenth
to the fifteenth centuries (remarkable because a Renaissance in
both art and letters could occur while the Empire itself was
collapsing on every side), have been termed by art historians the
Macedonian and Cretan schools of painting. Macedonian refers
in general to the shorter-lived, more realistic art of the end of the
thirteenth and first decades of the fourteenth century radiating
primarily from the center Thessalonika. The so-called Cretan

[78] A. Grabar, *Byzantine Painting* (Geneva, 1953) 45–46. Diehl, *op. cit.*, 743–44.
Cf. V. Lazarev, 'Duccio and Thirteenth Century Greek Icons', *Burlington Magazine*,
LIX (1931) 159. See also bibl. below, Chaps. 4–5.

refers to the reversion to (or in some cases continuation of) the more traditional modes of painting, found especially at Mt. Athos or on Crete itself, and extending through the sixteenth century and even later. Because of a growing awareness today of the complexity of Byzantine painting in this period, however, such a distinction between the two schools seems too rigid and is indeed often difficult to make clear in the paintings that have survived. It may therefore be better, as some scholars are now doing, to scrap the use of these particular terms which were originally coined a half century ago by the French art historian Millet.[79]

Sometimes overlooked even by art historians is the presence of Greek painters in Italy after the fall of Constantinople in 1453—men who continued to produce works in the more or less traditional Byzantine manner until as late as the seventeenth century. Their paintings, often referred to as belonging to the Cretan school, are admittedly not of primary importance. But they are frequently of quality, especially those produced by the group of painters living in the Greek community of Venice (about which we shall speak in Chapter 4).

It is the opinion of modern Greek art historians as well as certain western critics that the celebrated El Greco, born Domenikos Theotokopoulos on the Venetian-held island of Crete some four or five decades after the fall of Constantinople, may be termed, from certain viewpoints, one of the last of the 'Byzantine' painters.[80] El Greco studied for four years in Venice and later

---

[79] There is a growing literature on this complex problem, the terms of which, Macedonian and Cretan, were first used in G. Millet, *Recherches sur l'iconographie de l'Evangile . . . d'après les monuments de Mistra, Macédoine, et du Mont-Athos* (Paris, 1916) who based his distinction *entirely* on iconographical considerations. D. Talbot Rice believes the two terms should be avoided, an opinion he expressed to me personally in Athens in 1964. He thinks the term Cretan in particular is used much too loosely to refer to (1) 'half-Italian' icons (2) wall paintings in Crete (3) paintings on Mt. Athos, which are much unlike those of Crete, though referred to as Cretan. See now Talbot Rice, *Art of the Byzantine Era* (New York, 1963) 219ff. Cf. also the views of A. Xyngopoulos, *Historical Sketch of Religious Painting after the Conquest* (in Greek) (Athens, 1957) 1–12, and esp. his *Thessalonique et la Peinture Macédonienne* (Athens, 1955), and M. Chatzidakes, 'Rapport entre la peinture de la Macédoine et la Crète au XIVe siècle', *Hellenika* (1954) esp. 138 f.; another recent work of Talbot Rice, *The Art of Byzantium* (New York, 1959) 334–37, and the old work of Byron, *The Byzantine Achievement*, 216–19.

[80] Talbot Rice, *Byzantine Art*, 256, and his *Art of the Byzantine Era*, 232. R. Byron, *The Byzantine Achievement* (London, 1929) 38, 218; F. Rutter, review in *Burlington Magazine*, IX (1932) 274; J. Willumsen, *La Jeunesse du Peintre El Greco* (Paris, 1927) 161ff., etc. For more on El Greco see below Chaps. 4 and 5 on the Greek painters in Venice, with bibliography.

adopted as his permanent residence the Castilian city of Toledo. But despite the undeniable influence of these two centers on the formation of his technic and style, he never seems to have forgotten his Byzantine heritage. Indeed a remarkable document very recently discovered seems to indicate that he lived in Crete until the age of 25, not merely until 18 as was previously believed.[81] The point is that this greatest of all Greek painters may have been more deeply influenced in his early years by the Cretan-Byzantine style of his native island than most western scholars have been willing to admit. In that period painters were apprenticed rather early, so that by the age of 25 'Maestro' El Greco should already have had some ten years experience in the Byzantine style.

Italy, then, the prime area of Byzantine artistic influence, owed much to Byzantium: not only the models from which many Italian artists worked, not only the bronze doors, gorgeous fabrics, enamels and richly illuminated manuscripts which were brought to the West, but, of more underlying importance, the symbolic pattern of church decoration and even the iconographical schemes for some of the more important religious motifs. Thus, it may be said that all through the medieval period, from the sixth century probably even to the beginning of the Renaissance in the fourteenth, Byzantine art profoundly influenced that of Italy and, through Italy, many areas of western Europe.

CONCLUSION

What may we say in conclusion about the impact of Byzantine culture on the West? How is its influence to be assessed? It must be pointed out, first, that such important facets of Western culture as parliaments, Gothic architecture, and Scholasticism, above all the *basic* institutions of feudalism, manorialism, and chivalry were essentially Germano-Latin in origin, there being little or no Byzantine influence whatever. Indeed in connection with feudalism, chivalry, and Scholasticism certain influences seem rather to have flowed from West to East. But though not a few examples may be cited of medieval Greek acculturation to individual western practices, especially among the Byzantine upper classes, the Byzantine influence on the West

[81] See below Chap. 4, note 47, article of Mertzios.

seems to have been far stronger than the reverse. This was partly because at least up to the twelfth or early thirteenth century western civilization in almost all aspects was markedly inferior to the eastern (in classical Greek learning of course few westerners could equal the Greeks until the High Renaissance), and also because owing to its developing antipathy to the West, the East in general—the lower classes, monks and lesser clergy in particular —strongly resisted the adoption of Latin customs.

Though it must be clear from our investigation that there was a more or less continuing influence of Byzantium on western culture from the fourth all the way to at least the end of the fifteenth century, it is no less manifest that the degree of influence varied greatly from field to field, depending not only on the pattern of contacts but on the attitudes and receptivity of the various western areas. Italy for example was more deeply influenced than more distant, rather conservative France and immeasurably more than England. Nor is it easy to ascertain how deeply the Byzantine influences we have discussed penetrated the various classes of the western social structure, though it would seem that because of greater contacts with the East and a generally more flexible attitude the upper classes and merchants were most affected. It should not be overlooked also that our judgements as to the degree of influence must of necessity be tempered by the scarcity of the evidence remaining as well as by the status of scholarly research at the moment. It is easier to show, on the basis of the extant artistic monuments, what the eastern influence may have been in art than, say, in the development of the guild system, where we are reduced to hypothesis or deduction. Similarly we should consider, I think (as is usually not done), the evidence of such phenomena as vocabulary borrowings—borrowings which in most cases would not have taken place unless there were at least some degree of cultural transfer involved. On the other hand, the mere presence in the West of a great many Byzantine luxury items should not mislead us into assigning the same importance to these as cultural agents as we would attach to the adoption of Byzantine ideas, institutions, or techniques—considerations which in the long run were to prove of more permanent value.

With these qualifications and bearing in mind that western

culture was at bottom Germano-Latin, we may then affirm our findings that Byzantium, through its amalgamation of classiciusm and the more original 'Byzantine' elements of its culture, above all its unique brand of Christianity which permeated every facet of medieval Greek life, was able, directly or indirectly, to influence a great many aspects of western cultural development: in certain types of art and architecture, in the sphere of industrial techniques, in law and statecraft, in navigational terms and regulations, the recovery of classical Greek literature and possibly the composition of the romance, in the development of a more refined mode of living and in some forms of religious piety and music as well as in religious thought. In these aspects of *most* of the cultural areas meaningful to medieval man there seems to have been some tangible specific evidence of Byzantine influence in one area or another of western European society. Once more, however, it should be emphasized that these influences ranged from the very minor in some spheres to the very substantial in others.

No doubt the Byzantine contributions were more passive and less creative in certain fields, for instance in literature, philosophy, and science, which had in the main been taken over from the ancient Greeks and which, especially in the case of Aristotle, were first transmitted to the West via the Arabs. Yet even in their vaunted preservation of the ancient literary masterpieces the Byzantines were able to make a few contributions of their own. For example they developed certain philological methods of scholarship—methods which if sometimes faulty, nonetheless had more impact than is usually realized on the development of Renaissance textual criticism and which therefore could not help but influence the meaning and interpretation of the ancient texts transmitted (the ancient tragedies for instance).[82] Even in the domain of science, despite their almost worshipful devotion to ecclesiastical tradition as well as to the authority of the ancient Greek writers, a few Byzantines seem to have broken out of

[82] See e.g. U. von Wilamowitz-Moellendorff, *Euripides-Herakles*, I (Berlin, 1889) 194, and Geanakoplos, *Greek Scholars in Venice*, 288, 290. Cf. also now P. Kristeller, 'Umanesimo italiano e Bisanzio', *Lettere italiane*, XVI (1964) esp. 8–9, who thinks the selection and order in which western Renaissance humanists read certain ancient Greek authors (e.g. Aristophanes beginning with *Pluto*, Euripides with *Hecuba*), and the tendency of treating Plato, Aristotle, and the patristic authors together with the poets and authors, was probably influenced to a large degree by Byzantine practice.

these restraints and at least to have anticipated certain later western scientific developments. Moreover, as we have observed, in several other areas there can be no doubt that the Byzantines were able to make truly *original* contributions, specifically in art and architecture, in forms of religious piety and ecclesiastical literature, and, perhaps not least, in providing to the West something often overlooked by historians—a living example of a state with a highly centralized administration and tradition of statecraft under the rule of public law. In view of these considerations it is obvious that Byzantine civilization was far from being the mere 'fossilization of antiquity' that western historians were wont to term it not many years ago.

In sum, then, it was the rich content, the diverse elements *both ancient and medieval*, of Byzantium's unique cultural synthesis, that enabled it to attract the interest of the westerners and, little by little and despite the frequent reluctance or outright hostility of the Latins, to provide them with inspiration and guidance. And so in 1453 when Constantinople finally succumbed to the Turks, not only had Byzantium handed over its previous legacy of ancient Greek culture to the West—now prepared in part by the East itself to receive it—but, no less important, the West had assimilated a good deal of the products of Byzantium's own creativity. As a consequence of what might be called this long-term process of cultural infiltration, Byzantium played a much more pervasive role than is generally realized in molding the civilization of the medieval and hence, indirectly, of the modern, western world.

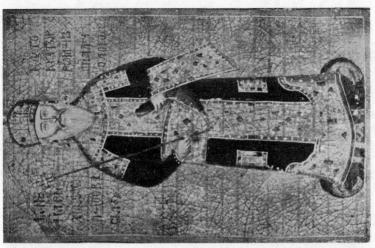

Byzantine Emperor Manuel II Palaeologus
(early 15th century). (See p. 153.)

Plate 3

King Roger II of Norman Sicily crowned by Christ. Mosaic
in the Martorana of Palermo (mid-12th century). (See p. 33.)

Emperor John VIII Palaeologus entering Florence on his way to the Council. Detail from fresco 'The Procession of the Magi' by Benozzo Gozzoli in Capella Medicea (c. 1459). (See pp. 96-7.)

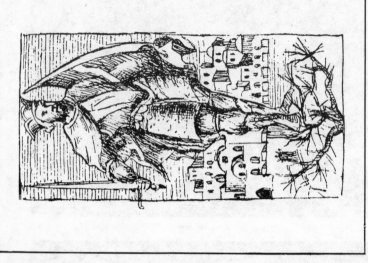

Emperor Michael VIII Palaeologus. Miniature in Greek Ms. VII, 22, of Marciana by George Klontzas (1590). Note western influence. (See p. 134.)

Plate 4

CHURCH AND STATE IN THE BYZANTINE EMPIRE: A RECONSIDERATION OF THE PROBLEM OF CAESAROPAPISM

I

INTRODUCTION: THE PROBLEM

IN the medieval theocratic societies of both the Byzantine East and the Latin West, where the influence of Christian precepts so strongly pervaded all aspects of life, it was inevitable that the institutions of church and state, of *sacerdotium* and *regnum* to use the traditional Latin terms, be closely tied to one another. But whereas in the West, at least after the Investiture conflict of the late eleventh century, the pope managed to exert a strong political influence over secular rulers, notably the Holy Roman emperor, in the East, from the very foundation of Constantinople in the fourth century, the Byzantine emperor seemed clearly to dominate over his chief ecclesiastical official, the patriarch.

Certain modern scholars, impressed by what they consider to have been the unlimited control exercised by the Byzantine emperor over the church, have applied to the imperial authority the term 'Caesaropapism'—meaning the concentration of complete civil as well as religious power in the hands of one person as if he were at once both emperor and pope. The implication here is that the Byzantine church was in effect a department of state. To be sure in recent years a number of authorities have become more cautious in the use of the term Caesaropapism, but the word is still not infrequently encountered in the works of important medievalists, western as well as Byzantine. It is the aim of this study to re-examine the relationship between imperial authority and the Byzantine church and by means of a new approach to and organization of the material, to define more clearly the degree and kind of control actually exercised by the emperor over the eastern church. As a result it is hoped that a more accurate appraisal will be possible of the validity of the term Caesaropapism as applied to Byzantium.[1]

A primary reason for the wide currency of the term Caesaropapism[2]—which by the way is of modern western coinage and is not to be found in the Byzantine sources—is that scholars have too often attempted to define Byzantine political theory from the western point of view. In the west, at least after the year 800, *sacerdotium* and *regnum* were in the hands of two different persons, pope and western emperor, separated geographically by the Alps and who, after the mid-eleventh century, were at times in violent conflict for political supremacy (through to be sure papal authority in strictly spiritual matters was seldom questioned by the emperor). In Byzantium, on the other hand, there was no such sharp dichotomy between the religious and secular spheres. Though two individuals, emperor and patriarch, held different offices, they resided in the same place and more often than not worked together. Indeed, throughout the Byzantine period a number of imperial legal enactments as well as pronouncements by leading canonists attest to the theory of close co-operation between emperor and patriarch for the well-being of the Empire. In the words of the oft-quoted statement from the *Epanagoge* of the Emperor Leo VI (which may well reflect the influence of the famous Patriarch Photius): 'As the polity (*politeia*) consists, like man, of parts and members, the greatest and most necessary parts are the emperor and the patriarch. Wherefore the peace and felicity of subjects in body and soul is [depends on] the agreement and concord of the kingship and priesthood in all things'.[3] More important from the pragmatic view (since the Epanagoge was never actually promulgated) is a statement that the historian Leo the Deacon ascribes to the tenth century Emperor John Tzimiskes: 'I acknowledge two powers in this life: the priesthood and the Empire; the Creator of the world has

[1] For bibliog. on the question of Caesaropapism see Appendix, Bibliographical Note B.

[2] The *Oxford Dictionary of the Christian Church*, ed. F. Cross (London, 1957) under 'Caesaropapism' says that the term means absolute control over all aspects of the church 'including matters (e.g., doctrine) normally reserved to ecclesiastical authority'. This is the interpretation of the term as used in this study.

[3] In E. Barker, *Social and Political Thought in Byzantium* (Oxford, 1957) 92.

entrusted to the former the care of souls, to the latter the care of bodies. If neither part is damaged, the well-being of the world is secure'.[4]

The above statements, which can easily be multiplied, express then the ideal relationship of *imperium* and *sacerdotium* in terms of a kind of symphonic duet between two divinely ordained institutions, the primary function of which is to preserve order and maintain harmony in imitation of the divine order in heaven. This constitution of two divinely appointed and in a sense parallel authorities is, it is clear, far from the concept of Caesaropapism or complete subordination of one power to the other.

Now even a cursory glance at Byzantine history reveals that this was an *ideal* principle; in actual fact conflict between emperor and patriarch was not infrequent. Indeed it would seem that in such cases the will of the emperor, with a few notable exceptions, prevailed. If we except the unique case of Patriarch Michael Cerularius with his exalted claims to religious and secular power,[5] the church as a whole generally accepted the authority of the emperor at least to share in the administrative control of the church to the point of his naming and even, though under strong protest, deposing patriarchs. To the superficial observer of Byzantine events, then, especially from the vantage point of the West (where by the twelfth century the pope had in the main triumphed over secular attempts to interfere in ecclesiastical administration) it is easy to understand why it seemed that an absolutist control of the Byzantine emperor over the church obtained. In western eyes the Byzantine emperor had usurped not only the function of the pope over church administration but even some of the spiritual powers of the clergy as well.

Before we begin our analysis it should be noted that there are certain fundamental difficulties inherent in the source material itself that make it difficult to reach consistent con-

[4] *Ibid.*, 96. Also cf. the famous novel 6 of Justinian (in Barker, 75) which likewise emphasizes the concord between the two powers. And see a letter of John II Comnenus to the pope on the division of spheres (in S. Lampros, *Neos Hellenomnemon* [in Greek] XI [Athens, 1914] 109–11).

[5] Not all critics agree about Cerularius' actual intentions; it is sometimes said, perhaps not quite accurately, that he aspired to be a Byzantine Hildebrand. On this see the qualifying remarks of J. Hussey, *Church and Learning in the Byzantine Empire* (London, 1937) 152–57 and esp. A. Michel, *Humbert und Kerullarios* (Paderborn, 1925–30); also L. Bréhier, *Le schisme orientale du XIe siècle* (Paris, 1899) (old but still useful); and Bury, 'Roman Emperors', in *Selected Essays* (Cambridge, 1930) 210–14.

clusions. In the first place, Byzantium, like other medieval states, never possessed an official written constitution summarizing the basic organization of government with its distribution of authority. No official document lists all the specific constitutional powers of the emperor. Not until near the very end of the Empire in fact was an official attempt even made by the imperial government to set down in writing the emperor's powers, or at least part of them, over the church.[6] To be sure there are the numerous scattered sources contained in both civil and canon law, such as the edicts of individual emperors, also the *nomocanones* and the acts of local or ecumenical councils. There are too the collections and interpretations of the great canonists Zonaras, Balsamon, Chomatianos, and especially of Matthew Blastares, all of whose pronouncements on church affairs, like those of the earlier Roman jurisconsults on civil law, came with the passing of time to assume a semi-official force of law—to form a kind of tradition in the church. What complicated the situation further was that each emperor, as the fountainhead of law, was able to legislate on his own, the usual practice in the event of objection to a predecessor's edict being to blunt the force of it through enactment of a new one. Moreover, with respect to canon law and its interpretation, there was nothing at bottom, except of course conscience, to prevent the individual canonist from expounding his own understanding of the existing canonical texts. Nor should we overlook the development of certain practices or customs in connection with church-state relations which in time also began to take on the force of law—practices such as the patriarch's demand of an orthodox confession of faith from the emperor at the time of his coronation.[7]

These conditions, then, sometimes make it possible to offer more than one seemingly valid interpretation of the same texts, especially of the ecclesiastical canons which are so fundamental in determining the extent of imperial power over the church. For example, some historians have emphasized that Theodore Balsamon, the authoritative twelfth century canonist, remarks in

[6] See below, text and note 69.
[7] See below, text and note 50. This seems to have been demanded by the patriarch first from the Monophysite-leaning Anastasius in the late sixth century. On the insistence of certain later patriarchs on the moral fitness of the emperor for his office see below, text and notes 31-32.

one passage that the emperor is 'subject neither to the laws of the empire nor to the ecclesiastical canons of the church'.[8] This statement certainly seems unambiguous enough. To judge, however, from the context in which this celebrated passage is to be found—a discussion as to whether priests and monks can, at the order of a bishop or the emperor, engage in secular types of work[9]—Balsamon's statement appears to fall under the rubric of disciplinary canons and therefore to have no connection with the area of dogma. (Alivizatos and other modern Greek theologians in fact maintain that the term ecclesiastical canon does not apply to dogma but only to ecclesiastical discipline and administration.)[10] Hence it would seem that the apparent significance of this particular passage, which is frequently cited in support of unlimited imperial power over all aspects of the church, has, in the light of its context, to be definitely qualified.

In trying to emphasize the extent of imperial power over the church one may point as evidence to certain religious titles given the emperor, especially in the works of the canonists—titles such as 'anointed of the Lord' (*Christos Kyriou*) or that of 'living icon of Christ' (*zosa eikon Christou*). Yet a scrutiny of the sources reveals that at least the twelfth century canonist Balsamon and especially the fourteenth century Matthew Blastares (whose work is considered to mark the culmination of all previous canonistic development)[11] sometimes refer also to the patriarchs in precisely these same words.[12]

[8] See Balsamon, 'In canonem XVI Concilii Carthaginiensis', ed. MPG, vol. 138, p. 93 (cited in this respect by A. Vasiliev, *History of the Byzantine Empire*, 470). In another passage Balsamon (in Rhalles and Potlis, *Syntagma of Divine and Holy Canons* [in Greek], IV, 544–45), says that 'the power and activity of the emperor concern body and souls while the power and activity of the patriarch concern only the soul'.

[9] Balsamon's conclusion is that since a bishop can order priests and monks to engage in certain secular work, so all the more can the emperor do so, as he can nominate bishops (Rhalles and Potlis, II, 229). But note again this does not here refer to dogma. Cf. Zonaras, *op. cit.*, III, 336.

[10] *Horos* is the Byzantine term for the decision of an ecumenical council regarding dogma. See H. Alivizatos, *The Holy Canons* (in Greek) (Athens, 1949) 21.

[11] See L. Bréhier, *Dict. d'histoire et geog. eccl.*, IX, cols. 160–61.

[12] John of Euchaita of the eleventh century refers to both emperor and patriarch as destined for rule by God. Both are ' "*Christoi*"—the anointed of the Lord' (MPG, vol. 120, cols., 1163, 1183). See title 3, pt. I, of *Epanagoge* (Barker, *op. cit.*, 91): 'The patriarch is a living animate image of Christ'. See Rhalles and Potlis, VI, p. 428 for Blastares, who calls the patriarch the 'living icon of Christ'. I cannot find this term used of the patriarch in the earlier canonists and its use during the later centuries may therefore be meaningful with respect to the imperial-patriarchal power relationship. See also Balsamon, in Rhalles-Potlis, III, 44–45.

More examples can be cited of ambiguities or seeming ambiguities in the source material. But these will perhaps suffice to indicate how difficult it is, in the absence of a comprehensive, official document which may be used as a constitutional frame of reference, to draw consistent conclusions on the basis of appeal to documents which express varying shades of opinion. An analogy with medieval England might be drawn. There as in Byzantium, there was no fundamental law which was superior to other statutes and by which laws could be tested for constitutionality. Since there was no formal definition of the king's power in one document, this meant that not only parliamentary statutes but developing tradition, as was the case in Byzantium, came to have virtually as strong a position as other types of law.[13]

Byzantine political theory as such may be said to begin in the early fourth century with Eusebius of Caesarea, the ecclesiastical adviser of Constantine the Great. Eusebius based his theories on scripture and Christian tradition, as well as on a strong influence of Hellenistic ideas of kingship (*Basileia*) and the Roman 'Caesaropapistic' idea of the emperor as Pontifex Maximus, highest priest.[14] (It must be observed that in pagan Rome civil officials served as priests during the period of sacrifices and that no priestly caste as such existed.)

According to Byzantine theory as based on Eusebius, the source of all authority in the universe, both religious and secular is God. The Divine Logos, that is Christ, is the supreme priest and king on earth, uniting in himself both *regnum* and *sacerdotium*. When Christ left the world the power was divided into two spheres, the spiritual being assigned to his apostles and the civil authority to Caesar. And throughout their history the Byzantines believed that the emperor derived his authority directly from God; hence the title *Christos Kyriou*.[15] It was the Byzantine view, furthermore, that the church hierarchy derived its authority from Christ through the Apostles. But this seeming indirection was, for the clergy, not a mark of inferiority; on the contrary,

---

[13] Cf. Bury, *Selected Essays*, 120–21, and Ensslin, 'The Emperor and Imperial Administration', 280.

[14] On 'Caesaropapism' and the Roman Pontifex Maximus see esp. Ostrogorsky, 'Relations between Church and State in Byzantium', (in Russian) 122 f. Cf. Sherrard, *Greek East and Latin West*, 91f. For bibl. on Eusebius see below, note 18.

[15] Title used by Balsamon, e.g., in Rhalles and Potlis, III, 44.

they could, in a certain sense, be considered even superior to the emperor because of the purely spiritual nature of their ecclesiastical authority.

What we would call the secular realm was presided over by the emperor. His realm was the universal Roman Empire which, having become the more perfect Christian Roman Empire after Constantine's conversion, was established by God on earth in imitation (*mimesis* is the famous Greek term) of the divine order or kingdom in heaven.[16] It was the emperor's sacred duty to seek the conversion of non-Christians outside the church, whence perhaps the application to Constantine of the term 'bishop of those without the church'.[17] As the representative of God over God's Kingdom on earth (*Basileia*) the emperor is responsible for the organization of the empire, for the establishment of justice and the maintenance of peace within the realm. He is the source of law, but as a Christian he must at all times base the laws of order and justice he establishes on Christian principles. As Eusebius envisioned it, the emperor was to frame his earthly government according to the model of the divine original in heaven. Following this conception, the emperor was a kind of mediator between God and man on earth, as it were the Vice-gerent of God.[18]

This in very brief outline is Byzantine political theory as based primarily on the assumptions of Eusebius and transmitted throughout the millenium of Byzantine history. Although there is disagreement among scholars as to Eusebius' precise meaning on certain points, it must be apparent that the realms of church and state are not here differentiated with complete clarity. There seems to be a certain interpenetration or even a blurring of the two spheres, a fact which was to lead to conflict between emperor

[16] See Eusebius' *Triakontaeterikos*, pt. I, p. 197, 11. 1-3, and pt. 3, p. 201, 11. 19-21, in *Eusebius Werke*, I (Leipzig, 1902) ed. by I. A. Heikel.

[17] This celebrated phrase has of course been variously interpreted. See J. Straub, 'Kaiser Konstantin als episkopos ton ektos', *Studia patristica*, I (1957), 678-95. See also the recent work of P. Demetropoulos, *The Faith of the Ancient Church as Canon of Life and the World* (in Greek) (Athens, 1959) 52.

[18] For a fine summary of certain aspects of Eusebius' political thought see N. Baynes, 'Eusebius and the Christian Empire', *Annuaire de l'institut de philologie et d'histoire orientales*, II (1933-34) 13-18. Cf. Ph. Sherrard, *Greek East and Latin West* (London, 1959) 92ff. Much fuller is E. Schwartz, *Kaiser Constantin und die christliche Kirche*, 2nd ed. (Leipzig, 1936); also F. Cranz, 'Kingdom and Polity in Eusebius of Caesarea', (*Harvard Theological Review*, 45 (1952) 47-66, and bibl. p. 48. And now cf. Y. Congar, *After Nine Hundred Years* (New York, 1959) 14-17.

and patriarch and makes it difficult for us to assess the degree of imperial control over the church.

Certain contemporary scholars take what seems at first glance a commendable approach to our problem, placing great emphasis on the results of a series of actual confrontations between emperors and patriarchs.[19] With this pragmatic approach one would find it difficult to take issue. Emphasis on immediate results is certainly a valid and important way to interpret power conflicts. Another method, however, with probably more to be said for it, would be to examine the long-range effects of these confrontations in order to see whether or not any *permanent* changes were effected in the church over the centuries.

In the early Byzantine period the most frequent issues involved in the clashes between patriarch and emperor were basically dogmatic—Arianism, Monophysitism, Monothelitism, Iconoclasm. And in these conflicts the will of individual emperors seems, temporarily at least, to have prevailed.[20] But a fundamental issue, as to whether an emperor unilaterally, that is by imperial decree, could alter the prescribed dogma of the church, was not really resolved. For despite triumphs during the lifetime of individual emperors, it is obvious that none of these heresies supported by the emperors was in the long run able to prevail in the church. On their own authority emperors did summon ecumenical councils and were able to 'pack' the assembly or otherwise to manipulate it.[21] But the basic question, whether, other than through such indirect methods, an emperor could bend the church to his will and actually alter dogma, was to appear again and again under later rulers, especially under the Palaeologoi.

[19] F. Dölger, review in *Byz. Zeit.* (1931) 449 of Ostrogorsky, 'Church and State' says 'The power balance of church and state was regulated according to the personalities who faced each other at various times'. For the celebrated western phrase 'Vicar of Christ' there seems to be no exact equivalent in Greek. E. Kantorowicz's suggestion, in a lecture, of *Christomimetes* ('imitator of Christ') is good but with not the same emphasis. The term commonly used on imperial Byzantine bulls, *Pistos Basileus*, is probably more or less equivalent to 'Defender of the Faith'.

[20] For a general account of these clashes (in English) see J. Bury, *Later Roman Empire* (London, 1923) and *Later Roman Empire*, 1st ed. (London, 1889). Constantius imposed Arianism during his reign, Zeno for a time leaned toward Monophysitism, and Heraclius imposed Monothelitism as a solution, while Leo III issued his edict outlawing the icons in 730 and Constantine V and Leo V continued this iconoclastic policy.

[21] Bury, *Later Roman Empire*, 403, notes cogently that Basiliscus by his Encyclical and Zeno by his Henoticon, virtually 'assumed the functions of an ecumenical council'.

A certain difference may be noted in the conflicts between emperors and patriarchs before and after the end of the Iconoclast struggle in the ninth century. Whereas in the earlier dogmatic conflicts strong emperors were frequently able to impose their will on the church, if only during their own reigns, after the ninth century and especially during the *filioque* controversy under the Palaeologoi, even this was usually to prove impossible. It seems reasonable to believe, as G. Ostrogorsky indicates in an early article dealing with the first nine centuries, that the dramatic protests in the seventh and eighth centuries of Maximos the Confessor, John of Damascus, and Theodore Studites during the struggles over Monothelitism and Iconoclasm, had something to do with the stronger opposition of the church, serving to inspire patriarchs to more active resistance of imperial demands. Ostrogorsky in fact cites evidence for what he terms the development of a dyarchy between imperial and ecclesiastical power after the earlier period.[22] One might, however, be hesitant about this part of his thesis if the term dyarchy is meant to convey the impression of an 'equal' partnership between emperor and patriarch. The relationship between the two powers would seem to have been a complex give-and-take of authority and influence on various levels —a kind of interdependence as it were,[23] characterized ideally in the civil codes and especially the pro-patriarchal Epanagoge as a *symphonia*, that is a concord or harmony.[24] In actual practice the relationship may well have been mixed, a blend of domination by the emperor over the church in certain areas, and perhaps an absence of imperial authority in other spheres. But how can we determine what the nature and extent of the emperor's authority in ecclesiastical affairs actually was, in particular in which spheres his control did or did not obtain?

If we attempt to analyze the complex of temporal and spiritual relations with reference to the problem as we have here set

[22] G. Ostrogorsky, 'Relations between Church and State' (in Russian), *Sem. Kond.*, IV (1933) 121 ff. (cf. Dölger review, *Byz. Zeit.*, 31 [1931] 449) cites artistic evidence to show that in the earlier period the emperor was portrayed as the priest-king Melchisedek, but later artists presented the emperor and patriarch standing side by side as Moses and Aaron.

[23] Cf. J. Hussey, *The Byzantine World*, 90–92. Cf. H. Moss, review in *Journal of Ecclesiastical History* (1960) 114, who favors the view of imperial absolutism over the church.

[24] See above notes 3–4.

it forth, it would seem that there are three different facets or spheres, each of which must be individually considered. First is the purely temporal realm for which the emperor alone made the laws, and which, historians would probably agree, was under the direct and complete authority of the emperor. The second sphere would include that area of the spiritual or ecclesiastical realm dealing essentially with the administrative or organizational matters of the church such as the establishment and redistricting of sees, disciplinary matters affecting the clergy (which we have no time to enter into here) and, perhaps most important, the appointment to or dismissal from patriarchal office. Control over these various aspects of what might be called the 'external' side of the church[25] was in case of conflict exercised in the last analysis by the emperor. It must be emphasized, however, that the church hierarchy normally shared, or the emperor let it believe it shared, in this control in a sensitive interplay of authority and influence.

The third facet of Byzantine church-state relations has to do with the most vitual aspect of the church. It concerns the holy sacraments and the most basic dogmas of the faith as set forth in the New Testament, the canonical epistles of the Fathers, and the first seven ecumenical councils—that is, what would be included in the tradition of the church.[26]

There is then a threefold division of spheres: first the secular falling entirely under the control of the emperor; second, that pertaining to the organization and administration of the church— that is, church polity. The third sphere, the inner or 'esoteric' form of the church, despite notable imperial attempts at interference, belonged as we shall see to the clergy alone. Of course none of the three spheres enjoyed a really separate existence in theocratic Byzantium. They were intertwined, interpenetrated, and together they formed an organic whole—in Byzantine eyes the Kingdom of God on earth. Nevertheless, only if we manage to keep these three realms differentiated can we hope to understand clearly the complexities of this ecclesiastical and imperial relationship, in particular the authority of the emperor over the church. A basic reason in fact for scholars' misunderstanding of the

---

[25] Phrase is from Ph. Sherrard, *Greek East and Latin West* (London, 1955), 93.

[26] On tradition (*paradosis*) see F. Gavin, *Some Aspects of Contemporary Greek Orthodox Thought* (London, 1923) 25–30 and esp. Ch. Androutsos, *Dogmatike of the Orthodox Eastern Church* (Athens, 1956) 7 ff.

emperor's role in the church is that they have not always clearly perceived the delimitation as well as the interpenetration of these three spheres.

Let us now examine in detail the function of imperial authority in each area. We need say little about the secular sphere. All scholars would be in essential agreement that the Christian emperor, as the fountain-head of law, was responsible for the temporal administration of the empire. The church in fact considered it a duty to follow imperial leadership in secular matters. But one should not forget that this sphere was permeated throughout by the moral influence of Christian ideals, the church deeming it a responsibility that imperial law should be humane and in accord with the moral teachings of the church.[27]

It is the second sphere, with its interplay of imperial and patriarchal authority, which formed the main point of contact between emperor and church and which witnessed some of the most dramatic encounters between emperors and patriarchs. This area, involving the question of control over the administrative form of the church and its delimitation from the 'esoteric' area, has caused the greatest misunderstanding among scholars. To this sphere we shall now turn.

II

THE 'EXTERNAL' FORM OF THE CHURCH AND IMPERIAL

AUTHORITY

As protector of the church the emperor took a very active, even dominant, role in its organization and administration. To be sure the degree of his influence depended to a considerable extent on the strength and personality of the particular emperor and patriarch of the moment.[28] Most striking of the imperial powers in this area was the authority to appoint the ecumenical patriarch of Constantinople, the highest official of the church. From a list of three names suggested by the *Synodos Endemousa*

[27] A. Gasquet, *De l'autorité impériale en matière religieuse à Byzance* (Paris, 1879). Sherrard, *Greek East and Latin West*, 92.
[28] See Dölger review, *Byz. Zeit.* (1931) 449. It is significant, according to Ensslin, 'The Emperor and the Imperial Administration', 255, that in the tenth century ceremonial *both* emperor and patriarch paid each other the tribute of formal *proskynesis*. Cf. Constantine Porphyrogenitus, *De cerimoniis* (Bonn) 159.

(the permanent Holy Synod in Constantinople) the emperor would select one. If none pleased him he could himself suggest that of another who, with the sanction of the Synod, would then be appointed patriarch.[29] No less important was his authority, but only in practice not in theory, to depose the patriarch. Again, however, this was supposed to be done with the approval of the Holy Synod—an approval technically not unduly difficult to obtain if the emperor were sufficiently determined.[30]

Of course the emperor not infrequently met with sharp opposition from the clergy, particularly in his attempts to depose a patriarch. But in the end, especially in the earlier centuries, his will amost invariably prevailed. We may cite the case of the most illustrious of all patriarchs, Photius, who for political reasons, was deposed by Emperor Basil I. Even when the Patriarch Nicholas Mysticus raised justifiable objections to the fourth marriage of the Emperor Leo the Wise on the grounds that it contravened the disciplinary canons of the church, the emperor managed finally to depose him.[31] The most ambitious of the Byzantine patriarchs, Michael Cerularius of the mid-eleventh century, despite the great authority he had succeeded in arrogating to himself and the popularity he temporarily enjoyed with the people of Constantinople even over the emperor, was also forced to abdicate. And later, in the thirteenth century, the monk Arsenios, because of his opposition to Michael Palaeologus' usurpation of the throne, was deposed as patriarch, but not before fomenting a virtual civil war against the régime.[32]

[29] Constantine Porphyrogenitus *De cerimoniis* (Bonn ed.) pt. 1, pp. 564–66. Pseudo-Codinus, *De officiis*, agrees (MPG., 156, col. 116–17). On the arbitrariness of the emperor's choice of patriarch, see V. Laurent, 'Le rituel de l'investiture du patriarch byz. au début du XVe siècle', in *Bulletin Sect. Hist. Acad. Roum.*, 28 (1947) 218–32. Also, Dölger, *Byz. Zeit.* (1931) 449 f.; 28 (1947) 218–32. Cf. L. Bréhier, 'L'investiture des patriarches de Constantinople au Moyen Age', *Studi e Testi*, no. 3 (Rome, 1946) 368–72, who points out that 'not a single patriarch was chosen except by the emperor's will'. (Yet witness the case of 1450, see note 33 below). Bréhier says that the imperial power of selection had been recognized by custom, if not by juridical act, since the ninth and tenth centuries.

[30] See Barker, *op. cit.*, 8. Emperor Anastasius in 495 had a synod of bishops depose the Patriarch Euphemius (P. Charanis, *Church and State in the Later Roman Empire* [Madison, 1939] 27.) There is no canon or canonist's opinion of course that the emperor explicitly had the right to depose a patriarch.

[31] On Photius see F. Dvornik, *The Photian Schism, History and Legend* (Cambridge, 1948). On Nicholas Mysticus, see Ostrogorsky, *Byzantine State*, 230–31.

[32] On Cerularius see above, note 4. On Arsenios see Geanakoplos, *Emperor Michael Palaeologus*, 235, 272, etc.

Even though in the last period of the Empire the Palaeologan emperors met with great difficulty in deposing incumbent patriarchs, following their policy of ecclesiastical rapprochement with Rome they were still usually able to prevail. One striking exception may be cited, however; in 1450, during the final miserable years of Empire, the unionist Emperor Constantine XI Palaeologus was overruled by the Holy Synod which, in defiance of the imperial will, not only deposed the incumbent pro-unionist patriarch but blocked the emperor's appointment of a pro-unionist replacement.[33]

Further privileges of the emperor in the realm of church administration and organization, both in theory and practice, were his power to redistrict dioceses in accord with political or ecclesiastical exigency, the right to translate bishops from one see to another, and the authority to alter the rank or honor (*time*, in Greek) of the relative sees. As the canonist Zonaras put it: 'The emperor can transform an episcopate into a metropolitan see, free him [the bishop] from the other metropolitans, and redistribute the episcopal districts'.[34]

We have yet to discuss an imperial privilege in the domain of ecclesiastical administration which, until the very end of the empire, the emperors always exercised as their own—the right to convoke ecumenical councils.[35] Today of course the pope claims it as his own privilege to summon general councils. But during

[33] See Bréhier, *Cambridge Medieval History*, IV, 624 and E. Pears, *The Destruction of the Greek Empire* (London-New York, 1903) 202. This was done under the influence of the anti-unionist George Scholarios. The synod deposed the Patriarch Gregory. It used to be thought erroneously that he was replaced by the monk Athanasius. See Ch. Papaioannou, 'The Praktika of the alleged final synod in St. Sophia', in *Ecclesiastike Aletheia* (in Greek), XV (1896); and Gennadios of Helioupolis, 'Was there ever a Patriarch Athanasios II?' *Orthodoxia* (in Greek), XVIII (1943) 117–23.

[34] Also Balsamon in Rhalles and Potlis, *Syntagma ton Hieron Canonon* (in Greek) (Athens, 1852) II, 23 ('It is given to the emperor to accomplish changes of episcopal sees.') We should mention here also the emperor's authority, in practice, to control ecclesiastical property. But though in this respect the emperor usually secured his aims, the church's opposition could at times be very strong. Note for example Nicephorus Phocas' edict of 964 (following the example of Romanus Lecapenus) issued in the aim of curbing the increase in ecclesiastical property. This had to be withdrawn, however.

[35] In a recent lecture (yet unpublished) Professor G. Florovsky set forth the view, certainly correct, that modern western scholarly views on Byzantine conciliar theory have been shaped far too much by the influence of the theories of the western Conciliar movement—theories of course alien to the Byzantine East. (He also maintains that the ecumenical councils are to be considered as ad hoc events rather than institutions.) See also Stephanides, 'The Last Stage in the Development of Church-State Relations in Byzantium,' *Ep. Het. Byz. Spoudon* (1953) 27–40.

the long existence of Byzantium the emperor jealously guarded
the precedent which he believed had originally been established
by Constantine the Great at the time of the first Council of Nicaea
in 325. Centuries later, at the Council of Florence, the ceremony
for the signing of the document of religious union was held up
over a severe argument between emperor and pope as to who
first should sign his name to the forms.[36] The argument hinged on
this very question of who had the authority to call the council into
being in the first place.

It should be stressed that according to the traditional Byzantine
view no council, even if summoned by the emperor, or by
emperor and pope together, could be considered truly ecumenical
unless all four eastern patriarchs, together with the pope, were in
attendance or at least represented. Thus Michael VIII Palaeologus
was never able to secure popular Greek approval of the ecumenicity of the unionist Council of Lyons in 1274 because of the popular
Byzantine conviction that all the eastern patriarchs had not been
properly represented.[37] The Greco-Italian monk Barlaam put it
well a few years later when, at the papal court of Avignon, he
addressed the pope on the objections of the Byzantine people to
religious union with Rome. He said:

> 'The Greek legates at Lyons were in fact sent there neither
> by the four patriarchs who govern the eastern church nor by
> the Greek people, but by the emperor alone who, without
> trying to get the support of his people, sought only by force
> to realize the union . . .'[38]

With respect to ecumenical councils, always a matter of
extreme concern to the East, there was still another practice—
evidently unspecified in the canonistic texts themselves—which
the Byzantines regarded as the sole prerogative of the emperor.
For a council to be considered valid it was required that its
proceedings be signed by the emperor. And before these conciliar decisions could go into effect as the law of the church, it was
necessary that they be promulgated as imperial law—that is, be

[36] See next Chapter, note 92. Also J. Gill, *The Council of Florence* (Oxford, 1959)
288.
[37] On the non-ecumenicity of Lyons for the Greeks, who considered it a 'Robber
Council', see Geanakoplos, *Emperor Michael*, 263 ff.
[38] See next chapter, text and notes 25–29.

incorporated into the civil law of the empire.[39]   As such they were
included in *nomocanones* and took on the force of civil statutes.
This is not to say that the canons, as a part of the civil law code,
could legally be revoked by the imperial authority. Certainly, as
we have seen, the emperor always had the power to revoke, or
rather to nullify secular law. But the question was quite different
when it involved the ecclesiastical canons. Even when the
emperor tried to encroach upon the purely disciplinary canons,
he might well meet with opposition—as was the case with Leo the
Wise's fourth marriage. But as we shall see, in the case of an
attempt on his part to change the more fundamental type of
conciliar decisions, the doctrine of the church, the emperor
always met with violent and intransigent opposition from most
of the clergy as well as the people.

Before we discuss this question which involves our third
category, the 'esoteric' form of the church, let us look at a related
problem which has caused a good deal of misunderstanding—the
emperor's so-called 'liturgical' privileges. These were religious
in nature and the emperor's possession of these special privileges,
so strange to modern western secular eyes, has further contributed
to the belief in the emperor's Caesaropapistic authority over the
church.

III

'LITURGICAL' PRIVILEGES OF THE EMPEROR

Because of the special position held by the emperor in Christian society as the representative of God on earth (as noted, the
Byzantines often called him 'the living icon of Christ'),[40] the
Byzantine church could not look upon him as an ordinary layman
and therefore bestowed upon him certain special privileges of a
religious nature. These extraordinary privileges have been
termed by modern scholars 'liturgical', or less accurately, 'sacerdotal'.[41]   Now these privileges, normally associated only with the

[39] E.g., the ecclesiastical *tomos henoseos* of a council in 920, signed by the emperor,
became part of the law of the land. (V. Grumel, *Regestes des actes du patriarchat de
Constantinople*, II, Reg. 669).

[40] See text and notes 11–15.

[41] See esp. L. Bréhier, 'Hiereus kai Basileus' (title in Greek), *Memorial L. Petit*
(Bucharest, 1948), 41–45. A. Gasquet, *L'autorité impériale*, 50–55, refers to the
emperor's 'sacerdotal' character with respect to these privileges. Also M. Mitard,

clergy, would seem to fall somewhere between what we have termed the external and the esoteric areas of the church. A useful analogy to these privileges might be what the Latin church calls the *sacramentalia* (in Greek, *mysteriakai teletai*, roughly 'lesser mystical ceremonies') as against the sacraments proper, the latter of which are exclusively the province of the clerics and may be said to form part of the inner or esoteric form of Christianity.

The most frequently mentioned liturgical privilege of the emperor was that of entering into the sanctuary of the church, that area where the altar is situated and the holy mysteries are performed. Striking as this privilege may seem, we should attach somewhat less importance to it if we recall that in the eastern church anyone in minor orders such as cantor, reader, porter, exorcist, has this right of penetrating into the sanctuary.[42]

The Byzantine emperor could also preach to the congregation. Leo VI the Wise we know took great pride and enjoyment in regaling the Byzantine populace with learned sermons delivered in person during church festivals.[43] At first glance this seems rather remarkable, given the fact that in the medieval period the western church looked with great disfavour, indeed generally prohibited, the activities of lay theologians (witness the Waldensians and their attempts to preach and explain the Gospel).

An even more impressive imperial privilege was that of receiving communion in the same manner as the priesthood. Thus the emperor would take the holy bread directly into his own hands from the paten and drink the wine immediately from the chalice —communicate himself, so to speak. This is to be contrasted with normal practice with respect to the Greek laity, which receives both the bread and wine from a spoon held in the hands of the officiating priest. An important qualification must be made, however, with regard to this privilege. The ability to effect the miraculous transformation of the bread and wine into the body and blood of Christ, the climax of the liturgy (in Greek, called

'Le pouvoir impérial au temps de Leon VI, le Sage', *Mélanges Diehl*, I (1930) 219: 'in certain respects he was a sacerdotal personage.' See Constantine Porphyrogenitus, *De Cerimoniis*, I, 621–22.

[42] On the cutting of a certain amount of hair from the head of the Porphyrogenitus in his infancy, a kind of tonsure or a sort of *koura*, see Bréhier, *loc. cit.*, 42–43. Source is *De Cerimoniis*, I, 621–22.

[43] H. Monnier, *Les Novelles de Leon le Sage* (Bordeaux, 1923) 211ff. Also Ostrogorsky, *Byzantine State*, 215–16.

Christ Pantocrator. Byzantine mosaic in dome of Norman palatine chapel in Palmermo (mid-12th century).
(See p. 47.)
Plate 5

Christ Pantocrator. Byzantine mosaic in dome of church at Daphni near Athens (11th century).

Christ Pantocrator. Byzantine mosaic in dome of St. Sophia, Kiev (11th century).

Plate 6

metabole or less correctly as a result of western influence, *metous-iousis*, roughly equivalent to the Latin 'transubstantiation')[44] belongs to the clergy alone. It should be noted, therefore, that before the emperor could partake of communion the services of a priest were required to consecrate the bread and wine.[45]

In addition the emperor could bless the congregation with the *trikir*, the three-candled candelabra symbolizing the Trinity, in the manner of the bishop, and also cense the icons and the people. A passage from the authoritative twelfth century Byzantine canonist Theodore Balsamon, whose attitude is generally pro-imperialist, describes most of these liturgical privileges of the emperor with these words:

'The Orthodox emperors (who choose the patriarchs) by the invocation of the Holy Trinity become the *christoi* of the Lord, unhindered and whenever they wish can enter into the holy sacrificial place (*hieron*) and cense and bless with the *trikir* like the bishop. It has also been given to them to preach to the people . . .'[46]

Lastly, we must mention a privilege of the emperor which was his alone and which he did not share even with the clergy. We refer to his anointment at the time of his coronation,[47] following the example of King David of the Jews. The most recent authoritative scholarship holds that this practice of imperial anointment first appeared among the Byzantines at the coronation of Theodore I Lascaris in the early thirteenth century at Nicaea, as a result of the influence of the nearby Latin Empire of Constantinople.[48] Another theory maintains that it was an

[44]Androutsos, *Dogmatike* (in Greek), 52. The sole significant difference between Orthodox and Catholics is the exact moment the miraculous transformation into Christ's body and blood takes place. Yet the eastern church objects to the western scholastic differentiation between accidents and substance.

[45] Rhalles and Potlis, II, 467.

[46] Rhalles and Potlis, II, 467. Cf. Balsamon, *ibid.*, IV, 544, which refers to *dikir* (two candles) not *trikir* (three candles). *Dikir* symbolizes the dual nature of Christ, *trikir* refers to the Trinity.

[47] Greek priests are not anointed at ordination, there being merely a laying-on of hands and prayer. This constitutes a sacrament, however.

[48] The most important recent authoritative works on this controversial question are by G. Ostrogorsky, 'Zur Kaisersalbung und Schilderhebung im spätbyzantinischen Krönungszeremoniell', *Historia*, IV (1955) 246–56 (cf. Ostrogorsky, *Byzantine State*, 380) and the earlier article of Ostrogorsky and E. Stein, 'Die Krönungsordnungen des Ceremonienbuches', *Byzantion*, VII (1932) 200, which affirms unction formed no customary part of the Byzantine coronation ceremony until the thirteenth century. Cf. F. Brightman, 'Byzantine Imperial Coronations', *Jl. of Theological*

accepted Byzantine practice to anoint the 'Basileus and Auto-crator' already under Basil I, that is, as early as the ninth century.[49] Be that as it may, it must be noted that even the act of imperial coronation and accompanying anointment was subject to a certain ecclesiastical restriction. For the patriarch could refuse to crown the emperor if he did not first approve his profession of faith. (This of course did not mean that the church had the right to elect the emperor.) The requirement of patriarchal approval of the imperial confession of faith dated from the accession of Anastasius during the Monophysitic troubles at the end of the sixth century.[50] At times certain patriarchs also attempted to impose moral requirements on individual candidates for the throne as in the case of the strong-willed Patriarch Polyeuctes, who in 969 refused to crown the usurper John Tzimisces until the latter had first put away his mistress, Theophano, his collaborator in the murder of his imperial predecessor Nicephorus Phocas.[51]

According to the most convincing judgment, at the coronation the patriarch acted in the capacity of the second most important 'civil' official of the Empire, while in the accompanying ceremony of anointment the patriarch's function seems primarily to have been sacerdotal.[52] As noted, anointment at coronation (whenever it first occurred) was a privilege of the emperor alone, and this act helped further to set him apart from all other men and give his reign the stamp of divine approval. It seems probable that the

---

Studies, II (1901) 383 ff. See also the very recent work of C. Christophilopoulou, *Election, Proclamation and Coronation of the Byzantine Emperor* (Athens, 1956). Cf. S Runciman, *Byzantine Civilization* (New York, 1933) 66, who says, however, that it was the Palacologan emperors who introduced the western custom of anointment. On the western custom of royal anointment see P. Schramm, *A History of the English Coronation* (Oxford, 1937) Chap. 1. Also E. Kantorowicz, *Lavdes regiae* (Berkeley, 1946) *passim*.

[49] See esp. W. Sichel, 'Das byzantinische Krönungrecht bis zum 10. Jahrhundert', *Byz. Zeit.*, VII (1898) 548 and B. Stephanides, *Ecclesiastical History* (in Greek) (Athens, 1948) 138, note 1, who believes anointment began probably under Basil I. Cf. also Ensslin, 'The Emperor and Imperial Administration', 273. A passage of Balsamon, in Rhalles and Potlis, IV, 544–45, seems to speak of emperors and patriarchs being anointed already in the twelfth century ('as the emperors are, so are the patriarchs great in the ability to teach through the power of the holy chrism.') But this is doubtless a metaphorical use of the term, since it is certainly clear that the patriarchs were never anointed.

[50] P. Charanis, *Church and State in the Later Roman Empire: The Religious Policy of Anastasius I* (Madison, 1939) 12.

[51] Ostrogorsky, *Byzantine State*, 260 (source, Leo the Deacon, Bonn ed., 98f.)

[52] Ostrogorsky, *Byzantine State*, 56; Bury, 'Constitution', 118; Charanis, 'The Crown Modiolus Once More', *Byzantion*, XIII (1938) 338–81.

oil (chrism) of baptism and of holy unction (*euchelaion*) was looked upon as different from that used in the ceremony of imperial anointment.[53]

Despite these impressive liturgical privileges of the emperor, most of which were shared by the Byzantine clergy, and notwithstanding the emphasis placed upon their importance by some modern historians, it must be admitted that the emperor always remained a layman. Even though earlier emperors such as Marcian and Justinian called themselves king-priest (*rex et sacerdos*), especially when dealing with the popes, and though emperors were not infrequently referred to by the Byzantine canonists as arch-priest (*Archiereus*),[54] the emperor in point of fact had no right to perform any of the sacraments. Thus although these liturgical privileges set the emperor above and apart from ordinary laymen, conferring upon him a kind of hieratic character,[55] in the last analysis they did not make him a cleric.[56]

THE 'ESOTERIC' FORM OF THE CHURCH AND IMPERIAL AUTHORITY

It was in the sphere of the inner or 'esoteric' form of the church that, in our view, the absolutism of the emperor was truly blocked. This is not to say that at a time of serious political crisis a host of emperors, from Justinian all the way to the last ruler Constantine XI Palaeologus, did not make resolute

---

[53] When a Protestant is converted to Orthodoxy he is not rebaptized but given the chrism. Greek priests cannot perform all the sacraments: they cannot ordain priests and only bishops have the right to bless the chrism of baptism, though priests of course can administer it.

[54] Rhalles and Potlis, II, 467. See Ensslin, *loc. cit.*, 275.

[55] The minor orders of the Greek church (cantor, reader, etc.) may be considered clerics of a lower type, but since they must receive the *heirothesia* which the emperor did not (being by c. 1250 anointed), the emperor cannot even in this sense be considered a cleric. It might be noted that in contrast to the *heirothesia* of the lower orders, the higher order of clergy—deacon, priest, bishop—receive the *heirotonia* which is a sacrament. However, Diehl, *Byzantium: Greatness and Decline*, 29, calls the emperor a priest. Stephanides, *Ecclesiastical History*, 138 (quoting Demetrius Chomatianos, from Rhalles and Potlis, V, 428ff.) says the emperor could do anything in the church except administer the actual sacraments ('*plen monon tou hierourgein*'). But cf. N. Baynes, 'The Byzantine State', *Byzantine Studies and Other Essays* (London, 1955) 49, who says (referring to the earliest Byzantine emperors): 'it took the Christian emperor many a year to learn he was not a priest.'

[56] I agree with Ostrogorsky, *Byzantine State*, 218: 'However strongly imperial influence might exert itself on the ecclesiastical organization, the emperor is still only a layman . . . and can be merely the protector, not the head of the church.'

attempts to exert control over the formulation or revision of dogma in the broader interest of the survival of the Empire.[57] To be sure, in accordance with the characteristic Byzantine concept of *oikonomia*, it was in some quarters accepted that in case of extreme political necessity the emperor was empowered to attempt the accommodation of the church to the exigencies of the state. But this seems to have held true only with respect to certain administrative or external aspects of the church and did not apply to the doctrinal, the more esoteric sphere.[58]

The esoteric form of the church contained within itself what we may call the more profound truths of the faith, essential fundamental truths which to the Orthodox were and still are considered necessary for salvation, the true end of human life. These truths include both the church's teaching on dogma and the sacraments. The dogmatic beliefs were those formulated in written form by the ecumenical councils and deal primarily with the nature of the Trinity and the Incarnation.[59] These in fact took such crystallized form as to become virtually inviolable; and any tampering with these dogmas or, as it was put, with the 'purity' of the faith, was considered *ipso facto* heretical.[60]

The sacraments (*mysteria* in Greek), so necessary for salvation, could be administered only by the clergy, one sacrament, that of

[57] M. Anastos, 'Political Theory in the Lives of the Slavic Saints', 13, says that 'in general the emperors prevailed even in the formulation of dogma'.

[58] On the peculiarly Byzantine concept of *oikonomia* there is little written. See now H. Alivizatos, *Oikonomia and the Canon Law of the Orthodox Church* (in Greek) (Athens, 1949). Also F. Dvornik, *The Photian Schism*, 8, 24, etc., J. Langford, *A Dictionary of the Eastern Orthodox Church* (London, 1923) 47 ff. To Runciman, *(Schism* and elsewhere, *oikonomia* is 'elasticity in the interest of the Christian community'. Alivizatos, *op. cit.*, shows *oikonomia* was 'a way out of the anomaly created by and proceeding from the imposition of extreme severity and precision in observance of canonical order'. (We might possibly compare *oikonomia* to the principle of equity in civil law.) *Oikonomia* is, we may say, the relaxing of disciplinary canons—regarding performance of the sacraments but *not* dogma—for the benefit, possibly political, of the community. See F. Gavin, *Some Aspects of Contemporary Greek Orthodox Thought* (London, 1936) 292. The Byzantine historians Pachymeres (Bonn) 387, and Gregoras (Bonn) 127, imply that the ecclesiastics of Michael Palaeologus' reign, disturbed over his unionist policy, believed that *oikonomia* did not, however, apply where dogma was involved, but only with respect to church organization.

[59] See Androutsos, *Dogmatike*, 294 ff., and the interesting points of view in Ph. Sherrard, *Greek East*, 54 ff. Also Gavin, *Orthodox Thought*, 272 ff. On the sacraments, Gavin, 305–75. C. Dyobouniotes, *The Dogmatics of Androutsos Reviewed* (Athens, 1907) thinks that the lower orders are *sacramentalia*. On *sacramentalia*, see also Gavin, 305.

[60] The Epanagoge (Barker, *op. cit.*, 90) reads that the Emperor must maintain all that is contained in the Scriptures and all set down by the seven ecumenical councils and at Byzantine law.

ordination, only by a bishop. In the case of baptism the chrism could be blessed only by bishops, then administered by a priest. (Incidentally, in the eastern church the number of the sacraments was apparently not officially fixed at seven until very late.)[61]

Although to be sure the question of the celebration of the sacraments by the emperors themselves never seems to have been raised in Byzantium, there were not a few imperial efforts made, in the interest of the state, to alter the traditional dogmas formulated in general council. Yet it is surely significant that in the more than ten centuries of Byzantine history, only one or two examples at most can be found of emperors who sought to alter church dogma when no pressing external danger threatened, that is, purely on intellectual grounds or in accordance with personal belief. Such seems to have been the case with Justinian's interest in the heresy of Aphthartodocetism in which he dabbled at the end of his reign.[62] The same was probably true even with respect to Leo III's issuance of his famous edict against the images in 730.[63] On the other hand Justinian's condemnation of the 'Three Chapters' and his insistence on certain views under the pressure of Monophysitism (several scholars believe that he even managed to incorporate his 'reinterpretation' of Chalcedonian doctrine into the acts of the Fifth Ecumenical Council)[64] were certainly motivated by political reasons. Now when an emperor, actuated by pressing political considerations, did attempt to reshape dogma, there was always a certain number of supporters—*politiques* we may call them—who were willing to go along for the sake of the state. Such was the case in the questions of Monophysitism, Monothelitism, possibly of Iconoclasm, and certainly with regard to the later Palaeologan emperors' attempts to foster religious union

[61] See Androutsos, *Dogmatike*, 314 ff., Gavin, *Orthodox Thought*, 278 ff. The first mention in the East of *seven* sacraments was by the monk Job in 1270, and by Michael Palaeologus at the Council of Lyons in 1274 (Androutsos, 314). Peter Lombard and Pope Alexander III apparently first enumerated seven in the West.

[62] Bury, *Later Roman Empire*, II, 375, 393.

[63] See G. Ostrogorsky, 'Les débuts de la Querelle des images', *Mélanges Diehl*, I (1930) 238 ff. Previously the date was considered to be 726 (Diehl, 'Leo III and the Isaurian Dynasty', in *Cambridge Medieval History*, IV, 9).

[64] See M. Anastos, 'Justinian's Despotic Control over the Church as Illustrated by his Edict on Theopaschite Formula and Letter to Pope John in 533', *Zbornik Rad. Viz. Inst.*, 8/2 (= *Mélanges Ostrogorsky*, II [1964] 1–11, a notable article the author kindly let me see before publication. Also see H. Alivizatos, 'Les rapports de la législation ecclésiastique de Justinien avec les canons de l'église', *Atti del congresso internazionale di diritto romano*, II (Rome, 1935) 79 ff.

with Rome in the face of the military threat of Charles of Anjou and, subsequently, of the even greater danger from the Ottoman Turks.[65]

One way, it would seem, of determining whether or not the emperor, in the mind of the Byzantine public at large, possessed the authority unilaterally to alter dogma would be to point to imperial successes in this area when no political motives were involved. But evidence for such successes cannot be found. And indeed the intransigent opposition evoked among the people even when the very fate of the Empire was at stake would indicate all the more that he did not have this right. Probably the best indication of the vulnerability of the emperors in their attempts to tamper with already crystallized dogma is the repeated failure of the Palaeologan emperors of the last two centuries to impose union with Rome on the eastern church when it was absolutely clear to those best familiar with the political realities that only through such a union could the Empire secure the military aid necessary to repel the Turks. The catch of course was the invariable condition that Rome always attached to unionist negotiations —insertion into the creed of the Latin *filioque* clause (the chief dogmatic difference between the two churches)—and in effect subordination of the Greek church to Rome. For most of the Byzantines, however—for the mass of the common people, most of the lower clergy, all the monks, and the greater part of the higher clergy and nobles—acceptance of the *filioque* would have constituted a fundamental change in the dogmatic basis of the faith. To them it meant not only apostasy but, as opponents of Michael Palaeologus, including Michael's own sister, termed it, a betrayal of the 'purity of the faith'. This in turn, the people believed, would lead not only to loss of God's favor but to inevitable destruction of the Empire itself.[66] Such was the conviction of most Greeks after the unionist Council of Florence in 1439[67]—a conviction borne out, they believed, by Constantinople's fall to the Turks only a few years later.

It is a striking fact that during the Palaeologan epoch and especially in the reigns of the three chief unionist emperors,

[65] Geanakoplos, *Emperor Michael, passim.*

[66] *Ibid.,* 270 and 274, which also cites G. Metochites, *Historia Dogmatica*, in A. Mai, *Patrum Nova Bibliotheca*, VIII (Rome, 1871) 38.

[67] Ducas (Bonn), 254 and 275.

Michael VIII, John VIII, and Constantine XI Palaeologus, there appeared no imperial propagandist, official or unofficial, to preach the legal right of the emperors to revise the church's dogma.[68] Such a claim is certainly not mentioned in that remarkable but little-known document of c. 1380, issued under John V Palaeologus and repeated under his son Manuel II, according to which the Holy Synod was constrained to list the powers of the emperor over the church. All of these, it should be observed, were of an administrative nature.[69] Whenever it was necessary for the Palaeologan supporters to mention doctrinal questions— and the pro-unionists always sought to avoid this—they stressed rather the political benefits to be derived from ecclesiastical union. Indeed they insisted that adoption of the Latin *filioque* clause entailed *no fundamental change in dogma*; rather a temporary administrative accommodation of the church to Rome. Even originally close friends of Michael VIII raised a storm of opposition to what they considered Michael's tampering with dogma, pointing out that the temporary political advantage to be gained could not outweigh what for them was to sacrifice the integrity of the faith.[70] To the clever argument of political expediency on the part of some extreme *politiques* in the reign of Constantine XI, just before Constantinople's fall to the Turks, 'let us unite with the Latins now and as soon as the danger passes we will quickly abandon the *filioque* and revert to Orthodoxy,' the future patriarch Gennadius Scholarios in effect replied: 'Do not fool yourselves; it is impossible to unite just a little bit with the Latins.'[71]

[68] Cf. Bury, *Later Roman Empire*, 403, who says that Basiliscus' Encyclical and Zeno's Henoticon assert the imperial right to dictate to the church and pronounce on doctrine. ('They virtually assumed the functions of an ecumenical council.') Nicetas (Bonn), 275, complains that the emperors set themselves up as 'definers of dogma'.

[69] For the list of nine powers (all pertaining to administration of the church and control over its prelates, administratively speaking), see V. Laurent, 'Les droits de l'empereur en matière ecclésiastique. L'accord de 1380–82', *Revue des études byzantines* (1954–55) 5–20. Cf. this article with B. Stephanides, 'The Last Stage of the Development of Church-State Relations in Byzantium', (in Greek), *Ep. Het. Byz. Spoudon* (1953) 29.

[70] On Michael's persecution of the monks, clergy and people see Geanakoplos, *Emperor Michael*, 264–76.

[71] See J. Gill, *The Council of Florence*, 384–85. Also N. Tomadakes, *George Scholarios and his Political Ideas* (in Greek) (Athens, 1954). In the *Acta Graeca*, ed. J. Gill, pt. 2, 433, the Emperor John VIII is quoted as saying that the emperor must follow the council's decision in dogma because he feels the council cannot err. (The *Acta Graeca* was pro-unionist.)

There is in fact, so far as I am aware, no official document from any period in which the emperor makes the flat claim to have complete power over the church in all spheres, including the doctrinal. Even such pro-imperialists as the canonist Theodore Balsamon and the historian Nicetas Choniates make no statement explicitly and categorically affirming the imperial right, unilaterally and without the agency of a general council, to alter or adjust the accepted dogma of the church.

Many of the emperors were theologians of considerable competence—Justinian, Leo VI, Alexius Comnenus, Manuel II Palaeologus, and others. But whenever an emperor attempted to alter dogma on his own there was invariably aroused a great public outcry. Justinian and Leo III, who sought to pronounce on dogma *ex cathedra*, to borrow the western phrase, were later forced by the popular reaction to convoke a council.[72] Basiliscus' attempt to revise the beliefs of Chalcedon was so violently rejected by the people that he was forced to repeal it and in fact to issue an anti-encyclical condemning his own views. And Zeno's *Henoticon* resulted in the schism of his patriarch Acacius, which brought upheaval to the church for some forty years, only to end later with the triumph of Orthodoxy. Heraclius promulgated his *Ecthesis* propounding Monothelitism, to be sure, with the help of his patriarch Sergius, but without reference to a council, a fact which immediately provoked an uproar. About ten years later, in connection with the same question, Constans II issued his *Typus* in an attempt to silence all discussion for or against the question of wills in Christ. The result of all this was the convocation of the Sixth Ecumenical Council (681) in which orthodoxy completely triumphed.[73]

Later emperors were wiser. It was more expedient for them to attempt to secure their ends by other means than by a frontal attack—the usual one with respect to dogma being the convocation of a council and an attempt to pack it or somehow to influence the passage of enactments imparting to their actions

---

[72] See Bury, *Later Roman Empire*, II, 383 ff. (on Justinian's edict over the Three Chapters). Also *ibid.*, 381–83 (on Justinian's edict in 543 against the Origenists, but here he was influenced by the attitude of many ecclesiastics). See also H. Alivizatos, *Die kirchliche Gesetzgebung des Kaisers Justinian I* (Berlin, 1913).

[73] On Basiliscus see Bury, *Later Roman Empire*, I, 403. On the other attempts to influence dogmatic formulation, *ibid.*, *passim*.

the sanction of legitimacy. They knew well that the people would accept only conciliar definitions of dogma. Two such examples were the attempts of Michael VIII at Lyons and John VIII at Florence. But even these emperors had a most difficult time in achieving their aims. For ultimately even their seemingly legitimate conciliar definitions were rejected—Lyons not only on the grounds of heresy in dogma but, as we have seen, that the four patriarchs of the East were not represented at the Council, and Florence on the basis that the Greek delegates had signed under duress despite the attendance of all five patriarchs of East and West (or their vicars) and long discussions on dogmatic questions.[74]

Florence in particular shows that even though the emperor appealed to a council to give his programme legitimacy and though he fostered open discussion of dogmatic differences, in the last analysis the final judgment as to acceptance of dogmatic change lay not even in the general council, as historians commonly believe, but in acceptance of the actions of the council by the great mass of the people. To be sure the question was complicated by the underlying Greek hostility for the Latins as a result of the Latin occupation of Constantinople in 1204 and the feeling of national pride and ecclesiastical independence from Rome.[75] But the fact remains that in the face of almost inevitable doom the great majority of the Greek populace chose to reject union with Rome, repeatedly fostered by their own emperors as the only possible salvation for the Empire from the Turks. In this most critical juncture, when effective imperial leadership over the church was most desperately needed, it not only revealed itself to be limited but was actively defied by the great majority of the people, clergy as well as laity.

Where in the final analysis then lay the ultimate authority or criterion for the preservation of the faith? Who was the final judge and defender, and what constituted the depository of the purity of the faith if it were not, as we have seen, the emperor? The obvious answer would seem to be—and the Byzantine sources, lay and ecclesiastical, are replete with such testimony—the ecumenical council. But, as we have noted, there were some cases where the representatives at councils were able to be swayed

[74] Gill, *Council of Florence*, 349 ff. Source is Ducas, 216.
[75] On this see below, Chap. 3, text and notes 73–85.

by imperial or clerical intimidation as at the 'Robber' Council of Ephesus in 449 or by imperial efforts to pack the assembly as in Constantine V's Iconoclastic Council of Hieria. If, however, the people felt that they had been betrayed by a council, then, as has not been adequately emphasized by historians, they might take it upon themselves to reject its decisions. This will of the people, a form of popular expression that reflected clerical as well as lay opinion and which is hard for us to grasp in concrete terms, has been referred to by some modern theologians as the 'conscience of the church'.[76] And, it is this, in the last analysis, even more than the general council, that was the true guardian or repository for the faith of the Greek church. Why did the Council of Florence in 1439 fail if not for the very reason that the masses, this 'conscience of the church', would not accept the decision as a true expression of the faith? The historian Ducas relates that on their return to Constantinople, after attending the deliberations over union with the papacy at Florence, the Greek representatives, when asked by the people why they had signed, replied: 'We have signed the union and sold our faith. . . .'[77] But this raises an even more fundamental question—had all the Greek representatives been convinced, as they clearly were not, of the truth of the Catholic position and proceeded voluntarily to sign the decree, would the masses then have accepted the union? The answer very probably would still have been the same.

CONCLUSION

What may we conclude from our analysis? It is clear to begin with that the emperor's power over the church was many-faceted. In the temporal realm he was a complete autocrat,

[76] See H. Alivizatos, 'The Conscience of the Church' (in Greek) (Athens, 1954). Also S. Tsankov, *The Eastern Orthodox Church*, trans. D. Lowrie (London, 1929) 90–92. He says the highest authority in the church is the community of the church, not the bishops alone nor the clergy nor the laity alone. 'The real guardian of piety is the body of the church, the people itself'. N. Zernov, *Eastern Christendom* (New York, 1961) 231: 'The Council's decisions require endorsement by the whole community.' This question of the conscience of the church was perhaps first put forth by the Russian scholar A. S. Chomjakov in several studies including *L'église latine et le Protestantisme au point de vue de l'église d'Orient* (Lausanne, 1872). Some modern Greek theologians subscribe to the theory (see above); others would place the final authority in the clergy as successors of Christ: cf. P. Trembelas, 'The Laymen in the Orthodox Church', (in Greek), *Ecclesia* (1930) 385 ff., and later issues. Also cf. Dyobouniotes in his dogmatic work. See finally Io. Kotsones, *The Position of Laymen in the Ecclesiastical Organism* (in Greek) (Athens, 1956).

[77] Ducas (Bonn) 216. Also cf. Gill, *Council of Florence*, 349.

limited only theoretically by the church in the application of Christian principles to civil law. In the external or administrative aspect of ecclesiastical affairs, it was the Byzantine ideal that the emperor as protector of the church work hand in hand with the ecclesiastical authorities. And this was normally the case. But when differences did arise—and they were not infrequent, especially with respect to the appointment or deposition of a patriarch—the imperial will seems almost invariably to have prevailed. It may therefore be said that in the sphere of ecclesiastical polity the emperor was able to exercise complete authority over the church, subject only to the relative strength of character of each incumbent emperor and patriarch.

Moreover, the emperor's so-called liturgical privileges bestowed upon him even the appearance of a kind of sacerdotal authority. It is primarily these two factors, virtually unlimited administrative control and his impressive liturgical privileges that have led some scholars to term the emperor Caesaropapistic. Yet, as we have shown, the emperor was never able successfully to penetrate into the church's inner core, the more spiritual form relating to dogma and the sacraments. Although his liturgical privileges raised him above all laymen, imparting to him almost a hieratic character, he could not assume the basic power of the clergy—to dispense the sacraments enabling man to achieve salvation. Nor, even more important, could he alter established dogma. In contrast to the post-1870 papacy pronouncing on dogma *ex cathedra*, he was not absolute or infallible in matters of faith.

Indeed, the frequency or infrequency of the repeated imperial attempts to redefine dogma in the church, either directly by imperial edict (as in the case of Leo III) or through the shield of an ecumenical council, is less significant than the ultimate failure of every single imperial attempt, in the long run, to revise the traditional dogma, with the possible exception of certain efforts of that most arbitrarily despotic of rulers, Justinian.[78] Imperial attempts to interfere in what we have termed the esoteric realm of the church, in particular the sphere of dogma, were never recognized by the will of the people, the true repository of the Orthodox faith. In view of the repeated imperial failures to

[78] See M. Anastos, 'Justinian's Despotic Control over the Church'.

control this vital, quintessential sphere of the church, it can hardly be argued that imperial authority over this area was a traditionally accepted imperial right, as was the emperor's role in the administrative sphere. With the authority of the emperor over the church thus restricted both theoretically and in actual practice to the administrative area of church polity and to certain liturgical privileges, we cannot speak of a truly absolute or Caesaropapistic master of the Byzantine church.

The term Caesaropapism, seen in this light, is thus not only inaccurate but extremely misleading. A new term is needed which would reflect the emperor's gradation of powers, from the absolute to the virtually non-existent, in the various spheres of the church-state complex. A possible suggestion for a new term might be Caesaroprocuratorism. As is well-known, in the reforms instituted by Peter the Great in the Russian church of the early eighteenth century, a new office, that of procurator, held by a layman, was created. This official was to control or share with the clergy in the administration of the Russian church but was to have no spiritual powers to interfere in dogmatic matters and, of course, he could not dispense the sacraments.[79] Through the application of the term Caesaroprocuratorism to Byzantium, the ambiguity of that misleading term Caesaropapism at first glance seems avoided with respect to the external and esoteric realms of the church. But, besides being rather unwieldy, Caesaroprocuratorism is inadequate in that the 'procurator' portion carries no connotation of association with the church.

Another suggestion might be Caesaropaternalism or Caesaro-cybernesis, the Greek word *cybernesis* pertaining to the act of governing. But the term paternalism is certainly too weak in scope and Caesarocybernesis on its side is overly strong and secular sounding. Some years ago Professor E. Kantorowicz, in a lecture concerned in part with this same question of Caesaro-papism, suggested as a substitute term the word *Christomimetes* ('imitator of Christ').[80] Though the term would seem accurately to

[79] In 1721 Peter established a kind of 'Spiritual Department' or Holy Synod to replace the old patriarchate. Peter tells us that this was established because the simple folk could not distinguish the spiritual from the sovereign power, believing the spiritual authority higher than the temporal.

[80] The term *Christomimetos* (made in the image of Christ) is found in Theophanes Continuatus (Bonn, 1938) 447.

reflect the position of the emperor as the Vicegerent of God on earth, it does not, at least explicitly enough, express his authority over the two institutions of church and state as such.

It is very difficult, unfortunately, to find one word that would reflect the shades of meaning that we have pointed out in the relationship of emperor and church. What is needed perhaps is a term that combines something of the kinds of titles applied to Queen Elizabeth I of England—Queen by the Grace of God, Defender of the Faith, and Supreme Governor of the church. But even these are not entirely accurate if applied to Byzantium. Supreme Governor of the church is perhaps too strong, nor do the titles convey the aura of sanctity, the profound mystique ascribed to the Byzantine emperor by his people. Nevertheless, though a satisfactory term is yet to be found, we should cease to apply the word Caesaropapism to Byzantine political theory if by that term is meant an all-pervasive imperial control not only over temporal activities but over all aspects of the life of the church as well. As we have tried to show in this chapter by means of a new approach to the material, the Byzantine emperor was not a true king-priest as implied in the term Caesaropapism.

CHAPTER THREE

THE COUNCIL OF FLORENCE (1438-1439) AND THE PROBLEM OF UNION BETWEEN THE BYZANTINE AND LATIN CHURCHES

1

For the medieval world the Council of Florence, held only fifteen years before the end of the Byzantine Empire, offered the last great opportunity to close the gap separating eastern from western Christendom. Not only was it the most brilliant convocation of Greeks and Latins in the entire Middle Ages, but it marked the first occasion in centuries that East and West assembled in ecumenical council to debate the differences separating their two churches.[1]

For almost four hundred years prior to the Council of Florence, from the schism of Patriarch Michael Cerularius and Pope Leo IX in 1054 to the convening of this Council in 1438, it had been a primary aim of popes and emperors to restore ecclesiastical communion. Negotiations with this object in view had, in fact, been conducted on approximately thirty different occasions.[2] Strong forces motivated the desire for union. To the papacy union was the most effective way to extend its ecclesiastical authority over East as well as West, while for the Byzantine emperors of the fourteenth and fifteenth centuries, union with the Latin church seemed the sole means to insure papal aid against the peril of either a Latin crusade or Turkish attack against Constantinople.[3] Of lesser importance but worthy of note was

[1] On this council's ecumenicity see the official decree of union in the so-called *Acta Graeca* (*Quae Supersunt Actorum Graecorum Concilii Florentini necnon Descriptionis Cuiusdam Eiusdem*, ed. J. Gill [Rome, 1953] hereafter referred to as *Acta*) 461. Cf. ed. Mansi, *Sacrorum conciliorum . . . collectio*, XXXIA, cols. 1027–28. At Florence, in contrast to the Council of Lyons in 1274, formal debate for the first time in centuries took place over ecclesiastical differences.

[2] Thus calculates L. Bréhier, 'Attempts at Reunion of the Greek and Latin Churches', *Cambridge Medieval History*, IV (1936) 594 ff.

[3] For bibl. on the complex problem of unionist negotiations in the period from 1054 to 1453 see Appendix, Bibliographical Note C.

the rare idealism of such thirteenth century figures as Pope Gregory X and Patriarch John Bekkos, or the western publicist Humbert of Romans and the Greek Franciscan John Parastron, to whom Greco-Latin religious accord was the supreme remedy for the problems of eastern and western Christendom.[4]

As a result of these considerations, union was actually declared at three separate times: first, following the Fourth Crusade of 1204 with enforced Greek conversion to Catholicism, then at the Council of Lyons in 1274 by personal agreement between Pope Gregory X and Emperor Michael Palaeologus, and, finally, at Florence itself through the convocation of a general council.[5] But although union thus seemed to have been achieved, it was in reality each time only ephemeral and without lasting effect. In view of the various forces conducing towards union, how can these repeated failures be explained? Why in particular did the Greek population, for whom the existence of the nation itself was often at stake, always repudiate union?

The answer to these questions lies partly in the nature of the motivations themselves. For to emperors and popes union was less a matter of merging two spiritual bodies than a means for the satisfaction of political ends. Religious sincerity, indispensable for permanent union, was too often lacking,[6] and if the objectives of the papacy remained generally constant, the enthusiasm of the emperors for union fluctuated in accordance with their need for western aid.[7]

[4] For recent works on Gregory X and Bekkos (who at first opposed union) see V. Laurent, 'La Croisade et la question d'orient sous le pontificat de Grégoire X', *Revue historique du Sud-est Européen* (1945) 105–37; and his 'Grégoire X et le projet d'une ligue antiturque', *Échos d'Orient*, XXXVII (1938) 257–273; G. Hofmann, 'Patriarch Johann Bekkos und die lateinische Kultur', *Orientalia Christiana Periodica*, XI (1945) 141 ff.; and my 'Michael VIII Palaeologus and the Union of Lyons', *Harvard Theological Review*, XLVI (1953) 79–89. Now also D. Geanakoplos, *Emperor Michael Palaeologus and the West*, 1258–82 (Cambridge, Mass.) 237–45 and 307–308. On the Dominican Humbert who acutely foresaw durable union only through pacific rapprochement and mutual education of both churches, see extracts from his 'Opus Tripartitum' in Mansi, *Conciliorum . . . Collectio*, XXIV, pt. 2, cols. 120–130; and cf. A. Michel, *Das Opus tripartitum des Humbertus de Romanis O. P.* (Graz, 1926) (inaccessible to me). On Parastron, a Constantinople-born Greek of Latin faith who declared he would gladly give his life for the success of union, see Viller, *loc. cit.*, XVI, 265, note 4; and my 'Michael Palaeologus and the Union of Lyons', 84. Also see Geanakoplos, *Emperor Michael*, 267–68.

[5] On these specific episodes see Appendix, Bibl. Note C.

[6] See Viller, *loc. cit.*, XVI, 280: 'negotiations were more political than religious (and) between two governments than two heads of churches.' Bréhier, *loc. cit.*, 596.

[7] For a convenient summary of the shifts in Greek imperial policy in accordance with the degree of external danger to Byzantium, see esp. Bréhier, *loc. cit.*, 695–696.

From the viewpoint of ecclesiastical government, a more fundamental reason for the failure of union was the conflict between two basic conceptions of the church. To the monarchical claims of the papacy was opposed the Byzantine concept of the pentarchy, what might be termed a kind of 'collegial' authority. In accordance with this theory the eastern patriarchs, while acknowledging the honorary primacy of Rome,[8] rejected papal assertions of universal disciplinary jurisdiction which would have permitted the papacy, on appeal, to intervene directly in affairs of the Greek church, in effect rendering the eastern bishops mere satellites of the Holy See.[9] While for the West, in accordance with medieval canonistic development, supreme ecclesiastical jurisdiction came to be vested in the pope alone, for the eastern church the highest religious authority was believed to reside in the ecumenical councils in which all five patriarchs of East and West had to be represented. It was this emphasis on the authority and canons of the first seven ecumenical councils, transmitted inviolate through the centuries, which constituted for Byzantium the essence of Orthodoxy.[10]

Complicating the difference in ecclesiastical polity from the Byzantine side, of course, was the traditional authority of the emperor over the Greek church—the so-called Caesaropapism. Whether the term is justifiable or not, it is clear that many emperors in times of political stress did use their authority in an attempt, successful or otherwise, to accommodate the Greek church to the needs of the state[11].

[8] On recognition of Roman primacy of honor see the treatise of the famous fourteenth century Greek theologian Nilos Cabasilas, 'De causis dissensionum in ecclesia', MPG, vol. 149, col. 685B. Cf. Heiler, *Urkirche und Ostkirche*, 141. Also on papal primacy F. Dvornik *Byzance et la primauté romaine* (Paris, 1964) and *The Primacy of Peter in the Orthodox Church*, by J. Meyendorff and others (London, 1963).

[9] On pentarchic theory see esp. Dvornik, *Photian Schism*, 150 and note 2; Jugie, *Le Schisme Byzantin*, 37–38; 222–223, 232; and Karmires, 'The Schism of the Roman Church', 30–31, 49, 56, and esp. 65–66.

[10] See Dvornik, *op. cit.*, 420, 423 and cf. Karmires, *loc. cit.*, 29.

[11] The role of Caesaropapism (see preceding chapter) has been the cause of much controversy. According to an important Catholic historian, M. Jugie, *Le Schisme Byzantin*, 3–9, and esp. 10, Caesaropapism 'incontestably should bear the chief responsibility for the preparation of the schism'. Cf. the typically Greek attitude of Ch. Papadopoulos, *The Primacy of the Bishop of Rome* (in Greek) (Athens, 1930) esp. 207 ff., who attributes the basic cause of the schism to papal attempts to impose primacy of jurisdiction over the Greek church. On the accommodation of the church to the state, the Byzantine theory of 'oikonomia', see above, Ch. 2, text and note 58.

The Lamentation of the Virgin. Byzantine fresco in church of Nerezi, Yugoslavia (mid-12th century). Plate 7 (See pp. 48-9.)

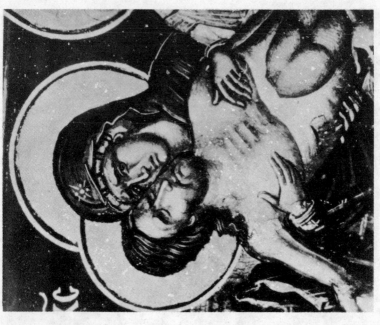

Descent from the Cross. Detail from fresco by Theophanes the Cretan in Catholikon of Laura Monastery on Mt. Athos (1535). (See p. 133.)

Plate 8

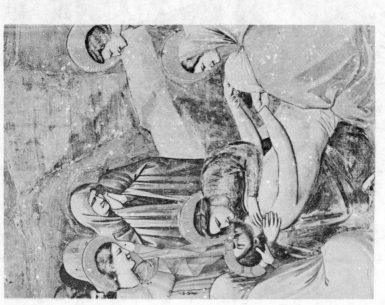

The Lamentation. Detail from fresco by Giotto in Arena Chapel, Padua (1303–05). (See p. 48.)

These politico-ecclesiastical considerations, however, were not the only obstacles to union. There was another factor, more difficult to define but of at least equal importance—the deep-rooted antagonism for the Latins felt by the Greek population of Constantinople on whom, in the last analysis, the success of union depended.[12] This popular antipathy for the Latins was more than religious in scope, but it tended, in the spirit of the age, to find expression in the church. For in that institution were reflected not only the basic difference of language, but the development of theories and practices characteristic of the mentality of each people.[13] It is therefore in the broad context of East-West antagonism that a full solution for the problem of union must ultimately be sought. Only thus can the endless and seemingly unproductive deliberations over such questions as the *filioque*, purgatory, the use of unleavened bread in the eucharist, or even the shaving of clerical beards acquire genuine significance. For apart of course from any dogmatic importance, these questions were symptomatic of the more underlying issues separating East from West, and it is this fact which made the problem of union so difficult.

It is not my purpose here to analyze the successive attempts at union. Rather it is my aim to focus on the disputations at the Council of Florence, which brought to a climax four hundred years of unionist efforts. Through an examination, necessarily brief, of certain aspects of the proceedings of the Council as well as of the circumstances which brought it about, I hope to provide some insight into the complexities of union and especially into the forces which prevented its successful conclusion. While I shall deal with some of the more generally known events of the Council I shall at at the same time touch upon several incidents, relatively unimportant in themselves, but revealing basic attitudes indicative of the underlying tensions between the two peoples and their churches.

[12] The Emperor Manuel II (d. 1425) realized this well when he warned his son John VIII that the pride of the Latins and the obstinacy of the Greeks would never agree, and attempts at union would only widen the schism (Sphrantzes [Bonn] 178–179). Cf. Syrop., 258.

[13] On identification of the Greek language with Orthodoxy, and the unfavourable Byzantine attitude to Latin see S. Runciman, 'Byzantine Linguists', *Prosfora to S. Kyriakedes* (in Greek) (1953) 577. For widespread Western prejudices against Greeks and their language, see Viller, XVI, 284–305. On reciprocal ignorance of Latin and Greek see Jugie, *Le Schisme Byzantin*, 39–42.

II

As no official acts as such survive for the Council of Florence, our information must in the main be drawn from three accounts of participants: first, the so-called *Acta Graeca*, written in Greek most probably by the pro-unionist Latinophile Bishop, Dorotheos of Mytilene;[14] second, the Latin account in dialogue form by the papal advocate Andrea of Santa Croce;[15] and, finally, the Greek history or memoirs of Silvester Syropoulos, Grand Ecclesiarch of St. Sophia in Constantinople. While the *Acta Graeca* has been considered most authoritative by western scholars, the work of Syropoulos, well known in the East, has long been neglected, indeed generally rejected, by the West. But this neglect was in part attributable to the adverse influence of its only editor, the Anglican Bishop Robert Creyghton, who in 1660 published the Greek text together with a frequently inaccurate, sharply anti-papal translation into Latin.[16] More important, however, was the attitude of leading Catholic historians, such as Hefele, Cecconi, and Allatius in particular, who violently attacked the work of

[14] The best edition is now that of J. Gill (see above, note 1). On Dorotheos as author of the *Acta* (or rather of the 'descriptive' sections as distinct from the 'acts') see Gill, *Acta*, pp. lxiii–lxix, and his 'Sources of the "Acta" of the Council of Florence', *Orientalia Christiana Periodica*, XIV (1948) 43 ff. Supporting Dorotheos' authorship are V. Laurent, 'Apropos de Dorothée Métropolite de Mytilène, *Revue des Études Byzantines*, IX (1951) 163–169 (a biographical sketch of Dorotheos); G. Hofmann, 'Die Konzilsarbeit in Ferrara,' *Orientalia Christiana Periodica*, III (1937) 110; and T. Frommann, *Kritische Beiträge zur Geschichte der florentiner Kircheneinigung* (Halle, 1872) 63–79; A. Vogt's article on the Council of Florence in *Dict. Théol. Cath.*, VI, col. 28 (cf. col. 49); and, recently, D. Balanos, *The Byzantine Ecclesiastical Writers* (in Greek) (Athens, 1951) 172, note 1. Cf. however, the older work of H. Vast, *Le Cardinal Bessarion* (Paris, 1878) 436–449, and Hefele-Leclercq, *Conciles*, VII pt. 2, 957, who ascribe authorship of the Acta to Bessarion.

[15] In Mansi, XXXIB, cols. 1431ff. On Andrea himself see T. Ortolan's article in *Dict. d'Hist. et Geog. Ecclés.*, II, col. 1662, and on weaknesses in Andrea's account owing to its dialogue form and dependence on interpreters at Florence see Frommann, *op. cit.*, 45.

[16] The full title assigned by Creyghton is S. Sgouropoulos (sic), *Vera historia unionis non verae inter Graecos et Latinos, sive Concilii Florentini exactissima narratio, etc.* (Hague, 1660). (A new edition of Syropoulos is eagerly awaited from V. Laurent.) S. G. Mercati's article in *Enciclopedia Italiana*, XXI, 910, says that Syropoulos' anti-unionist tendencies are accentuated by Creyghton, whose inexact translation in turn provoked the confutation of L. Allatius, *In Robert Creygtoni apparatum, versionem . . . scriptam a Silvestro Syropulo . . . exercitationes* (Rome, 1674, earlier ed. 1665). See further the recent article of J. Gill, 'The "Acta" and the Memoirs of Syropoulos as History', *Orientalia Christiana Periodica*, XIV (1948) 300–341. For a Greek point of view on Syropoulos see A. Diamantopoulos, 'Silvestros Syropoulos and his *Memoirs* at the Florence synod', (in Greek) *New Zion*, XVIII (Jerusalem, 1923) 241ff. and later issues.

Syropoulos for its anti-unionist views, considering the author to be a kind of Sarpi of the Council of Florence.[17]

For these reasons, not to mention the relative unavailability of Creyghton's edition,[18] comparatively few western scholars have been even aware of the remarkable store of information Syropoulos provides. Yet his work is practically the sole record of what went on behind the scenes among the Greek delegation. Beginning with the diplomatic preliminaries to the Council, Syropoulos describes in detail the dangerous journey of the Greeks from beleagured Constantinople to Venice, their day-by-day activities at the Council, their hopes, frustrations, and petty quarrels, and, above all, their private discussions both among themselves and with the Latins. In short, Syropoulos draws a remarkably complete picture of the Greek mentality, especially of the deep conflict between the unionist Latinophiles and the anti-unionist Orthodox during this critical period of Byzantium's dying days.

Recently Professor Joseph Gill of the Pontifical Institute in Rome (who has published a valuable edition of the *Acta Graeca* and more recently a book on the Council of Florence),[19] has demonstrated the accuracy of a number of Syropoulos' statements, hitherto considered false or grossly exaggerated. On the basis of comparison with newly discovered documents, Gill analyzes, for example, the correctness of Syropoulos' numerous figures regarding the daily subsistence promised by the papacy to the Greek delegates at Florence.[20] Some use of Syropoulos has also

[17] On this see Frommann, *op. cit.*, 37–58. Also Cecconi, who, in his long 224-page introduction generally impugns Syropoulos' accuracy (esp. pp. 14–15, 32, 36, 45 and 50). Cf. Hefele-Leclercq, *Conciles*, VII pt. 2, 958–959, and, on Allatius, see preceding note. See finally the harsh invective of Ph. Labbé, in Hardouin, *Concilia Generalia*, IX, 1079, who places Syropoulos in the company of such notorious heretics as Arius, Nestorius, and the Albigensians.

[18] The only avilable printed copies in America to my knowledge are at Harvard University and the Library of Congress.

[19] See above notes 1 and 14. Add now J. Gill, *The Council of Florence* (Cambridge, Eng., 1959) and his *Personalites of the Council of Florence* (Oxford, 1965).

[20] Gill, 'The "Acta" and the Memoirs of Syropoulos as History', 330–341, esp. 339: '(The Acta Camerae Apostolicae) reveal that Syropoulos' dates of payments and sums recorded as paid are often exact and that the Greeks had real grounds for complaint.' Also now Gill, *The Council of Florence*. Cf. Cecconi, *op. cit.*, 478–486 and also Syrop., who makes very numerous references to papal subsistence or payments (see 105, 205 ff., 225, 302, 318, and esp. 105, where he records that no money or subsistence was ever given to the Greeks without ulterior motives). The Acta says almost nothing about the penury of the Greeks except that the pope's financial embarrassment was the cause of the council's transfer from Ferrara to Florence (220; Mansi, 696).

recently been made by other notable Catholic scholars, such as
G. Hofmann, V. Laurent, and R. Loenertz, while several modern
Greek historians have found corroboration for statements of
Syropoulos in passages of contemporary Byzantine writers.[21]
Syropoulos' remarks are, to be sure, often partisan, but is it not
necessary for the historian to understand the anti-unionist as well
as unionist views at the Council? It is indeed these very attitudes
which may best explain the failure of lasting union. Provided
Syropoulos' statements can be controlled by other Byzantine
writings or, whenever possible, by contemporary Latin accounts,
there is no justifiable reason to reject his history as an important
and basic source for certain aspects of the Council.[22]

Seven years of diplomatic negotiation preceded the assembling
of the council at Florence,[23] during which the papacy, after
centuries of refusal, finally accepted the conditions of the Greek
people and clergy for the establishment of valid union — namely,
the convocation of an ecumenical council.[24] This stipulation is
perhaps nowhere more clearly defined than by the celebrated
Barlaam of Calabria, who in 1339, exactly a century before
Florence, had been secretly sent by the Emperor Andronikos III

[21] G. Hofmann, 'Die Konzilsarbeit in Ferrara', *Orientalia Christiana Periodica*, III
(1937) 110ff. and later issues; V. Laurent, 'Apropos de Dorothée, Métropolite de
Mitylène', 163–166; and R. Loenertz, 'Les Dominicains Byzantins Théodore et
André Chrysobergès et les Négociations pour l'union des églises de 1415 à 1430,'
Archivum Fratrum Praedicatorum, IX (1939) 5–61, esp. 32, 46. Also Gill, *Council of
Florence*. Cf. also M. Jugie, 'Note sur l'histoire du concile de Florence de Sylvestre
Syropoulos', *Échos d'Orient*, 38 (1939) 70 ff. and J. Décarreaux, 'L'arrivée des grecs en
Italie pour le concile de l'union d'après les Mémoires de Syropoulos', *Revue des études
italiennes*, VII (1960) 27–58. Among modern Greek historians see esp. Diamanto-
poulos, 'Silvestros Syropoulos, etc.', 265 ff.; P. Kalligas, *Studies and Speeches* (in
Greek) (Athens, 1882) 1–186; and Demetrakopoulos, *Historia schismatis*, 99–174.

[22] F. Dölger, review in *Byzantinische Zeitschrift*, 47 (1954) 154 and Frommann, *op.
cit.*, 6, note 1, consider Syropoulos the second important source for the Florentine
council, after the *Acta Graeca*.

[23] Unionist pourparlers had been going on intermittently since long before this,
but the Turkish conquest of Salonika in 1430 and the accession of Pope Eugenius
IV in 1431 marked a new stage in the negotiations. See Loenertz, 'Les Dominicains
Byzantins', 5, and Diehl-Guilland, *L'Europe Orientale* (Paris, 1945) 359.

[24] This Greek attitude was expressed only a short time after 1054, the date usually
considered as marking the definitive schism (see my article with bibliography, 'On
the Schism of the Greek and Roman Churches', *Greek Orthodox Theological Review*
[1954] 17–18), when the emperor wrote to the pope that union could be realized
only through the convocation of a general council (see Norden, *Papsttum und
Byzanz*, 48). The popes of the fourteenth century themselves seemed to favour a
council, but never gave their full support until the western conciliar movement
forced their hand (Viller, XVIII, 20–35 and see below, text and note 30).

to the papal court at Avignon to plead the cause of union.[25] Inasmuch as Barlaam's discourse reflects the sentiment prevailing among the Greek people also later during the period of Florence,[26] it is worth quoting. Barlaam said to the pope:

'. . . That which separates the Greeks from you is not so much a difference in dogma as the hatred of the Greeks for the Latins provoked by the wrongs they have suffered. It will be necessary to confer some great boon on them to change their feeling. . . . There is only one effective means to bring about union: through the convocation of a general council to be held in the East. For to the Greeks anything determined by a general council has the authority of law. You may object and say that a council has already met at Lyons to treat of union. But no Greek recognizes the ecumenicity of the Council of Lyons, since no subsequent council has declared it so. The Greek legates at Lyons were, in fact, sent there neither by the four patriarchs who govern the eastern church, nor by the Greek people, but by the emperor alone, who, without trying to gain the support of his people, sought only by force to realize the union.[27] To the four patriarchs therefore send legates, and under their presidency a general council will convene which will achieve union. Then all of us present at the council will say to the Greek people: Here is what the Holy Ecumenical Council

[25] Barlaam's discourse is printed in MPG, vol. 151, col. 1332. On Barlaam's mission see C. Gianelli, 'Un projetto di Barlaam Calabro per l'unione delle chiese', *Miscellanea Giovanni Mercati*, III (Vatican, 1946) 171 and note 22; and Viller, XVIII, 21-24. See further on Barlaam, Jugie's article in *Dict. Hist. et Géog. Ecclés.*, VI, cols. 817–834.

[26] The idea of an ecumenical council to end the schism was expressed by many Greeks between the period of Barlaam and the Council of Florence: Nicephorus Gregoras, X, 8; John Cantacuzenos, IV, 9; Nilos Cabasilas, MPG, vol. 149, cols. 684 ff. (for a recent article touching on Cabasilas see M. Paulová, 'L'Empire Byzantin et les Tchèques avant la chute de Constantinople', *Byzantinoslavica*, XIV [1953] 164); and Joseph Bryennios (who died just before the convocation at Florence), *On the Union of the Churches* (in Greek) ed. Bulgaris, I (Leipzig, 1768). Noteworthy, on the western side, is the attitude of the Dominican Humbert of Romans, who just before 1274 had favoured the convocation of a council but in the East (Mansi, XXIV, col. 128). Cf. Viller, XVIII, 23, note 1, and 20–35, for mention of representatives of the University of Paris like Jean Gerson in the early fifteenth century who demanded a council to treat of the Greek union. Finally see Loenertz, *loc. cit.*, 42–43.

[27] As Jugie, *Le Schisme Byzantin*, 259, justifiably emphasizes, there were only two Greek bishops at the council, and the union was concluded 'without psychological preparation and theological discussion on the disputed points'. In fact, the concessions mentioned in letters borne by the imperial envoys had been forcibly extorted from the Greek clergy.

has decreed: It is your duty to obey its decisions, and all will submit. . . .'[28]

Barlaam's appeal at the time was ignored, for the Avignonese papacy had no intention of compromising its absolute authority by the assembling of a council to debate differences with the 'schismatic' Greeks.[29] But the subsequent decline of papal prestige in the West as a result of the Great Schism and the increasing western emphasis on conciliar supremacy, eventually induced the Holy See to view the Greek demands in a more favourable light.[30] This change of attitude coincided with an even more pressing need of the Greek Emperors for western aid in order to salvage their last remaining territories of Constantinople and the Morea from the Turks, now practically at the gates of the capital.[31]

The situation became three-sided, however. For besides the Holy See, its bitter rivals, the western conciliarists sitting at Basle, also looked upon a Greek union as the best means of establishing ecclesiastical superiority in the West. Thus the Byzantine emperor and patriarch were courted by both Pope Eugenius IV and the assembly of Basle, each promising military aid for Constantinople together with the payment of all expenses for the journey of a Greek delegation to a general council to be held in the West.[32]

The contest for Byzantine favour grew increasingly severe. Indeed, the account of Syropoulos, corroborated by a report of the legate of Basle, John of Ragusa, and by papal documents, describes the rival western delegations at Constantinople com-

[28] This passage follows the quotations conveniently cited in Viller, XVIII, 22–23. For text see MPG, vol. 151, cols. 1332 ff.

[29] For Pope Benedict XII's refusal of Barlaam's proposal see MPG, vol. 151, cols. 1255 ff. The chief point at issue was the *filioque* (on which see below, text and note 64). The Pope and Curia did not want to question an article of the faith already defined (see Viller, XVII, 23 and Jugie, *op. cit.*, 251).

[30] On this see Paulová, 'L'Empire byzantin . . . ', 164–167; Loenertz, 'Les Dominicains Byzantins', 42–43; Viller, XVIII, 20–35; and Jugie, *op. cit.*, 251. On the Great Schism see also O. Halecki, 'Rome et Byzanz au temps du grand schisme d'occident', *Collectanea Theologica*, XVIII (1937) 476–532.

[31] Bréhier, *loc. cit.*, 617 ff.; Vasiliev, *op. cit.*, 640, 672; etc.

[32] See Syrop., 32 ff. E. Cecconi, *Studi Storici sul Concilio di Firenze* (Florence, 1869) 478–486. For the papal-Basle rivalry over Byzantine favor see Frommann, *op. cit.*, 7ff.; Paulová, 'L'Empire Byzantin et les Tchèques', 164–167; W. Waugh, 'Councils of Constance and Basle', *Cambridge Medieval History*, VIII (1936) 35 ff., and the work of J. Haller, *Concilium Basiliense*, I–V (Basel, 1896–1905) *passim*. Of interest here also is a little-known Greek work on the Greek-born, pro-unionist pope of the early fifteenth century Alexander V, by M. Renieris, *The Greek Pope Alexander V; Byzantium and the Basle Council* (Athens, 1881).

peting with such intensity as to be restrained from blows only by imperial intervention.[33] Previous to this, an even more violent scene had occurred at Basle itself, where the papal and conciliar adherents created so great a tumult in disputing the question of the Greek union that in the revealing phrase of Aeneas Silvius (later Pope Pius II), 'You would have found the drunkards of a tavern better behaved.'[34]

Why in the end did the Greeks prefer the offers of the papacy to those of the Basle fathers, when Byzantine tradition itself, at least from the standpoint of the pentarchy, would seem to be conciliar in emphasis? Would it not have been more advantageous, as several modern Greek scholars question, to have preferred the Basle assembly?[35] This problem has not yet been fully elucidated by historians,[36] but we may suggest several reasons for the selection of the papacy. Besides the fact that both emperor and patriarch stipulated the personal presence of Pope Eugenius at the council[37]—a condition uncertain of attainment at Basle[38]— the Greeks naturally preferred as a site for the council the papal choice of Ferrara in Italy as opposed to more distant Basle, Avignon, or Savoy, places insisted upon by the Basle conciliarists.[39] Added to this, probably, was the Greek familiarity with the

[33] See Syrop., 54 ff. For the report of the Basle envoy John of Ragusa see Cecconi, *Studi Storici*, 487 ff. and esp. pp. dxi, dxii. On John of Ragusa's account see Diamantopoulos, *loc. cit.*, 274–275. On John also see F. Dölger, 'Ein byzantinisches Staatsdokument in der Universitätsbibliothek Basel: ein Fragment des Tomos des Jahres 1351', *Historisches Jahrbuch* (1953) 218–220; and cf. Gill, *op. cit.*, 63–66, 74–83. As for the papal embassy's account, see Cecconi, *op. cit.*, esp. p. dlxxvii: 'ad vitandum quondam motionem galiotarum nostrorum (!) contra gentes illarum galearum. Imperator fecit dictas galeas transire ad portum ante palatium suum. . . .'

[34] See *Der Briefwechsel des Eneas Silvius Piccolomini*, ed. R. Wolkan, pt. I, vol. I, *Briefe aus der Laienzeit* (Vienna, 1909) letter 24, p. 58 ff., dated May 21, 1437. (English transl. in W. Boulting, *Aeneas Silvius* [London, 1908] 82.) Cf. Mansi, XXXI, cols., 223 ff.

[35] See esp. Diamantopoulos, 'Silvester Syropoulos', 265 ff.; and Kalligas, *Studies and Speeches* (in Greek) (Athens, 1918) 11–32.

[36] See Paulová, *loc. cit.*, 167 ff.

[37] See documents published by G. Hofmann, in *Orientalium Documenta Minora*, III, fasc. III (Rome, 1953) nos. 9–10, pp. 13–15, dated Nov. 11 and 26, 1435, letters of Patriarch John II and Emperor John VIII to Pope Eugenius IV: 'cognoscimus, quod presentia vestre beatitudinis multum necessaria est in futura synodo' (ed. Cecconi, *op. cit.*, 154–155 and 166–167). Cf. Paulová, *loc. cit.*, 167.

[38] Just before the convocation of the Council at Ferrara-Florence, the Basle fathers had suspended the pope from his functions. See also Hofmann, *Orientalium Documenta Minora*, III, fasc. III, p. 29, letter of John Palaeologus to the Basle synod declaring himself free of obligation because Basle had not carried out its promises.

[39] On these sites see the reports of the papal embassy in Cecconi, *op. cit.*, no. 188, esp. pp. dlxxvii–dlxxx; and of the Basle envoy John of Ragusa, *ibid.*, p. dxvii. Cf. Syrop., 19. Acceptance of the cities specified by Basle would have permitted exercise of great influence by the conciliarists.

traditional prestige of the papacy in contrast to the relatively
recent emergence of western conciliarism. Not to be overlooked,
finally, is the role of the Greek emperor. In line with Byzantine
autocratic ideas, he may well have preferred to negotiate with a
single absolute authority instead of the notoriously factious
assembly at Basle.[40] We must be careful in this connection, however, not to overstress the concept of an all-pervasive Caesaropapism on the part of the emperor during this period, inasmuch
as the very failures of the many unionist attempts initiated by the
emperors themselves militate against such a theory.[41]

On the 24th of November, 1437, in ships provided by the
pope, a huge Byzantine delegation of seven hundred ecclesiastics
and laymen, headed by the Emperor John VIII Palaeologus, the
Patriarch Joseph of Constantinople, and representatives of the
three other patriarchs, finally set out for Italy. After a long,
hazardous voyage of three months[42] the Greeks reached Venice.[43]
But almost immediately after their arrival, the Council was
threatened with disruption over a question of protocol. On the
entrance of the Patriarch Joseph into Ferrara, he absolutely
refused, despite the demands of the papal representatives and his
own pro-unionist convictions,[44] to salute the pope in the western

[40] Syrop., 79 and 85 ff., reports that as late as his arrival in Venice the emperor
was still undecided whether to go to Basle or Ferrara, the latter being the site fixed
by the pope for the Council. According to Syrop., he was advised by the Doge to
select that most advantageous to him. But news of the death of the western Emperor
Sigismund, a supporter of Basle from whom the Greek emperor expected aid,
probably helped to induce the Greeks to go directly to Ferrara. On the accuracy of
this report see Frommann, op. cit., 9; and B. Stephanides, 'The Last Stage of the
Development of the Relations between the Byzantine Church and State' (in Greek)
(1953) 27–40, both of whom seem to accept its authenticity. Cf. Hefele-Leclerq,
VII, pt. 2, 961, which denies its accuracy.

[41] The popes tended to over-emphasize the power of the emperor over the Greek
church, and therefore often wrongly attributed Greek popular hostility toward
union to imperial perfidy. See Viller, XVI, 264, note 4 and XVIII, 20–21. Also A.
Fliche, 'Le problème oriental au second concile oecumenique de Lyon', Orientalia
Christiana Periodica, XIII (1947) 4.

[42] On the preparations for departure and the voyage itself see Syrop., 60–80.
Little important information is added by other Greek historians. But cf. the report
of the Bishop of Digne (who participated in the papal embassy escorting the Greeks
to Venice) in Cecconi, op. cit., no. 188, esp. p. dlxxxi.

[43] For the arrival at Venice see Syrop., 80 ff. Note his moving account (87) of
Greek emotion at seeing the former treasures of Hagia Sophia exhibited at San
Marco. On the reception at Venice see Acta, 1–5 (Mansi, 466–467); and Ducas
(Bonn) 212.

[44] On his unionism see even Syrop., 92, who reports that the patriarch confided
to intimates his hope that papal co-operation would permit him to cast aside the
Greek church's servitude to the emperor and 'to recover the authority proper to

manner of genuflecting and kissing his foot. According to Syropoulos, the patriarch exclaimed indignantly to the papal legates: 'Whence has the pope this right? Which synod gave it to him? Show me from what source he derives this privilege and where it is written? The pope claims that he is the successor of St. Peter. But if he is the successor of Peter, then we too are the successors of the rest of the Apostles. Did they kiss the foot of St. Peter? . . .'[45]

To these remarks the Latin bishops replied that it was an ancient custom for all to kiss the pope's foot—'bishops, kings, and even the emperor of the Germans and the cardinals who are holy and superior to the emperor.'[46] The response of the patriarch is significant: 'This is an innovation and I will not follow it. . . . If the pope wants a brotherly embrace in accordance with ancient ecclesiastical custom, I will be happy to embrace him, but if he refuses, I will abandon everything and return to Constantinople.'[47] (It is interesting to observe that at the first meeting of pope and patriarch since the Council of Florence— the historic one of Pope Paul VI and the Patriarch Athenagoras in Jerusalem in 1964—each prelate embraced the other, giving him the kiss of peace. The lesson of the meeting at fifteenth century Florence had evidently been well learned!)

In the end the patriarch's inflexibility prevailed. Yet the victory was not entirely his, for Pope Eugenius, instead of welcoming the patriarch and his prelates in public ceremony, received them in his private quarters, where few western eyes could witness the omission of this mark of subordination.[48]

This initial difficulty, suggested obliquely by the *Acta Graeca*[49]

me'. On this curious passage see B. Stephanides, 'The Last Stage', 38 ff.; and Diamantopoulos, 'Silvester Syropoulos', 275-276. But the patriarch was disillusioned, says Syrop., 93, when he heard of Eugenius' demand that he kiss the pope's foot.

[45] Syrop., 92-95. [46] Syrop., 95. [47] *Ibid*.

[48] Syrop., 96. Also see Andrea da Santa Croce, col. 1435: 'in secreto camera', and *Acta*, 9 (Mansi, 474): 'in palatium papae'.

[49] The *Acta Graeca*, 9-10, pointedly omits mention of the footkiss, but for evidence that similar practice was current at this time see elsewhere in the *Acta*, 467 (Mansi, 1040), where immediately after the reading of the decree of union at Florence, Greeks as well as Latins 'kissed the knee and hand of the Pope'. (cf. Andrea da Santa Croce, col. 1702). Andrea, col. 1435, does not explicitly mention the footkiss on the Patriarch's arrival in Ferrara. But see G. Hofmann, 'Die Konzilsarbeit in Ferrara', pt. 2, *Orientalia Christiana Periodica*, III (1937) 410, who seems to accept Syropoulos' statement that it was demanded, as does Hefele-Leclercq, VII, 962. See also Stephanides, *Ecclesiastical History* (in Greek), 359.

and of which the form of salutation is prescribed in papal ponti-
ficals,[50] vividly symbolizes Greek insistence on the essential
equality of the bishops of Constantinople and Rome, a fundamental principle of pentarchic theory as opposed to the claims of
the pope to be the vicar of Christ and successor to Peter, *first*
among the Apostles.[51] In the word 'innovation', moreover, as
used by the patriarch, there is expressed a difference in concept,
the significance of which lies at the heart of the conflict between
the churches. To the medieval Latin mind, what the Greeks
might term innovation in rite and even in dogma—for example
the doctrine of the *filioque*—was not necessarily *change* in ecclesiastical truth but rather a logical *development* and was permissible
particularly if sanctioned by the papacy. For the Greeks, on the
other hand, anything other than undeviating adherence to the
doctrines and traditions as established by the first seven ecumenical councils (apart of course from Holy Scripture) was to be
considered innovation and hence reprehensible.[52]

This contrast between what we might term Greek conservatism and the more flexible western attitude toward ecclesiastical
development first becomes clear in the conflict between Patriarch
Photius and Pope Nicholas I in the late ninth century, and even
more distinct after the pontificates of Leo IX and Gregory VII

[50] See M. Andrieu, *Le Pontifical Romain au Moyen Age*, II, *Le Pontifical de la Curie Romaine au XIIIe Siècle* (Vatican, 1940), 386, stating that during certain ceremonies king, archbishop, and bishop 'osculetur pedem ipsius'. Also cf. 357, par. 16. It is of interest that, while the Dictatus Papae of Gregory VII required the emperor to kiss the foot of the pope and that, according to western custom, the emperor should hold the bridle and lead the mule of the seated pope, none of the sources of the Council of Florence allude to such a performance on the part of the Greek Emperor, recording rather that he rode into the papal palace. See *Acta*, 7 (Mansi, 470–471). Such a practice was the object of acute criticism in the East, being considered highly degrading to the imperial dignity. See esp. G. Ostrogorsky, 'Zum Stratordienst der Herrschers in der Byzantinisch-slavischen Welt', *Seminarium Kondakovianum*, VII (1935) 189–192; and cf. Ch. 2 of my *Emperor Michael Palaeologus and the West*, 44, note 61.

[51] See F. Dölger, 'Rom in der Gedankenwelt der Byzantiner', *Byzanz und die Europäische Staatenwelt* (1953) 105, who emphasizes that the Greeks (especially of the later period, after 1204) considered *Christ Himself, not the pope*, as head of the Church —obviously to denigrate papal claims to primacy. Also Dvornik, *Byzance et la primauté romaine*, 142 f. Gill, in his *Council of Florence*, 105 n. 3, minimizes the import-ance of the incident of the foot-kiss. But it is, I believe, symptomatic of an important difference of tradition and mentality in the two churches.

[52] Note the typical statement of the Patriarch Joseph at Florence (*Acta*, 438; Mansi, col. 1001) that he would never change the dogmas handed down from the fathers. On Greek retention of traditional practices and Latin innovations see also Barlaam's second Greek discourse, ed. by C. Gianelli, 'Un projetto di Barlaam per l'unione delle chiese', *Miscellanea Giovanni Mercati*, III (1946) 165 and text 202.

in the latter part of the eleventh, when papal claims to universal jurisdiction underwent their great expansion at canon law.[53] It is important to observe, therefore, that when, subsequently, representatives of the two churches confronted each other to discuss union, they argued from basically different premises. The Greeks expected the papacy to conform to conditions *before* the schism of 1054. The Holy See, on its part, insisted upon all the prerogatives of papal power developed since that period—in other words subordination of the Greek church to Rome virtually in the manner of the Latin churches of the West.[54]

Of greater significance at the Council of Florence than the conflict over patriarchal salutation of the pope was the dispute between emperor and pope over the problem of seating in the cathedral at Ferrara where the council was first to convene. In his desire to assume the role of arbiter, Pope Eugenius insisted that his throne be placed in the middle of the church, with the Greek representatives at his left and the Latins on his right. The Emperor John Palaeologus, however, considered this an infringement of imperial rights, for in accord with Byzantine tradition reverting to Constantine the Great, he believed it the prerogative of the emperor, as Vicegerent of God, to preside over ecumenical councils.[55]

After prolonged argument a solution was achieved whereby, as the Greeks insisted, the papal throne was placed on the side of the Latins. But it was, at the same time, elevated above all others including that of the emperor. Moreover, another throne, corresponding in every respect to that of the Greek Basileus, was set up on the Latin side for the emperor of the West, despite the vacancy of the throne caused by the recent death of the western

[53] See a hitherto unknown Greek discourse of Barlaam, also dated 1339, in which he maintained that to achieve union the pope should return to the traditional form of the creed as it existed before the schism, that is, without the *filioque*. In Gianelli, *loc. cit.*, 167 and 187. On Photius and Nicholas see Dvornik, *Photian Schism, passim*. Also Heiler, *Urkirche und Ostkirche*, esp. 141.

[54] See my article, 'On the Schism of the Greek and Roman Churches', 23. Not to be overlooked here also are the imperfect contacts between Rome and Constantinople which kept each side at least partially ignorant of the precise course of events in the other. It is probably true, nevertheless, that more frequent contacts existed than is generally believed.

[55] On the seating see *Acta*, 11 (Mansi, 474E); Syrop., 101–103; and Andrea da Santa Croce, 1435 ff. On the imperial presidency over ecumenical councils see Dvornik, 'Emperors, Popes, and General Councils', *Dumbarton Oaks Papers no.* 6 (1951) 1–23.

Emperor Sigismund.[56] The poor patriarch of Constantinople, his protests overruled, was in the meantime relegated to a place below both pope and emperors, a position, according to Andrea of Santa Croce, corresponding to that of the highest ranking cardinal.[57] Thus, contrary to traditional Byzantine theories, not to mention of course Greek ethnic pride, the Greeks at least symbolically were forced to recognize the supremacy of papal theocratic theory over both their emperor and patriarch. As for the equality indicated between western and eastern emperors, it touched upon even more sensitive feelings of the Byzantines, whose rulers had never really become reconciled to the existence of a rival imperial title in the West.[58]

It is worthy of note that in the heated debates which followed, papal champions made no use of the famous Donation of Constantine to support papal claims of supremacy. One wonders in this respect what may have been the role of Nicholas of Cusa, who already in 1431, some years before Lorenzo Valla, had attacked the authenticity of the Donation.[59] Cusanus was one of the legates who escorted the Greek delegation from their capital to Venice,[60] and while in the East (where we know that he searched for manuscripts),[61] he probably learned that a Greek translation of the Donation was in circulation at Byzantium. Since the Greeks, or at least a strong body of Byzantine opinion, in the aim of diminishing papal authority, interpreted the document to mean that Constantine had transferred to Constantinople not only the entire

[56] *Acta*, 11 (Mansi, 474E); Syrop., 103; and Andrea, XXXIB, col. 1436.

[57] Andrea, col. 1436: 'In oppositum primis cardinalis sedes patriarchae fuerat constituta.' The *Acta* does not specify the exact position.

[58] Cf. Humbert of Romans (Mansi, XXIV, pt. 2, col. 124) who says that the chief cause of the schism was rivalry over the claims to the Empire. On the beginnings of this problem see W. Ohnsorge, *Das Zweikaiserproblem im früheren Mittelalter* (Hildesheim, 1947). A very curious passage is contained in Syropoulos, indicating that the Emperor John VIII had hopes of co-operating to achieve union with the western Emperor Sigismund in the aim eventually of succeeding him on the western throne. It is certain at any rate that the two emperors were on cordial terms and that John had at one time even visited Sigismund's court. See Syrop., 8, 57; *Regesta Imperii: Die Urkunden Kaiser Sigismunds*, ed. W. Altmann (Innsbruck, 1896) II, nos. 12226 and 11367; and cf. Kalligas, *op. cit.*, 8.

[59] See E. Vansteenberghe, *Le Cardinal Nicolas de Cues* (Paris, 1920) 27–28. It should be noted that at the time of Cusanus' attack on the Donation he was a supporter of the western conciliar movement.

[60] On this embassy see the reports of the Basle and papal ambassadors in Cecconi, *Studi Storici*, pp. dix ff. and pp. dlxxvi ff. Cf. Syrop., 54. See also Gill, *op. cit.*, 73, 77.

[61] See M. Honecker, 'Nikolaus von Cues und die griechische Sprache', *Sitzungsb. Heidelberger Akad. Wissen. Phil.-hist. Kl.*, XXVIII (1938) 13.

Roman government but with it ecclesiastical primacy,[62] Cusanus may possibly have seen the danger of trying to support claims through an appeal to such a double-edged weapon as the Donation of Constantine.[63]

When the negotiations at the Council at last got under way, as in the past a great part of the discussions centered on such perennial dogmatic and liturgical questions as the nature of the pains of purgatory, the use of leavened or unleavened bread in the Eucharist, the precise moment at which the Eucharistic miracle occurs, and most important, the procession of the Holy Spirit, commonly called the *filioque*, which has for centuries been the greatest doctrinal stumbling block between the two churches.

The Latins believed that the third person of the Trinity, the Holy Spirit, proceeds from the Father *and the Son* (*filioque*)—a double procession as it were. The Greeks maintained, on the other hand, that the Holy Ghost proceeds from the Father alone. These two views were the result of basically different approaches to the concept of the Trinity. Of course both were in complete agreement on the fundamental question of the identity of substance in the three persons. To the Greek mind, however, most important was the theological truth of one principle or source (*arche*) in the Godhead—that is in the person of the Father. The Latin view rather took as the point of departure the unitary nature of the 'trinity' of persons in the one Godhead. Very simply put, one side tended to emphasize what might be referred to as the 'three in one', the other the 'one in three'. Thus for the Latins the Greek view, which stressed the 'monarchy' of the Father, seemed to subordinate the Son to the Father. And to the

[62] On this significant Greek attitude see esp. F. Dölger, 'Rom in der Gedankenwelt der Byzantiner', *Byzanz und die europäische Staatenwelt* (1953) 109–110, who shows that the twelfth century Byzantine canonist Theodore Balsamon and the historians Cinnamos and Anna Comnena (among others) reveal a good knowledge of the Donation, but that they turn this against the papacy. Surprisingly, as Dölger notes, Pope Nicholas I did not use the Donation against the Greeks, although Cardinal Humbert subsequently employed it against Cerularius in the events of 1054.

[63] It may be true, on the other hand, as Professor Stephen Kuttner points out to this writer, that by the early fifteenth century the Donation had lost much of its potency even in the West. See the recent work of W. Ullmann, *The Growth of Papal Government in the Middle Ages* (London, 1955) 416–420; and S. Williams, 'The Pseudo-Isidorean Problem Today', *Speculum*, XXIX (1954) 703. Cusanus himself was not at the Council of Florence, having at the time been sent on a papal mission. See now also P. Alexander, 'The Donation of Constantine at Byzantium and its earliest use against the western Empire', *Mélanges G. Ostrogorsky I* (Belgrade, 1963) 11–26.

Greeks, the Latin view, which placed the source of the Holy Spirit in the common nature of the Father and the Son, seemed to indicate the existence in the Trinity of two first principles, or, crassly put, of two gods.[64]

Preliminary proposals for the debate of this problem disclosed the basically different Greek and Latin attitudes toward the church. The Orthodox, led by Mark, fiery Metropolitan of Ephesus and exarch of the patriarch of Antioch,[65] tried to cut the ground from the Latin position by insisting that the dogmatic aspect of the *filioque* was here irrelevant and that the question for debate should be simply the legality of adding anything at all to the creed as originally established at the ecumenical councils of Nicaea and Constantinople.[66] The Latins, especially their spokesmen the Greek Latinophile Bessarion, Archbishop of Nicaea, and the Greek-born Dominican Andrea of Rhodes,[67] maintained, on the other hand, that the argument should focus directly on the question of the truth or falseness of the dogma itself,[68] since, as they insisted, the addition of the term *filioque* merely made explicit what was already implicit in the writings of important fathers of the early church.

[64] See *Acta*, 413 (Mansi, 973), where the Latins remark of the Greeks: 'They suspect . . . that we affirm two sources, and two causes for . . . the Trinity . . . but we believe in one source [archic principle].' On the *filioque* in general see esp. A. Palmieri's article in *Dict. Théol. Cath.*, V, col. 2309 ff.; Gennadios Scholarios, 'According to the addition, there was in the symbol', in Dositheos, *Tomos of Love* (in Greek). (Jassy, 1698) 291–307; and on the Greek and Latin positions at the end of the eleventh century, B. Leib, *Rome, Kiev, et Byzance* (Paris, 1924) 331–344.

[65] According to the *Acta*, 12 (cf. Syrop, 66 and 110) both Mark and Isidore of Russia represented the patriarch of Antioch. Cf. Andrea da Santa Croce, col. 1436. On Mark's significant role see the full length work of A. Diamantopoulos, *Mark of Ephesus and the Council of Florence* (in Greek) (Athens, 1899) and L. Petit's article in *Dict. Théol. Cath.*, IX², cols, 1968 ff.

[66] See Syrop., 166 ff.; *Acta*, 56 (Mansi, 517), where Mark says that the cause of the schism is the illegal addition of the *filioque*. Elsewhere in the *Acta*, 67 (Mansi, 529), Mark emphasizes the decree of the Council of Ephesus in 431 which forbade any change whatever in the creed.

[67] On Bessarion, later Cardinal of the Roman church, see esp. H. Vast, *Le Cardinal Bessarion* (Paris, 1878); and L. Mohler, *Kardinal Bessarion als Theologe, Humanist, und Staatsman* (Paderborn, 1923). On his role at Florence see E. Candal, 'Bessarion Nicaenus in Concilio Florentino', *Orientalia Christiana Periodica*, VI (1940) 416 ff.; and E. Udalcova, 'The Struggle of Parties in fifteenth century Byzantium and the Role of Bessarion of Nicaea' (in Russian), *Vizantiysky Vremennik*, II (1949) 294–307 and III (1950); cf. R. Coulon's article in *Dict. Hist. et Géogr.*, II, col. 1696 ff., and cf. R. Loenertz, 'Les Dominicains Byzantins', 5–61.

[68] See *Acta*, (Mansi, 556), where the *filioque* is termed an explanation, not an addition: 'explanation . . . not . . . addition.' Also Andrea da Santa Croce, cols. 1459 and esp. 1463 ff. and 1475 ff.

GREEK AND LATIN VIEWS OF THE TRINITY, TO ILLUSTRATE THE *FILIOQUE* QUESTION

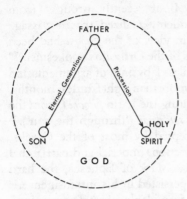

Attempt to depict traditional Greek view, showing procession of Holy Spirit from the Father. A dotted line between Son and Holy Spirit might indicate the temporal procession from the Son as viewed by the Greek unionist Margounios. See below, Chap. 6. [Drawn by Geanakoplos.]

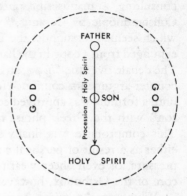

Attempt to depict compromise position on *filioque* accepted by some Greeks at Florence. The Holy Spirit proceeds *through* the Son. [Drawn by Geanakoplos.]

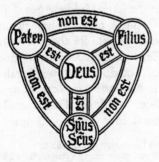

Medieval Latin view of the Trinity, found on stained glass of western cathedrals. Holy Spirit proceeds from *both* Father and Son.

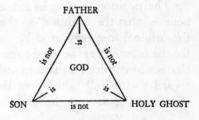

Modern Catholic depiction of the Trinity. [From R. Garrigou-Lagrange, O.P., *The Trinity and God and the Creator: A Commentary on St. Thomas' Theological Summa*, St. Louis, Herder, 1952.]

N.B.—No diagram, of course, can be entirely accurate in depicting the 'mystery' of Trinitarian doctrine.

Both sides appealed for support to old manuscript texts of the Greek church fathers—a method of striking modernity. To the embarrassment of the Greeks, an uproar occurred when the Latins, consulting a manuscript of St. Basil recently brought from Constantinople by Cusanus,[69] suddenly realized that a passage which seemed to support the Latin view of the *filioque* had been expunged from a copy in the hands of the Orthodox spokesmen.[70] The debate over the *filioque*, an endless labyrinth of arguments and counter-arguments, continued for more than eight fruitless months, until a formula was approved equating the Latin *filioque* ('from the son') with the Greek phrase *dia tou hyiou* ('through the son').[71] This compromise was finally accepted by most of the Greeks, either as a result of personal conviction, imperial and patriarchal pressure, or even sheer weariness. Mark of Ephesus, the hard core of the Orthodox, however, persisted in his intransigence.[72]

Why was the *filioque* such a formidable obstacle to union? What fear motivated the fanatic Orthodox so that they would not yield before entreaties from all sides to accept a solution which could insure aid for their city, now almost the sole remnant of Byzantine territory unconquered by the Turks. The answer to this question is fundamental for understanding the failure of unionist efforts in the entire period of the later Middle Ages.

The position of the Latins is of course clear. They firmly believed that the 'addition' to the creed, despite its absence from the original formulation at Nicaea-Constantinople and adoption for the first time at the local council of Toledo in 589, was a valid clarification of dogma made in order to preclude Arian errors with regard to the full divinity of the Son. And the Latins could not accept it as unauthorized doctrinal innovation without of

[69] *Acta*, 297 (Mansi, 769) and Andrea da Santa Croce, esp. cols. 1585 ff.

[70] On the long involved conflict over MSS and their interpretations in which texts of St. Basil played an important part, see *Acta*, 250–390 (Mansi, 720–876). On the problem of corruption of texts in particular see esp. *Acta*, 296–298, 308, 326 ff., 354, and 401 (Mansi, 769–772, 783, 840 ff., 836, and 888). Also letter of Bessarion in MPG, vol. 161, cols., 325 ff. Cf. Vast, *op. cit.*, 81–82; Vogt, *Dict. Théol. Cath.*, VI, col. 36; and M. Creyghton, *History of the Papacy*, II (London, 1892) 184.

[71] See decree of union in *Acta*, 461 (Mansi, 1029); Andrea da Santa Croce, col. 1696; Mark of Ephesus, MPG, vol. 159, col. 1076. Cf. Stephanides, *op. cit.*, 362. This identification of terms was largely the work of Bessarion.

[72] Particularly useful here is Syropoulos' knowledge of behind-the-scenes activities. See Syrop., *passim*, and *Acta*, 393, 402, 416, 450 (Mansi, 879, 888, 976, 1016). J. Gill, 'The "Acta" and the Memoirs of Syropoulos', 303–355. Also Gill, *Council of Florence, passim*.

course implying that for centuries they had been reciting heresy.[73] What the pro-Orthodox on the other hand seemed most to have feared in accepting the *filioque*, was not merely alteration of the traditional Orthodox dogma, of what in their view had been established as inviolate by the first seven ecumenical councils, but, by extension, loss of their national identity—in other words the beginnings of a Latinization of the Greek church and people.[74] They could not erase from their memories the experiences of fifty-seven years of Latin occupation in Constantinople and the continuing western domination of their islands and other Byzantine areas.

After the Fourth Crusade of 1204 many of the Greek clergy had been dispossessed of their ecclesiastical properties and the people forced to accept the supremacy of the Roman church. In particular it was required that the creed be recited with the *filioque* and the liturgy celebrated with unleavened bread.[75] In addition, certain feudal practices characteristic of the Latin church had been imposed upon the Greek clergy, such as the taking of a compulsory personal oath recognizing papal authority through the clasping of one's hands within those of a Latin superior. Finally, a papal legate had even been dispatched to Constantinople to dictate ecclesiastical, and in effect influence political, decisions.[76] Eloquent testimony of the deep Greek resentment towards their Latin

[73] For a good example of Latin inability to accept invalidity of the *filioque*, see Giannelli, 'Un projetto di Barlaam, etc.', 172 and esp. 176.

[74] See in *Acta*, 400 (Mansi, 885) the revealing remark of a Greek bishop at Florence: 'I will not give up our dogma and become Latinized.' It is to be noted that certain western theorists, esp. of the fourteenth century, had proposed elaborate schemes for forcibly Latinizing the Greeks. That set forth in the *Directorium*, written by Brocardus or possibly by the Dominican Guillaume d'Adam, planned to convert¯ the Greek churches into Latin, suppress the fanatically Orthodox Greek monks, burn the heretical Greek books and, perhaps most important, to force certain male Greek children to learn Latin letters. The plan would even have abolished the Greek language had it not been used at Christ's crucifixion! See Prologue, note 3.

[75] On Greek experiences under Latin domination in Constantinople see article cited of R. L. Wolff, 'Organization of the Latin Patriarchate of Constantinople', 33–34. At the start of the conquest, however, Innocent III had directed that the Greeks be permitted to retain their rites (MPL, vol. 215, cols, 959ff.) but this was not observed. In Cyprus for example the Greeks were not permitted during the fourteenth century to retain their liturgical usages (Raynaldi, 1338, no. 72; 1368, no. 20; 1370, no. 4). The Greeks of southern Italy, in 1284, were enjoined by Pope Martin IV to chant the creed with the *filioque* under pain of excommunication (Viller XVI, 265 and note 2).

[76] On the practice of an ecclesiastical feudal oath see Bréhier, 'Attempts at Reunion', 606. On the significance to the Greeks of a Latin legate in Constantinople, see my article, 'On the Schism of the Greek and Roman Churches', 19–23.

conquerors is provided by a canon of the Fourth Lateran Council (1215), according to which the Greeks were accustomed to purify their altars following each use by the Latins, and to rebaptize their children after performance of the equivalent Latin rite.[77]

These experiences of a dominated people had remained vivid in the minds of the Greek laity as well as the clergy, and the possible restoration of similar conditions through submission to the Pope was a great fear of the vast majority of Greeks. Not all the people shared this feeling, it is true.[78] For some, primarily among the intellectuals and the bureacracy, were ready to accept the Latin union, either as a result of sincere conviction or, more probably, in order to save themselves from what seemed the even greater danger of Islamization.[79]

It was the view of the majority of the Orthodox that the danger of Latinization threatened not only their religion but their political, social, and economic life as well. For gradually, since even before the First Crusade, Byzantium, more perhaps than is generally realized, had been penetrated by Latin influences. Latin officials participated in the administration, Latin commanders and mercenaries fought in its armies, and everywhere were the Gas-mules, children of mixed Greco-Latin marriages. More important even was the virtual strangle-hold exercised by the Venetians and Genoese over almost the entire economic life of the capital.[80]

[77] Hefele-Leclercq, *Conciles*, V pt. 2, 1333. Cf. the remark of Petrarch (in 1366): 'These tricksters call the Roman church their mother, but they treat our Latin rites as foolishness, and purify their basilicas after one of our people has entered them' ('Rerum sinilium', in *Opera Omnia* [Basle, 1554] Bk. VII, ep. 1. Cf. ed. G. Fracassetti, *Lettere Senili di F. Petrarcha*, I [Florence, 1869] 422–424.

[78] Jugie, *Le Schisme Byzantin*, 263, believes that the increasing number of Greek translations of Latin theological works (of Thomas Aquinas, etc.) explains the development of pro-unionism among certain of the Greek clergy.

[79] On the fear of Latinization and particularly that union would restore Latin domination, see N. Kalogeras, *Mark of Ephesus and Cardinal Bessarion* (Athens, 1893) 57–102; the oration of Barlaam in MPG, vol. 151, col. 133; and the *Directorium of* Brocardus (or Guillaume d'Adam). Cf. Viller, XVI, 274; and my 'Michael VIII Palaeologus and the Union of Lyons', 86–87. On the preference of some Greeks for the Turks see Kalogeras, *op. cit.*, *passim.*; H. Evert-Kapessova, 'Le Tiare ou le Turbain', *Byzantinoslavica* (1953) 245–255; and, finally, Udalcova, 'The Struggle of Parties in fifteenth century Byzantium . . . ,' *Viz. Vrem.*, III (1950) 106–132, who analyzes the views toward union of the various classes in Byzantium. Regarding Latin military aid for Byzantium see the treatise of Demetrius Cydones (late fourteenth century), *De admittendo latinorum subsidio*, in MPG, vol. 154, cols. 1028D, urging the acceptance of Latin aid against the Turks. For discussion of this see D. Zakythinos, *La Grèce et les Balkans* (Athens, 1947) 46–56.

[80] On Latin penetration in general see Vasiliev, *op. cit.*, 680 and 684, and my *Emperor Michael Palaeologus and the West*. On the Gasmules' importance see the

Some anti-unionists became so extreme in their fear of Latin influence that they openly declared their preference for 'the turban of the sultan to the tiara of the pope'.[81] This was no idle talk, since it was observed that in Asia Minor, the Turks, in accordance with Mohammedan precepts, had generally permitted to the conquered Byzantines the exercise of their religion and retention of their ecclesiastical hierarchy.[82]

It may be too much to speak of a genuine Byzantine 'nationalism' in this period, though to be sure, with the loss of the non-Greek areas, it seems to have been more evident than in earlier centuries. But it cannot be denied that the Greeks regarded themselves as a people very distinct from the Latins. The crusades and especially the years of subjugation had greatly sharpened this awareness, turning it into overt hostility. It is no wonder, then, that a Greek supporter of the union came to be looked upon as a traitor. Striking confirmation for this statement exists already from the year 1274, when one of the imperial envoys, returning to Constantinople after espousing the religious union at Lyons, was taunted by the rabble with the words, 'You have become a Frank' (that is, a Latin).[83] To the Orthodox party religious union thus came to mean not only ecclesiastical apostasy but a betrayal of the Greek heritage and sense of national pride.

In the light of this explanation it would appear that the question of the *filioque*, so bitterly debated at Florence, masked the vital, underlying problem of the hostility between Greeks

---

Byzantine historians Gregoras (Bonn) 98 and Pachymeres, I (Bonn) 188, 309. For Italian economic domination in Constantinople see R. Guilland, 'Les appels de Constantin XI Paléologue à Rome et à Venise pour sauver Constantinople (1452–1453), '*Byzantinoslavica* (1953) 226–227, and W. Heyd, *Histoire du commerce du Levant au moyen-âge* (Leipzig, 1885–6; new edn. Leipzig, 1936) I, 427–527 and II, 257–313.

[81] Statement attributed to the Grand Duke Lukas Notaras not long before Constantinople's fall (in Ducas [Bonn] 264). Evert-Kappesova, 'La Tiare ou Le Turbain', 245–257, shows that this sentiment, usually cited as the expression of a blind hatred, constituted a political program. Cf. the interesting remarks of I. Sevčenko, 'Intellectual Repercussions of the Council of Florence', *Church History* (1955), p. 315, n. 47. Also S. Runciman, 'Byzantine and Hellene in the Fourteenth Century', *Tomos Harmenopoulos* (1951) 30–31. Cf. the statement of Jean Gerson, chancellor of the University of Paris, in his discourse to the king of France after the Council of Pisa (1409), that the Greeks prefer the Turks to the Latins (see A. Galitzin, *Sermon inédit de Jean Gerson sur le retour des Grecs à l'unité* [Paris, 1859] 29 and cf. Manuel Calecas, MPG, vol. 152, col. 239).

[82] The Koran prescribed toleration to Christianity. See L. Bréhier, *Vie et Mort de Byzance* (Paris, 1947) 498.

[83] Quoted in my *Emperor Michael Palaeologus*, 271.

and Latins.   To the anti-unionist Orthodox, union, with submission to papal authority, was, in brief, the prelude to assimilation by the Latins.[84] In the words of a leading Orthodox polemist
of the fifteenth century, Joseph Bryennios: 'Let no one be
deceived by delusive hopes that the Italian allied troops will come
to save us. If they pretend to rise to defend us, they will take arms
only to destroy our city, our race, and our name.'[85]

We must pass over other differences, liturgical and disciplinary,
debated at Florence and which may also have disguised the fear
of Latinization,[86] in order to discuss the final act of union at the
Council. Urged on by the Latinophiles, under pressure from the
pope, who, owing to policy, financial difficulties, or both, did
not pay the Greek subsistence for five months[87]—pushed by the
emperor, who in the end ordered Mark himself to remain silent,[88]
and goaded even by reports of an imminent Turkish attack on
Constantinople,[89] the last of the Orthodox finally yielded.[90] With
their surrender and Greek concessions on the most important
questions at issue,[91] preparations were begun to draw up the decree

[84] On the Greek fear of Latinization see further *Acta*, 400 (Mansi, 885), where a
Greek bishop, objecting to acceptance of the *filioque*, says pointedly: 'I prefer to die
than ever to become Latinized'. George Scholarios, subsequently an arch-foe of
union, refers to the union as 'Latinism', and warns the Greeks that by accepting it
'all of you and this assembly will become Latins . . .' (cited in Demetrakopoulos,
op. cit., 168). Also a curious letter of Bessarion, written after the Turkish conquest to
the tutor of the children of the last representative of the Byzantine imperial family.
He instructs them to live in all respects as Latins, wearing Latin clothing, attending
Latin churches, even praying in the Latin manner (Sphrantzes, [Bonn] 418 ff.).

[85] Quoted in Kalogeras, *op. cit.*, 70. On Bryennios, who died just prior to the
Council of Florence and who was in attendance at the Council of Constance, see
Bréhier's article in *Dict. Hist. et Géog. Ecclés.*, X, cols. 993–996; and Ph. Meyer, 'Des
Joseph Bryennios Schriften, Leben und Bildung', *Byz. Zeit.* V, (1896) 74–111.

[86] It is significant that when Pope Eugenius asked the Greeks at Florence to
abandon the use of leavened bread ('enzymes'), the Greeks, according to the *Acta*,
446 (Mansi, 1012), responded that the practice was handed down from their ancestors
(*patroparadoton*), as was the use of azymes for the Latins.

[87] On this see Syrop., 142, 207, 292, and see above, note 20. In justice to the Pope
it should be noted that his financial difficulties were doubtless aggravated by attacks
in the area by the condottieri Niccoló Piccinino (Syr., 142), and also because the
Council of Basle had deprived him of many ecclesiastical revenues (W. Boulting,
Aeneas Silvius [London, 1908] 69).

[88] *Acta*, 393 ff. (Mansi, 880 ff.). Cf. Vast, 85 and 87–90.

[89] Syrop., 125–129.

[90] Syrop., 290 ff. But cf. a letter of Bessarion in MPG, vol. 161, 424CD., stating
that at Florence union was agreed to 'absque quocumque violentia sponte et
voluntarie'.

[91] On the final definition of the *filioque* and other disputed points see the discussion
and official decree of union in both Greek and Latin versions as printed in the *Acta*.
440–472, esp. 495 ff. (Mansi, 1004–1045). It may be noted that each church retained
its own rites and usages, esp. the azymes and enzymes (unleavened and leavened

of union. But as was perhaps inevitable, a conflict arose even over the signing of the document itself, for both pope and emperor claimed the honour of having their name inscribed at the begining of the text. In true western theocratic fashion, Eugenius affirmed the superiority of his rank to that of the emperor, while John Palaeologus, in a last assertion of authority, maintained that, as from the time of Constantine it had been an imperial right to convoke synods, his name should take precedence.[92]

Before the desperate need of his capital for aid, however, the emperor gave way, and the signing of the *horos* began. But one Greek prelate did not sign. While the Patriarch Joseph had died only a short time before[93] and another bishop had fled from Florence,[94] Mark of Ephesus alone resolutely refused to affix his signature.[95] As Pope Eugenius indicated at the time, this omission would prove fatal for the success of the union.[96] It was a prophetic remark, as on the return of the Greek delegation to Constantinople, Mark became the soul of the violent Orthodox opposition to union.[97]

The most significant aspect of the unionist decree was its emphasis on the crucial problem of papal supremacy, acceptance of which would, in effect, mean surrender of the independence of the Greek church.[98] In the document the authority of the pope as universal head of the churches of both East and West was clearly affirmed,[99] although it was stated in the passage immediately

---

bread), while the Latin teaching of purgatory prevailed. On the settlement of the specific points at issue cf. the various opinions of Jugie, *op. cit.*, 267; Frommann, *op. cit.*, 18; and Stephanides, *op. cit.*, 326–363. For the crucial problem of papal supremacy see below notes 98–101. Significant is a passage in the *Acta* quoting the Pope as saying after signing of the union: 'I do not know what more to ask of the Greeks, for what we asked for and sought, we have.' But cf. Syrop., 307–308.

[92] Syrop., 280 ff.

[93] *Acta*, 444–445 (Mansi, 1008–1009).

[94] The *Acta* does not mention the flight of Isaias, Bishop of Stravropol, but his signature is missing from the tomus and Syropoulos, 292, explicitly mentions his secret departure before the signing of union.

[95] Syrop., 284; *Acta*, 460–471 (Mansi, 1041–1045).

[96] Syrop., 291–294. Cf. Frommann, *op. cit.*, 26 ff.

[97] See Syrop., 330 ff. At Mark's death George Scholarios (later as monk named Gennadios) became the leading anti-unionist (Ducas, 254–264).

[98] See *Acta*, 451 ff. (Mansi, 1016ff.) and Syrop., 278 ff. The key point was the right of appeal to the pope against the patriarchs.

[99] The decree reads that the pope possesses the 'primacy over the whole world,' and is 'successor to the blessed Peter first of the Apostles, true vicar of Christ, head of the entire church, and father and teacher of all Christians, with complete power received from our Lord Jesus Christ via Peter to teach, rule, and govern the universal

following that 'all the rights and privileges of the patriarchs of the East are excepted'.[100] Despite the lack of precise information in the sources, it seems likely that the curious latter phrase was interpolated to assuage Orthodox feeling by at least the appearance of limiting papal absolutism. As Edward Gibbon put it so well, ironically but accurately, in his famous *Decline and Fall:* 'To satisfy the Latins without dishonoring the Greeks . . . they weighed the scruples of words and syllables till the theological balance trembled with a slight preponderance in favor of the Vatican.'[101]

On the sixth of July 1439, in the cathedral of Florence under the recently-completed dome of Brunelleschi, the solemn ceremony of union took place, with Cardinal Cesarini reading the decree in Latin and Bessarion in Greek. Almost immediately afterwards, Pope Eugenius, mindful of the recent death at the Council of the Patriarch Joseph, urged the election of a new patriarch for Constantinople while the Greek clergy was still at Florence. This fact, mentioned by the principal sources, is recorded by Syropoulos with the additional statement that Eugenius proposed the enthronement of the titular *Latin* patriarch of Constantinople, already appointed by the pope.[102] If

church. . . . ' See *Acta*, 464 (Mansi, 1032); Syrop., 293 ff., and Andrea da Santa Croce cols. 1697–1698. For various opinions regarding papal jurisdiction as expressed in the decree see Frommann, *op. cit.*, 18; Hefele-Leclercq, *Conciles*, 1049–1051; Stephanides, *op. cit.*, 361–364; and G. Hofmann,*Papato, conciliarismo, patriarchato (1438–1439)*, *Teologi e deliberazioni del concilio di Firenze* (Rome, 1940) 69–73.

[100] The Latin text of the *Acta*, 464 (Mansi, 1032) reads: 'salvis videlicet privilegiis omnibus et iuribus eorum (patriarcharum)'. The Greek: 'reserving, that is, both all their rights and privileges'. Cf. Gill, *Council of Florence*, 286 ff. and his *Eugenius IV Pope of Christian Union* (Westminster, 1961) 125 f.

[101] E. Gibbon (ed. J. Bury, 1909), VII, Ch. 66, p. 111. The fact that the same clause also appears in a canon of the Fourth Lateran Council of 1215 (at which time the Greek church was forcibly united to Rome) would seem to indicate that no great importance should be attached to the phrase. Indeed at Florence the same words doubtless conveyed different meanings to each side (cf. Frommann, *op. cit.*, 18; and Stephanides, *op. cit.*, 363). A severe argument, of course, developed over the addition of this clause. See *Acta*, 475 (Mansi, 1025). Cf. the attitude of Hofmann, *Papato, conciliarismo, etc.*, 69–73. Also on the decree of union itself note esp. the opinion of Frommann. *op, cit.*, 19: 'There took place no union, in fact not even a compromise but a silencing of the differences by means of a brilliantly indefinite and ambiguous definition.' See also Frommann, *Zur Kritik des Florentiner Unionsdecrets* (1870); my'Edward Gibbon and Byzantine Ecclesiastical History', *Church History* (June 1966).

[102] Syrop., 299 and *Acta*, 468–471 (Mansi, 1041–1044). The titular Latin patriarch of Constantinople was then Pope Eugenius' nephew, Francesco Condolmaro (see L. de Mas Latrie, 'Patriarches Latins de Constantinople,' *Revue de l'Orient Latin*,' III [1895] 444. Cf. Frommann, *op. cit.*, 187).

Syropoulos' remark is correct[103] and the suggestion of Eugenius had actually been carried out, a certain Latinization of the Greek church would thus already have begun at the very top of the Greek hierarchy.

The story of the return of the emperor and his clergy to Constantinople and the repudiation of the union by the great majority of the people is well told by the Byzantine theologians and historians as well as by Syropoulos.[104] The popular opposition was based not only on the underlying attitudes already described, but, more immediately, on the belief that union had been obtained under duress, that the military aid agreed to by the Holy See would, like previous papal promises, be ineffectual,[105] and, finally, on the conviction that the Byzantine people themselves would suffer the judgment of God if the purity of the faith were altered.[106]

So strong was the Orthodox opposition to the union that it persisted to the very capture of the capital by the Turks in 1453. Indeed, even the Turkish conquest did not destroy the ethnic Greek feeling, for it was the church, significantly, which preserved this spirit throughout the long centuries of Ottoman domination.[107]

III

One wonders, in retrospect, what the course of Byzantine history might have been had the Greek and Latin churches been

[103] That this appointment was at least under discussion may be inferred from a statement of the Pope, cited in *Acta*, 471 (Mansi, 1044), that he wanted selection of the best man, *neither relative nor friend*, as the new patriarch. (A certain nephew of Eugenius, named Condolmaro, is mentioned in Syrop., 54, as having commanded the papal fleet in Constantinople just before the convocation of the Council.)

[104] Syrop., 346 ff, lists seven factors for the failure of union in Constantinople. See also Ducas, 215 and 252 ff.; Mark of Ephesus, MPG, vols. 160–161, *passim*, and his works in L. Petit (ed.), *Patrologia Orientalis*, XV, 1-170 and XVI, 307-524.

[105] This is an argument of Joseph Bryennios in his 'Concerning the union of the churches' (in Greek), ed. Bulgaris, I, 469 (cited in Viller, XVI, 283). See esp. the speech of George Scholarios quoted in Demetrakopoulos, *op. cit.*, 161ff. On Scholarios, who became the first Greek Patriarch after the Turkish conquest, see his *Oeuvres complètes*, ed. Petit-Siderides-Jugie (Paris, 1928ff.). For a recent sketch of Scholarios' life see Paulová, *loc. cit.*, 192–203.

[106] On the judgment of God see Ducas, 254 ff., and for similar disturbances over the Union of Lyons in 1274, see my *Emperor Michael Palaeologus and the West*, 264–76.

[107] Vasiliev, *op. cit.*, 675–676; K. Paparregopoulos, *History of the Greek People*. V (Athens, 1903) (in Greek) 497 ff.

able successfully to consummate union at Florence.[108] Is it possible that the deepening chasm between East and West might have been bridged and the conquest of Byzantium averted?[109]

Probably the only way to have achieved union at this time with even remote chance of success would have been to adopt the kind of policy suggested by Barlaam: in essence, recognition of pentarchic equality by the papacy[110] and the holding of a council in Constantinople itself,[111] so that the Greek populace, by following the discussions at first hand, could allay its deep suspicions of the Latins and especially of its own Latinophiles. On the other hand, a convocation in Constantinople might well have provoked immediate retaliation from the Turks.[112] But even more important, the papacy could hardly have accepted terms which would have been contrary to the entire monarchical tradition of the western church and at the same time have deprived the Holy See of a decisive victory over the Greeks, so necessary for its triumph over the conciliarists of Basle.

Even had the Greek people accepted the Florentine union, there seems little likelihood that the Latin princes would effectively have responded to papal appeals for a crusade against the Turks. For the West, always doubtful in any case of the sincerity of Greek conversion, was now deeply engrossed in its own

[108] It should be pointed out that although the Greek church as a whole repudiated union, it is on the basis of the act of union at Florence that certain eastern Christians termed Uniates are today in communion with Rome.

[109] On the inevitability of Byzantium's fall cf. S. Runciman, 'Byzantine and Hellene in the Fourteenth Century', *Tomas K. Harmenopoulos* (in Greek) (1951) 29–30, and *Byzantinoslavica* (1953) p. v.

[110] See Giannelli, 'Un projetto di Barlaam,' *Miscellanea Giovanni Mercati*, III,175–176 On his return from Avignon Barlaam wrote a treatise against papal primacy of jurisdiction. Nevertheless, he subsequently became closely identified with the Roman church. On Barlaam see above, text and notes 25–29.

[111] The suggestion of a Constantinopolitan council is mentioned several times by Syropoulos. He notes, 13. that the Patriarch Joseph favoured this proposal because in the West the Greeks would be at the mercy of the Latins for their subsistence. Syrop., 155, also records that in 1426 the famous philosopher Gemistos Plethon had advised the Emperor to insist on Constantinople as the site for a council. Cf. on this Demetrakopoulos, *op. cit.*, 103. Though the Latins were in general unwilling to go to Constantinople, it is noteworthy that Humbert of Romans (13th century), who understood the Greek mentality well, had already suggested that 'papa in Graeciam debere descendere, si spes esset probabilis, quod propter hoc reuniretur ovile' (Mansi, XXIV, col. 128).

[112] Ducas (Bonn) 215, says that the Emperor had stressed to the Sultan the religious aims of the Council of Florence, but the Sultan no doubt realized the political considerations involved. According to Sphrantzes, 178–180, the first and greatest cause of the Turkish attack and slavery of the Greeks was the Council of Florence. Cf. Syrop., 14.

problems and therefore in general almost indifferent to the fate of the East.[113] Thus in 1453 when Constantinople finally succumbed to the Turks, only a few humanists, their passion for Hellenism inflamed by their contacts with Greek intellectuals at Florence, lamented the fall of the capital. Significantly, however, they mourned more what they termed 'the second death of Homer and Plato' than the passing of medieval Byzantium.[114]

[113] How, cried some of the Greeks, could the Latin princes help them in view of their inability to aid even the Latin states in the East? The great western states were not yet seriously menaced by the Turks and felt no compulsion to help. Most threatened were Hungary, Albania, Venice and Genoa with territory in the east. France and England, still involved in the Hundred Years' War, did not respond effectively to papal appeals, not participating in the unfortunate crusade of Varna (1444), which seemed to seal the fate of the Greek Empire. No secular prince, in fact, except the Duke of Burgundy had sent representatives to the Council at Florence. (For the insulting attitude of the Burgundian envoys to the Greek Emperor, see Syrop., 175–177; cf. *Acta*, 212–213). The absence of western princes at Florence was a profound disillusionment for the Greek Emperor.

[114] See especially the eloquent letter of Aeneas Silvius (the later Pope Pius II), in *Opera Omnia* (Basle, 1571) 712 (cf. E. Vansteenberghe, *Le Cardinal Nicolas de Cues* [Paris, 1920] 228): 'Secunda mors ista Homero est, secundus Platonis obitus!' On western disinterest in Constantinople's fall and rhetorical laments of the humanists see R. Cessi, 'La Caduta di Costantinopoli nel 1453', *Atti del Reale Istituto Veneto di Scienze Lettere ed Arti* (1937–1938) 565, and M. Gilmore, *The World of Humanism 1453–1517* (New York, 1952) 15–21.

PART II

BYZANTIUM AND THE RENAISSANCE

THE GRECO-BYZANTINE COLONY IN VENICE
AND ITS
SIGNIFICANCE IN THE RENAISSANCE

The old theory that the Renaissance was caused by the great influx of Byzantine refugees coming to the West after Constantinople's fall in 1453 is today of course accepted by no reputable scholar. Indeed, some social-economic historians, pushing the pendulum far in the other direction, have tended to reduce almost to a minimum the significance of the part played by the Byzantine refugees. Now it is indisputable that the Renaissance, whether its roots were Italian or French or a combination of both, was at the outset a Latin, not a Greek movement. Yet there can be no doubt that ancient Greek literature and philosophy, which more than anything else expanded the intellectual horizon of the Renaissance, could have come to the West only from their principal medieval depository, the Byzantine East, including southern Italy. And in the transmission of this learning to the West, the role of the Byzantine refugee was decisive.

The history of the dissemination of Greek learning westward is now reasonably well-known, at least in broad outline. And a number of good biographies of the leading Byzantine or post-Byzantine humanists involved have been written,[1] though a host of lesser but not insignificant figures still await investigation. Nevertheless, western historians, in their focus on the western activities of the more famous Byzantine individuals such as Bessarion, Pletho, and Chrysoloras, have failed to notice a factor which, directly or indirectly, affected the lives of most of these emigrés—that is, the existence of a large, cosmopolitan Greek colony in Venice. This is particularly true with respect to the

[1] For bibl. on Byzantium and the Renaissance see Appendix, Bibliographical Note D.

later period when Venice displaced Florence as the leading centre of Greek studies in Europe. Of course scholars are fully cognizant of the work of the famous Aldine press of Venice in producing first editions of the Greek classics, and they recognize a certain influence of Byzantium on the later brilliant art of Venice. But either because of undue concentration on the achievement of Aldus or because it has not generally been realized that the remarkable diaspora of Greeks to the West just before and for long after 1453 focused on Venice, historians have not viewed the lives of the Greek scholars, as many of them should be viewed, in the context of the thriving Greek community of Venice. It is the purpose of this essay, insofar as time permits, to reconstruct the more important events in the history of this colony, and then, having provided a more complete background to the activities of the Greek refugees in Venice, to attempt to draw a few conclusions as to the significance of the colony for the development of Greek learning in the Renaissance.

I

Because of the development of a long-range international trade, the city of Venice seems early to have attracted a considerable foreign element. Among the first to settle there were probably Greek merchants. We know that until the ninth century the patron saint of Venice was not Mark but the Greek Theodore, and that in the eleventh century Byzantine workmen were summoned by the Doge in order to embellish, perhaps entirely to construct, the church of St. Mark. Venetian-Byzantine contacts became more frequent in the twelfth century as a result of the growth of the large Venetian commercial colony in Constantinople, numbering some ten to twenty thousand persons. So close did relations between the two peoples become that intermarriage now became common, and the Venetians of the home city adopted Byzantine habits of dress, Greek titles and ceremonies, and even introduced Greek words into the Venetian dialect.[2] Yet that the Greek merchants, craftsmen, and occasional

---

[2] On the Greek settlement in Venice before 1453 and its influence on Venice in general no work has been written: see allusions in A. Frothingham, 'Byzantine Art and Culture in Rome and Italy', *American Journal of Archaeology*, X (1895) 160 ff. and M. Armingaud, *Venise et le Bas-Empire* (Paris, 1868). Byzantine art, of course, and its influence on the Venetian has been studied.

diplomat then living in Venice were numerous enough or organized to form what may be called a colony is doubtful. A more substantial number of Greeks do not seem to appear in Venice until the Franco-Venetian capture of Constantinople in 1204, after which there came or sometimes were summoned to the lagoons many Byzantines, including skilled artists and artisans seeking employment.

But it was the danger threatening the Greek East by the advancing Ottoman Turks that brought the greatest influx into Venice. In the half century or so before Constantinople's fall in 1453, a gradually increasing number of refugees from the East poured into the West. Venice, as lord of important territories in the Greek East, especially the island of Crete, and as the chief port of debarkation in Italy, received the major part of these refugees. This stream quickened rapidly after 1453, and now a veritable flood of Greek emigrés, often well educated, in many cases indigent or in rare instances wealthy, entered Venice, there to become members of the growing Greek community. By the end of the fifteenth century this Greek colony had so burgeoned as to become one of the largest contingents of foreigners and certainly, from the political, economic, and intellectual view, the most significant in the city.

These Greek residents of Venice in the century and a half following 1453 seem to have come at first from Constantinople and the Morea, and then increasingly from Crete, the economic and social structure of which did not offer sufficient opportunities for its more energetic and talented individuals. Other Greeks also came from such Venetian-held areas as the islands of Corfu, Zakynthos, the Archipelago, Cyprus, and the Peloponnesian city of Monemvasia. From these Venetian colonies the Greek inhabitants found it only natural to gravitate to Venice itself, which always maintained close contact with its eastern possessions. The journey from Crete to Venice usually took about three weeks, a relatively short time in the period, and we know from letters of Cretan intellectuals working in Venice that such voyages were very frequent. Not all of course, especially after the first waves fleeing the Turks, were refugees. Young Cretans and, later, Cypriotes would go to seek their fortune in Venice where opportunities beckoned. If they failed to find work they could be secure in the knowledge that provisions could easily be sent them and that in any event return home would not be difficult.[3]

Before we proceed to examine the motives, aside from the obvious desire to escape the Turks, which induced the emigrés to come to Venice and the extent to which they were able to make use of the opportunities available, let us briefly trace the history of the Greek colony from shortly before 1453 until 1600, the limits of this essay. We might begin with the convocation of the famous council held at Florence in 1439 in the aim of reuniting the Greek and Roman churches.[4] This was to have a far-reaching effect not only on the history of the colony but on the relations of all Greeks who found themselves in the West. On its way to Florence the large Greek delegation stopped first in Venice. The delegates were greatly impressed by the beauty and splendor of the city of the lagoons.[5] And indeed this memory served to induce many Greeks to return later to Venice for permanent settlement. What had impressed them was not only the material riches of the city but the evidence of a continuing appreciation for the Byzantine ways and habits. Most prominent of the Greeks who later returned to Venice was Bessarion, Archbishop of Nicaea and subsequently Cardinal of the Roman Church. As a leading member of the Curia he lost no time in preaching to the Pope and especially to the Venetian Doge, the necessity of launching a western crusade to recover Constantinople from the Turks. Of significance is the fact that, despite his many years of residence in Rome and the great reputation of Florence as the leading humanistic center, he chose Venice as the permanent respository for his collection of manuscripts, most important of

---

[3] The only study on the history of the Greek colony (extending to the nineteenth century) is the old one of the Greek librarian of St. Marks, G. Veludo: *Hellenon Orthodoxon apoikia en Venetia* (in Greek) (henceforth referred to as *Greek Colony*) (Venice, 1893), and a brief Italian version, 'Cenni sulla colonia greca orientale', *Venezia e le sue lagune* (Venice, 1847) I, 78 ff. (Veludo was not, as some say, a Greco-Italian but a Greek born on Tinos). See now the recent work of Geanakoplos, *Greek Scholars in Venice*, Chap. 3, on the Greek colony.

[4] See above Chapter 3.

[5] See their reactions in J. Gill, *Quae supersunt Actorum Graecorum Concilii Florentini* (Rome, 1953) pt. 1, pp. 4–5. Also M. Creyghton's ed. of S. Syropoulos, *Historia vera unionis non verae . . . Concilii Florentini* (Hague, 1600) sect. 4, Chapter 16, for the impressions of two Greek delegates to the Council, Dorotheos of Mytilene and Syropoulos. Cf. account in Ducas (Bonn ed.) 212.

which were some 500 written in Greek.[6] As is well-known, the latter constituted the greatest single collection of Greek manuscripts in the period of the Renaissance. In a letter Bessarion wrote in 1468 to the Doge of Venice, he expressed his intention of donating his manuscript collection to Venice. The letter indicates Bessarion's awareness of the growing significance of the Greek community there and reflects also the rapport developing between Venetians and Byzantines—a sharp contrast to the mutual hatred of the previous centuries as a result of the Latin sack of Constantinople in 1204. Bessarion wrote:

'As all peoples of almost the entire world gather in your city, so especially do the Greeks. Arriving by sea from their homelands they debark first at Venice, being forced by necessity to come to your city and live among you, and there they seem to enter another Byzantium (*quasi alterum Byzantium*). In view of this, how could I more appropriately confer this bequest upon the Venetians to whom I myself am indebted and committed by obligation because of their well-known favors to me, and upon their city which I chose for my country after the subjugation of Greece, and in which I have been very honorably received and recognized.'[7]

The union signed by the Greek and Roman churches at Florence is also of significance because it induced the Venetian state to look with special favour upon the so-called Uniates—those Greeks who had accepted the union with its provision for papal supremacy while retaining the Byzantine rite. But the attitude of the Greeks of Venice toward the western church and their adherence to it oscillated in accordance with their need for support from the Venetian government. As their political and economic condition improved, they were gradually emboldened to cast aside even their usual lip-service allegiance to the patriarch of Venice and finally, openly, and with even the tacit sanction of the Venetian government, to proclaim their adherence to the Orthodox patriarch of Constantinople.

[6] On Bessarion's Ms collection see H. Omont, 'Inventaire de manuscrits grecs et latins donnés à Saint-Marc de Venise (1468)', *Revue des bibliothèques*, IV (1894) 129–87. More recent is L. Labowsky, 'Manuscripts from Bessarion's Library found in Milan', *Medieval and Renaissance Studies*, V, 108–31.

[7] My translation, from Omont, *loc. cit.*, 139. Also on Bessarion's donation see preceding note, Labowsky article.

This religious problem runs like a thread throughout the history of the Greek colony during the entire fifteenth and sixteenth centuries. As refugees who had lost their homeland and whose nation no longer existed, the Greeks clung tenaciously to the religion of their forefathers as the most tangible evidence of their unity as a people. Indeed, in 1456, soon after the fall of Constantinople and with the reinforcement of the community through the continuous arrival of more refugees from the east, the Greek colonists petitioned the Venetian Council of Ten for the right to establish a church 'for their own use'. Previous to this, Orthodox monks or priests had been able, unofficially it would appear, to hold services at times in certain Venetian churches—at St. Servilius, St. Lorenzo, St. Severus, St. Biagio, St. John Chrysostom, St. Agatha, St. John in Bragora, and also at St. Eustathius, where there was an altar to the ancient Byzantine St. Demetrius. Moreover, we know that as early as the second decade of the fifteenth century Orthodox priests secretly performed services in private homes—a practice forbidden by Venetian law.[8]

The spokesman for the Greek community in its petition to the government in 1456 was the Uniate Isidore, former Byzantine Metropolitan of Kiev, and now an influential Cardinal of the Roman Church. On June 18 of the same year, the Venetian Senate replied favorably to the request, granting the Greeks not only the use of a Latin church but, if this proved unsatisfactory, the right to construct their own. But circumstances were not yet ripe for the erection of a church of the Greek rite. Probably the Venetian patriarch protested. In any case later, in 1470, when the Venetians had just lost the Greek island of Euboia to the Turks and had need of the military prowess of the able Greek cavalrymen, the so-called *stradioti*, the Serenissima granted the colony the use of a side chapel in the Venetian church of San Biagio along the Riva dei Martiri. The proviso was made, however, that no Greek priest could celebrate the liturgy elsewhere under penalty of a fine. It might be noted that an exception to this rule was made for the famous Anna Notaras, wealthy daughter of the last Byzantine Grand Duke Lucas Notaras.[9] (It was he who reportedly said

[8] Veludo, *Greek Colony*, 5.
[9] On this first Venetian ecclesiastical concession see now M. Manousakas, 'The first permit (1456) of the Venetian Senate for the church of the Greeks in Venice and Cardinal Isidore' (in Greek), *Thesaurismata* (Venice, 1962) 109–18.

'Better the turban of the Turk in Constantinople than the tiara of the Pope.') She was permitted to have religious services performed in her own home. Regarding Anna it is interesting to note—and this is little known—that, moved by the unhappy fate of her compatriots, whose country had now been blotted out of existence, she had developed elaborate plans to establish an independent Greek enclave in Tuscany in the territory of Siena. This particular project, the remarkable aim of which was probably the first step to the formation of a kind of small Greek nation in the West, was never realized.[10] It was rather in the Greek community of Venice that the dream of Anna seems to have acquired a certain substance.

Again and again the colonists requested permission to begin the construction of their own church. But the answer was always that they should instead 'frequent the Latin churches'. Evidently the Venetian government, influenced by its episcopate, feared that the Greeks, once in possession of their own building, would cast off any pretence of subordination to the Venetian patriarch and revert to schism.

Nevertheless, on November 28, 1494, the Greeks were finally accorded significant recognition. Following the example of the communities in Venice of Slavs, Albanians, and Armenians, as the document reads, the Greeks petitioned for and received permission to establish a 'Brotherhood of the Greek nation' (*Scuola e Nazione greca*). This was to be a kind of philanthropic and socio-religious society to administer to the various needs of the Greek people, under the protection of the famous Byzantine Saint Nicholas of Myra. This is perhaps the most significant date in the entire history of the colony. For it marked the formal recognition of the community as a corporate body before the law. The Venetian government, however, always wary, stipulated that the initial membership was not to exceed 250, apart from women and children. A constitution was thereupon drawn up in imitation of the Venetian, with provisions for voting procedures, representation, and the formation of a council. This organization was

[10] On this project see Geanakoplos, *Greek Scholars*, 62 and note 26. Also details in G. Cecchini, 'Anna Notaras Paleologa: Una Principessa greca in Italia e la politica senese di ripopolamento della Maremma', *Bolletino Senese di Storia Patria*, XVI (1938) 1–41. References in M. Manousakas, 'Recherches sur la vie de Jean Plousiadenos', *Revue des études byzantines*, XVII (1959) n. 78. The Maremma project may not have been carried out because the area is marshy.

maintained down to the very end of the colony, although minor modifications in the constitution were at times admitted.[11] Thus in 1563 the number of the councillors, the governing body of the colony, was set at forty and later, still higher. The officials, headed by a president called *Gastaldo*, were salaried by the community but were under the supervision of the Venetian government. It should be emphasized that the success of the Greek petition in securing formal recognition from the Venetian government was probably due in large part to the increasing dependence of the Venetian state on the military services of the *stradioti*.[12]

Still not content without their own church, the Brotherhood in 1511 again petitioned the Council of Ten for permission to buy land to build a church, to be dedicated to St. George, the patron saint of the soldier. The reasons cited in the request reveal something of the relations existing between the emigrés and Venetians at the time. The Greeks emphasized the troubles arising between the two religious groups, especially the fact that the Greeks in attendance at Latin churches failed to understand what was being said during the mass. Moreover, the colonists wanted to provide proper burial for their dead. Evidently, hitherto they had been compelled to bury their dead in Latin cemeteries, where not infrequently the bones were exhumed, violated, and perhaps thrown into the sea. Finally and most important, the Greek petition declared that the chapel of San Biagio then in use could not accommodate all the worshippers, now increasing greatly in number, especially in view of the many *stradioti* and their families recently brought in by the Venetian government.[13]

Not until three years later, on April 30, 1514, did the Council of Ten approve the request for a church and cemetery. It was stipulated, however, that the Greeks must remain *veri e Cattolici cristiani* and secure also the approval of the pope for their projects.

[11] Geanakoplos, *Greek Scholars*, 62–63; Veludo, *Greek Colony*, 9.

[12] The constitutional changes are reflected in the still extant *Mariegola* (archives) of the Greek community. Cf. Veludo, 11. On the importance of the *stradioti* to both the Greeks and Venice, no really satisfactory study has been made. See C. Sathas, 'Greek Stradioti in the West and the Revival of Greek Tactics', (in Greek) *Hestia*, XXIX (1885) 371–76 and later issues. Also his *Documents inédits relatifs à l'histoire de la Grèce au Moyen Age*, IV (Paris, 1882) esp. liv ff. and *passim*.

[13] Petition printed in F. Cornelius, *Ecclesiae venetae antiquis monumentis* (Venice, 1749) pt. I, 372–73. See Greek transl. in K. Bires, *Arvanites, the Dorians of Recent Hellenism* (in Greek) (Athens, 1960) 186–87.

This was granted by Pope Leo X, who in addition accorded the Greeks the right to choose a priest who would officiate according to the eastern rite (*'juxta ritem et morem vestrum'*). Most important, he granted them freedom from local clerical interference. The words of Pope Leo clearly indicate that in his eyes the Greeks were not to be considered Orthodox schismatics but bona fide members of the Catholic church of the Uniate rite.

Understandably, the Venetian patriarch Antonio Contareno contested the papal decision on the grounds that the Greeks would revert to schism and might even lead Latins astray. But his efforts were unavailing. For Pope Leo, always sympathetic to representatives of Greek culture and probably influenced by the growing circle of Greek humanist scholars around him in Rome, enjoined the Venetian patriarch and episcopate from interfering in the affairs of 'Catholics of the Greek rite.'[14] After further trouble representatives of the colony, led by the old stradiot, Theodore Palaeologus, who for years had fought gallantly for Venice, decided on the purchase of a plot for the church in the section of San Antonin. Construction began and the first service took place on March 4, 1527. Yet this was only a provisional church, quickly constructed to enable the removal of the congregation from San Biagio. The famous church of San Giorgio dei Greci, which still exists, was begun in 1539. Construction took 34 years, being completely finished only in 1573 at a cost of 15,000 ducats. Much of this sum was raised by a tax which the officials of the Greek community were in 1546 permitted by the Venetian government to levy on all Greek ships entering the port of Venice.[15] This is a strong testimonial to the Greek sense of patriotism, since most of the Greek ship owners, as Turkish subjects, had no obligation to contribute. Several architects, among them the noted Italians Sante Lombardo and Zanantonio Giovo (Chiona) directed the building of the church, on the foundations of which not only Greek workers but, as the documents relate, old men and children were eager to contribute their labor. Built of fine stone and adorned with paintings by artists of Greek, particularly Cretan origin, and

[14] On this whole episode see now Manousakas, 'The First Permit of the Venetian Senate'. Cf. Veludo, 20.

[15] On the tax see S. Antoniadis, 'Porismata apo ten meleten procheiron diacheiristikon biblion ton eton 1544–47, etc.' (in Greek), *Praktika Akademias Athenon*, XXXIII (1958) 466–87. On the construction of the church see esp. Veludo, 19 ff.

precious old icons, some brought earlier from Byzantium, this remarkable edifice still stands today as a monument to the efforts of the Greeks of the diaspora to preserve unbroken the traditions of their lost homeland. Other Greek churches were later constructed in Naples, Ancona, Livorno, and elsewhere in Europe. But San Giorgio of Venice, besides being the oldest of the Greek churches of the diaspora in the West, is most symbolic for the preservation of the Hellenic identity in the crucial period when the Greek nation had disappeared.

There is no time here to relate in detail the intensified religious persecution undergone by the colony at the hands of the Venetian episcopate. The latter feared, rightly, that the community was slipping away from its jurisdiction. At one point the patriarch Girolamo Quirino, if we can believe one source, excommunicated the entire congregation and even locked the communicants in their church during the days of Holy Week. In the 1530's the noted Cretan scholar Arsenios Apostolis, a Uniate Greek and fanatical pro-Catholic who had been imposed on the community as its priest by the Venetian government, created the most serious difficulties. The conflict grew increasingly severe until 1577 when the Venetian government finally reversed its policy and, at least unofficially, permitted the Greeks to place their church directly under the authority of the Orthodox patriarch of Constantinople. Their priest Gabriel Severus was permitted to assume the title of Metropolitan of Philadelphia, a title henceforth to be borne by all his successors in Venice. The triumph of the colony over the Venetian patriarch may have been due, as one modern scholar believes, to the fear the Greeks might ally with the new Lutheran movement.[16] But more important, it seems to me, was the traditional Venetian attitude of expediency (recall the famous Venetian saying, 'Siamo Veneziani poi Cristiani'), based on the benefits accruing to the Venetian state and society from the services of the Greek stradioti and mariners, and from the thriving commercial activities of Greek merchants and shipowners. Finally, not to be overlooked is the contribution made by the emigré Greek intellectuals to Venetian cultural life— a contribution we shall turn to presently.

[16] P. Pisani, 'Les Chrétiens de rite oriental à Venise et dans les possessions vénitiennes (1439–1791)', Revue d'histoire et de littérature religieuses, I (1896) 209 ff.

The Greek colony was located in virtually the heart of Venice. It encompassed the area immediately surrounding the church of San Giorgio dei Greci, only a few hundred meters to the east of St. Mark's Basilica itself, on the Rio dei Greci in the area now termed Campo dei greci and in the quarter of San Antonin. In 1478 the population of the colony was between four and five thousand persons, a fairly large number when one considers that in 1509, according to the authority of Beloch, Venice itself had no more than 110,000 inhabitants. There was a continuous increase of the Greek population as a result of infusions from the Venetian possessions in the East, newly conquered by the Turks. By 1580, according to the testimony of Andreas Darmarios, a contemporary Greek copyist from Monemvasia who had come to Venice, no less than 15,000 Greeks were living in Venice. This number, he says probably with exaggeration, swelled to 30,000 with the arrival in port of many Greek ships from Alexandria, Constantinople, Crete, and the Greek islands.[17]

What was the social structure of the colony? What opportunities or professions were open to Greeks that might induce them to emigrate to the Serenissima? The archives of the Greek colony (called *Mariegola*), many documents of which await reading and interpretation, are still preserved in the chancery of the church of San Giorgio and reveal to us the wide range of occupations adopted by the emigrés. It would be a mistake to believe that the community consisted mainly of intellectuals. Actually it embraced a wide stratum of society, from merchants, intellectuals and artists, to soldiers, mariners, shipowners and captains, tailors, iron workers and goldsmiths, laborers perhaps in glass works or the arsenal, women in charge of aristocratic Venetian households, and an occasional judge and doctor.[18]

Among the earliest occupations was that of *stradiot* (from the Greek *stratiotes*, soldier). The *stradioti*, as noted, were a body of light cavalry troops consisting of youths from the Greek and Albanian territories held by Venice in the East, and constituted one

---

[17] For opinion of G. Beloch, 'La popolazione di Venezia nei secoli XVI e XVII', *Nuovo archivio veneto*, n.s. III, p. 1. On the size of the Greek colony see Veludo, *Greek Colony*, 60 and S. Antoniadis, *Museo di Dipinti sacri* (Venice, 1959). Also for Darmarios' remark see E. Legrand, *Notice biographique sur Jean et Theodose Zygomalas* (Paris, 1889) 254–55.

[18] See Antoniadis, 'Porismata', 477 ff.

of the most important arms of Venice in the fifteenth and sixteenth centuries. They were noted for their daring and swiftness, and their *esprit* was doubtless inspired by pride in their Byzantine heritage and revenge against their traditional enemy the Turks. The Venetian humanist Pietro Bembo has left us a description of a band of Cretan *stradioti* who held a joust on a frozen canal in 1491 in honor of the ex-Queen Catherine Cornaro of Cyprus. The exploits of the *stradioti* against the Turks as well as western enemies of Venice, such as the Germans in the early sixteenth century, became legendary. Frequently mentioned in the official Venetian documents, the services of the *stradioti* to the Venetian state, it should again be emphasized, were in large part responsible for the gradually increasing favor shown to the colony by the government of Venice.[19]

The Venetian Republic also recruited sailors from its Aegean island possessions to fight against the Turkish navy. But the exploits of the Greek mariners, while of significance, have attracted less attention than those of the *stradioti*. Research reveals that the Greek colony included among its inhabitants also those who performed life's more menial tasks—common laborers, tailors, stone workers, and so on, who in fact comprised the majority of the population. Pisani would have us believe, and perhaps rightly in view of the number of Greeks who were what we would now call 'displaced persons,' that some assumed the less savory professions of spying, counter-spying, or acting as go-between for questionable purposes.[20] On the other hand we know that not infrequently highly educated Greeks were used by the Venetian government as interpreters, as for example the humanist-professor at the University of Padua, Marcus Musurus, and the high-born leader of the *stradioti*, Theodore Palaeologus, who for his services as Venetian envoy and interpreter before the Sultan was paid by the Venetian Senate 360 ducats a year. At his death in 1532, we are told, he was honored by his compatriots with burial in the church of San Giorgio.[21]

Except for the conspicuous cases of the Byzantine aristocrats

[19] See note 12 above and Geanakoplos, *Greek Scholars*, 55–56. Many references to *stradioti* may be found in M. Sanuto's famous *I diarii di Marino Sanuto* (1496–1533), ed. R. Fulin, etc., 58 vols. (Venice, 1879–1903).

[20] Pisani, *loc. cit.*, 202.

[21] See Veludo, 14–18 on Theodore and other *stradioti*.

Anna Notaras, Eudocia Cantacuzene, and Nicholas Vlastos, we have little record of the presence of wealthy Greeks in the colony during the earlier period. Often fleeing the Turkish advance, many refugees could carry few, if any, possessions with them—perhaps a precious manuscript or two, or a valuable Byzantine icon. Beginning in the later sixteenth century, however, and extending through the seventeenth, the period which marks the colony's greatest prosperity from the economic point of view, there gradually emerged a surprisingly large number of wealthy Greek merchants, and, more commonly, of Greek ship captains and owners. Some had probably worked for others until they had amassed sufficient funds to venture on their own. Others had made their fortunes through trade with Constantinople and other areas of the Turkish occupied East. A striking example is that of the wealthy merchant, Thomas Flanginis, who in 1626 presented to the Greek community a large sum of money which enabled it to add to its existing elementary school a kind of college.[22]   There many of the outstanding Greeks of his and the following century, from all over the Greek world, were to receive at least part of their education before continuing perhaps at the University of Padua. A number of these students later returned to the East, to take up positions as teachers and priests.[23]

II

So much for the social-economic and religious background of the colony and its role in the life of Venice. Let us now turn to its contribution, direct or indirect, to the development of humanistic studies. As is well-known, Venice at the end of the fifteenth and the first quarter of the sixteenth century became indisputably Europe's principal center of Greek studies. Previously the primacy in Greek studies had long been held by the Florence of the Medici, beginning with the teaching there in 1396-97 of the Byzantine diplomat-scholar Manuel Chrysoloras. His instruction

[22] See esp. C. Mertzios, 'Thomas Flanginis kai ho Mikros Hellenomnemon', (in Greek), in *Pragmateiai tes Akademias Athenon*, IX (1939) 47–52 and *passim*.

[23] See the recent article (with little on this subject however) of C. Tsourkas, 'Gli scolari greci di Padova nel rinnovamento culturale dell'Oriente Ortodosso', (Padua, n.d.) 36 pp. Also G. Typaldos, 'The Greek Students at the University of Padua' (in Greek), *Epeteris Hetaireias Byzantinon Spoudon* (1929).

had brought to Florence for study some of the leading humanists of the day, some of whom later went also to Ferrara to work under his great pupil Guarino of Verona. Both Chrysoloras and Guarino lectured for a brief time in Venice. But the rise of Venetian interest in humanistic studies, in its initial stage, was owing rather to the influence of the nearby university of Padua, which after 1409 became the state University of all Venetia. Padua rather early had developed an interest in classical Latin letters through the activities of such persons as the jurist Lovato dei Lovati and the rhetorician and poet Mussato. And it was the combination of this interest with the age-old relations of Venice with the Greek East that eventually induced the Venetians to turn their attention to Greek studies.[24]

Scholars have emphasized the significance of Venice's eastern colonies in this respect but they have overlooked the importance of the Greek community in Venice itself. The celebrated Venetian Cardinal Pietro Bembo put it well when, probably in 1539, he delivered a speech before the Venetian Senate panegyrizing the study of Greek in his native city. He said:

'There are special reasons and the most cogent of motives which impel the Venetians to undertake and constantly to strive to bring to a happy conclusion the revival of Greek letters. You have been provided most liberally with the means of bringing to fruition this very noble undertaking; you have living among you Greeks as your neighbors, you have under your hegemony not a few of the Greek cities and islands, and you suffer from no lack of as many teachers and books as are needed for this task.'[25]

Bembo was referring here not only to Venetian possession of various Greek territories in the East, but more specifically, it would seem, to the Greek colony *within* Venice with its inhabitants of all types, including teachers of Greek, who, as he put it, 'live among you as your neighbors'. In the Greek community, then, the Venetians had, so to speak, a built-in natural resource.

---

[24] On Chrysoloras see G. Cammelli, *Manuele Crisolora* (Florence, 1941). On Chrysoloras and Guarino in Venice and the origins of Greek studies in that center see Geanakoplos, *Greek Scholars*, 24 ff.

[25] My translation. Text in J. Morelli, 'Intorno ad un orazione greca inedita del Cardinale Pietro Bembo alla Signoria di Venezia,' *Memorie dell' R. Istituto dèl regno Lombardo-Veneto*, II (Milan, 1821) 251–62.

As pointed out, the colony was in close communication with the Greek East, especially Crete, and its population was constantly being replenished by new arrivals from the East. It was these Greeks, those that is with an extensive knowledge of Greek literature, who helped to carry Greek letters from Venice to many of the principal areas of western Europe. To cite only two examples: that of the Cretan, Demetrius Ducas, who was summoned from Venice to Spain to teach Greek at the University of Alcalá and there supervised the Greek New Testament version of Cardinal Ximenes' celebrated Complutensian Polyglot; and also the Cretan Calliergis, who after establishing a press in Venice moved to Rome, where he became the pioneer printer of Greek in the papal capital.[26]

The historian may point out that centuries earlier merchants of Venice living in her colony at Constantinople had possessed some knowledge of Greek. But that was the spoken vulgar Greek, necessary for commercial transactions, rather than the classical literary language which was considerably different. As we have noted, it was rather the inspiration affecting Venice from the early Latin humanism of Florence and neighboring Padua that seemed first to have induced Venetian noblemen to turn from the business of trade to the contemplation of literature and philosophy. But if the initial impetus to Latin humanistic studies in Venice came from elsewhere in Italy, it was from the environment of the Greek colony there, with its close connections with the East, that the Greek scholars who were so important in gaining for Venice the primacy in Hellenic letters received much of their stimulus and inspiration.

The most prominent name associated with this brilliant period of Venetian primacy is of course that of the Italian, Aldus Manutius. Before inaugurating his press Aldus had realized that only one city in Italy, Venice, could fulfil all the complex requirements of a Greek press. Venice possessed a class sufficiently wealthy to buy, and the leisure to read, the printed classics. Venice was less subject to papal pressures than other Italian cities. Important too in Aldus' thinking must have been Venetian possession of the precious collection of Greek manuscripts bequeathed by Bessarion—manuscripts which could serve

[26] For the only biographies on Ducas and Calliergis, see Geanakoplos, *Greek Scholars*, Chaps. 7 and 8.

as paradigms for his books. And hardly less significant for him must have been the presence in Venice of a large, thriving Greek community, from which he could secure the services of copyists, typesetters, and editors in the difficult work of preparing textual editions. His principal editor was to be the Cretan Musurus (who edited no less than 11 or 12 of the 30 Greek first editions of Aldus), while Aldus' compositors were in large part Cretans (the chief being John Gregoropoulos),[27] given the difficulty of finding persons competent to read the Greek script from which the printing was done.

We have no wish to diminish the importance of the extraordinary contribution of Aldus to the development of Greek letters. He was after all the central figure around which most of the Hellenists of Venice revolved.[28] But it is not generally realized that in the publication of Greek works he was anticipated in Venice by certain little-known Greek emigrés, the Cretans Laonikos and Alexander, at least one of whom seems to have been a priest in the Greek colony, and quite possibly also by the Cretans, Zacharias Calliergis and Nicholas Vlastos. In instituting his own Greek press Calliergis was, in part at least, influenced by a desire to preserve the Greek masterpieces as a heritage for his countrymen, while for Aldus of course it was more of a business proposition. Calliergis' staff consisted exclusively of Greeks, all of whom were drawn apparently from the Greek community of the city.[29]

Aldus was certainly the leading force behind the establishment of his celebrated press. He himself edited or collaborated in printing the works of Greek authors. And, of course, he offered a means of employment, an outlet as it were, for the talents of the Greek emigrés. On the other hand, it is improbable that without the reservoir of talent provided by his Byzantine workmen and associates, with their mastery of the language and technical skill,

[27] Most recent biography of Musurus, in Geanakoplos, *op. cit.*, Chap. 5. On Gregoropoulos see now M. Manousakas, 'The Correspondence of the Gregoropouloi Dated (1493–1501)' (in Greek), *Epeteris tou Mesaionikou Archeiou*, VII (1957) 156–209.

[28] The best source on Aldus' career is now E. Pastorello, *L'epistolario Manuziano Inventario cronologico-analitico* (1483–1597 (Florence, 1957). For a synthesis see the old and faulty work of A. Firmin-Didot, *Alde Manuce et l'hellénisme à Venise* (Paris, 1875). See recently C. Dionisotti, 'Aldo Manuzio Umanista', *Umanesimo Europeo e Umanesimo Veneziano* (Florence, 1963) 213–243.

[29] See Geanakoplos, *Greek Scholars*, 19, 58, 204–12.

he could have offered to the public, in the relatively short period of less than two decades, as much as he did of the corpus of classical authors. As Aldus himself said about one of his Greek collaborators: 'The aid of Musurus in the edition of texts is so precious to me that, had Greece produced two more of his merit as councillors of mine, I would not despair of giving before long to people of taste, in very correct editions, the best work of both Greek and Latin.' By the time of Aldus' death in 1515, his press had given to the world practically all the major Greek authors of classical antiquity.

With the Cretan John Gregoropoulos and the Italian Scipio Carteromachus as a nucleus, Aldus gathered around him a group of western and Greek Hellenists and established a *Neakademia*, where it was prescribed that at meetings the Greek language alone could be spoken. There the problems involved in the projected publications of his press were analyzed. There western Hellenists, in friendly cameraderie with eastern exiles, could exchange manuscripts and ideas, while often western visitors could benefit from their association, to return later to their homelands enriched by their experience. The great Erasmus profited in this manner. Erasmus was very fond of Musurus and expressed his amazement at the generosity of Musurus and other Greek emigrés, who, without hestitation, presented to him valuable manuscripts in their possession, along with advice on literary problems. As I have shown in a recent work, a great deal of the material for Erasmus' famous Aldine edition of his *Adages*, the book which made his European reputation, was acquired from the Greeks of Venice.[30]

It is true that in the archives of the Greek colony we find almost no mention of the names of the more illustrious Greek humanists of the late fifteenth and early sixteenth centuries— Musurus, Calliergis, Ducas, Janus Lascaris. (Those of the later sixteenth and seventeenth centuries, however, do appear.) But this should not be taken to indicate that they had no connection with the colony. The colony's official records were not regularly kept until 1549, and even then generally only vital statistics such

---

[30] On Aldus' *Neakademia* see D. Geanakoplos, 'Erasmus and the Aldine Academy of Venice: A Neglected Chapter in the Transmission of Greco-Byzantine Learning to the West', *Greek, Roman, and Byzantine Studies*, III (1960) 107–34. Cf. also *Greek Scholars*, 263–66.

as baptisms, marriages, and deaths were recorded. Moreover, the church of San Giorgio had not yet been built. Finally, it was only natural that the more important of the Greek scholars, like their western humanist counterparts, were drawn to and for practical reasons often lived in, the households of their Italian patrons. Thus Musurus, to judge from Erasmus' colloquy *Opulentia Sordida*, resided for a time, along with Erasmus and some thirty others including many Greeks, at the press of Aldus at San Paterniano. And another Greek with the most prestigious position of all, Janus Lascaris, ambassador of King Francis I to Venice, probably lived in quarters provided by the French government.[31] Yet, from sporadic references I have been able to collect from the sources (for example, that Erasmus later visited Musurus and his father at their home with the Cretan scholar John Gregoropoulos present; a statement that Calliergis lived for a time with Musurus at the Borgo Zocco in Padua; a reference that George Trivizios, the scribe and employee of Cardinal Bessarion, was the very first priest of the Greek colony),[32] there can be absolutely no doubt that these Greeks, even if they did not always live strictly within the limits of the Greek quarter, frequently corresponded and in general had a very close rapport with one another.

With the death of Aldus in 1515, then of Musurus in 1517, and finally of Janus Lascaris and Arsenios Apostolis in 1534 and 1535 respectively, the hegemony in Greek studies moved to northern Europe. Across the Alps in France, Budé came to the fore, and in Germany and England Reuchlin and Erasmus had already become important. But the role of Venice was not ended. Because of her economic prosperity, the fact that she was still the main center of the book and manuscript trade, and not least because of the growth of her Greek colony, she continued to remain a center for the dissemination of Greek learning. Many more presses were now established in the city by Greeks. Some of

[31] For Erasmus' colloquy see *Colloquies of D. Erasmus*, trans. N. Bailey, III (London 1900) 180–95. Cf. P. Smith, 'Key to the Colloquies of Erasmus', *Harvard Theological Studies*, XIII (1927). On Lascaris see B. Knös, *Un ambassadeur de l'héllenisme: Janus Lascaris* (Upsala-Paris, 1945).
[32] On Erasmus at Gregoropoulos' house see P. S. Allen, *Opus Epistolarum Des. Erasmi Roterodami*, V, no. 1347, p. 245. On Calliergis with Musurus see Geanakoplos, 210, and on Trivizios, see Manousakas, 'The First Permit . . . to the Greek Colony, etc.', *Thesaurismata*, I, 118 note. Also Ch. Patrinelis, 'Greek Codicographers in the Years of the Renaissance', (in Greek) *Epeteris tou Mesaionikou Archeiou* (Athens, 1961) 63–124.

these, like the Glykys, specialized, as Calliergis (unlike Aldus) had done earlier, in the publication of Greek ecclesiastical texts.[33] Indeed, until the very end of the nineteenth century almost all the Orthodox ecclesiastical books printed in Greek emanated from the presses of Venice. Prayer books, psalters, gospels, liturgical and pietistic works, homilies—all these, in a format strongly reminiscent of Byzantine manuscripts, the Venetian Greek presses spread throughout the Greek world, thereby helping also to preserve the Byzantine tradition. Some of the Greek scholars of lesser importance who continued to come to Venice from the East in the sixteenth and seventeenth centuries, many of whom were copyists, were Anthony Eparchos, Nicholas Sophianos, Angelos Vergikios, Andreas Darmarios and Constantine Palaeokappas. Not all, to be sure, remained in Venice. Some, like Vergikios and Eparchos, went north to France and elsewhere. And others even returned to the East. But the fact remains that they resided for a time at least in the Greek community and it was through the Greek colony that they made their way to other areas of Europe.[34]

Another consideration to be mentioned in this respect, hitherto briefly alluded to, was the attraction of the nearby University of Padua. This Venetian-owned institution, with its long intellectual tradition, became the center of studies of higher learning for students coming from the entire Greek East.[35] There in fact several of their countrymen held high professorial posts. In 1463 Demetrius Chalcondyles of Athens was appointed the first professor of the newly established chair of Greek.[36] There the Uniate Greek priest Alexander Zeno also taught. Most important, Marcus Musurus, in the early sixteenth century, made this Greek chair the Mecca for students from all areas of Europe. More than a score of western students who benefited from his teaching at Padua or Venice later became leaders in the humanistic

[33] See Veludo, *Greek Colony*, 129.

[34] On these Greeks mentioned above see references in Legrand, *Bibl. hell.*, *passim.* Also Patrinelis, *op. cit.*

[35] For Paduan documents see J. Facciolatus, *Fasti gymnasii patavini*, 2 vols. (Padua, 1757). Also on Greeks at Padua G. Fabris, 'Professori e scolari greci all'università di Padova', *Archivio Veneto*, XXX (1942) 120–65. The recent article of C. Tsourkas, 'Gli scolari greci di Padova nel rinnovamento culturale dell' Oriente Ortodosso' (Padua, n.d.) is a popularization.

[36] I hope shortly to publish Chalcondyles' discourse at Padua (in Latin), on the inauguration of Greek studies there in 1463.

movements of their own countries.[37] At Padua, following the customary practice, Cretan *stemmata* or crests of the chief Cretan families held a place of honor in the aula of the university far into the seventeenth century.[38] It seems that there was also a kind of small Greek colony in Padua (though apparently without a church), and relations between it and the community in Venice were close.[39] Indeed, because of the constant intercourse between the two cities, Venice and Padua formed virtually a single center of culture.

In the later sixteenth century, when the Greek colony of Venice began to reach its zenith from the point of view of numbers and economic wealth, the colony was under the leadership of the forceful Bishop of Philadelphia, Gabriel Severus. At this time Greek ships came regularly from the east to load and unload their cargo on the Rio dei Greci, the canal running adjacent to the community. '*Stratiotesch*' Greek songs such as the famous 'Barzellette dei quattro compagni strathioti', in a kind of mixed Greco-Venetian dialect, were often to be heard in the Greek quarter and in other sections of the city. The Greek costume of the East was the typical mode of dress in the colony, and in the church of San Giorgio men, women, and children crowded on feast days to participate in the colorful religious celebrations conducted by a bishop, at least three priests and as many deacons and chanters, while pious nuns and monks from San Giorgio were more than mere spectators. On ordinary days children would attend classes in Greek and Latin in the school established nearby.[40] Some Greeks had become more or less assimilated to the Venetians through intermarriage and were living in other sections of the city. But they, too, often returned to the quarter to consort with their fellow countrymen. Indeed many of the emigrés had now achieved the coveted honor of Venetian citizenship.

In this period the chief Greek scholarly figure was Maximos

---

[37] On Musurus' teaching see Geanakoplos, *Greek Scholars*, 135 ff. On Zeno see Facciolatus, *op. cit.*, 12.

[38] These can still be scrutinized in the great hall (*aula*) of the University. See on the *stemmata* G. Gerola, 'Gli stemmi cretesi dell'Università di Padova', *Istituto Veneto di Scienze Lettere ed Arti*, in *Atti del R. Istituto Veneto di Scienze Lettere ed Arti* (1928–29) 239–78.

[39] Tsourkas, 'Gli scolari greci di Padova'.

[40] On the scene see Geanakoplos, *Greek Scholars*, 69, and other works cited above.

Margounios, the Cretan ecclesiastic. Forbidden for political reasons by the Venetian government to assume the bishopric of Cythera to which the patriarch of Constantinople had appointed him, he had been granted a yearly pension by the Venetian senate. He spent his time teaching Greek publicly in Venice and, perhaps earlier, in the school of the community of San Giorgio. Or he might busy himself with preparing editions of classical Greek or ecclesiastical works, translate Greek works into Latin, engage in polemics with Bishop Gabriel Severus over the question of the *filioque*, or even correspond with learned western scholars such as the German Protestant humanist Martin Crusius of Tübingen University. Margounios, it seems, lived within the confines of the Greek colony. From his will we observe that he bequeathed his fine library of Greek books to the monastery of St. Catherine of Sinai in Candia, Crete, his birthplace, 'for the benefit', as he put it, 'of the students of this monastery and universally of all the Greek nation'. Other books in Latin, as we shall see in a later chapter devoted to his carer, he willed to the monastery of Iviron on Mt. Athos. Still other bequests he made to various Greeks of Venice, specifically to the monks attached to San Giorgio, and as executors of his estate he appointed Greeks living in the colony headed by Metropolitan Severus. Although his career has been generally overlooked by western scholars, Margounios, who spent all his later years in close relation with the colony, was probably the most significant figure in the intellectual life of the Greek colony, and in fact of the Orthodox church, in the later sixteenth century.[41]

Besides intellectual activity we may cite examples of an extraordinary artistic production in the Greek colony. Indeed still being clarified in the development of Venetian art is the influence of late Byzantine painting, especially of the so-called 'Cretan school', which extended from approximately the fourteenth to the seventeenth century and was the last great flowering of the traditional Byzantine manner. The term 'Cretan school' (to be distinguished from the more realistic 'Macedonian') is a broad one, referring loosely to several related but distinguishable areas or aspects of late Byzantine painting—to the half-Italian icons of the post-Byzantine period, to the wall frescoes of churches on the

[41] On Margounios and esp. his residence in the Greek colony, see below, Chap. 6, note 23.

island of Crete itself, and to the remarkable sixteenth century frescoes on Mt. Athos, especially those at Lavra of the monk called Theophanes the Cretan.[42] Some scholars regard the 'Cretan' influence on Venetian painting as of importance. (We must not forget that with Crete a Venetian possession communications were easy.) Others are less impressed, or believe that the influence flowed rather from Venice to Crete.[43] In any case we know that in the post-Byzantine period under discussion there was a large number of Greek painters in Venice who plied their craft in the Greek colony and often exhibited their works on the Rialto.[44] Among these were many commercial, that is generally inferior artists called *Madonneri*, who on demand could produce icons of the Virgin in the old Byzantine style and of which practically every Venetian family of any means possessed at least one specimen.[45] An important collection of *Madonneri* paintings, that of Likhachev, consisting of some 250 icons, is preserved today in the Hermitage Museum in Leningrad. It is striking to note the similarity of many of these icons (most are from Venice, others from another center of *Madonneri* painting, Otranto in southern Italy) to the late thirteenth and early fourteenth century pre-Renaissance icons of Italy.[46]

[42] On the Cretan tradition see above, Chap. 1, text for note 79, and esp. A. Xyngopoulos, *Historical Sketch of Religious Painting after the Conquest* (in Greek) (Athens, 1957) esp. 80–190. Also Chatzidakes' article 'The Cretan Artists in Venice'. Further, K. Kalokyris, 'Byzantine Monuments of Crete' (in Greek), *Kretika Chronika* (1952), and more recently his *Byzantine Wall Paintings of Crete* (Athens, 1957). On the Cretan tradition on Athos, esp. regarding Theophanes, see now K. Kalokyris, *Athos, Themes of Archaeology and Art* (in Greek) (Athens, 1963) 55ff. and esp. M. Chatzidakes, 'The Painter Theophanes Strelitzas the so-called Vathas', *Nea Hestia* (1963) 5–16. Also see A. Xyngopoulos, 'Rapport entre la peinture de la Macédoine et de la Crète au XIVe siècle', *Hellenika* (1954), 136 ff.

[43] Esp. S. Bettini, *La pittura di icone Cretese-Veneziana* (Padua, 1933), and his work listed in note 45, below.

[44] Most recent on the Greek artists of Venice is Chatzidakes, *Les icones de Saint-Georges des Grecs et la collection de l'institut hellénique d'etudes byzantines et post-byzantines* (Venice, 1962), which shows that in the first half of the sixteenth century the influence flowed from Crete to Venice and not the reverse. Also his 'The Cretan Artists in Venice', (in Greek), *Kretika Chronika*, XV (1961) 211 ff. See also Xyngopoulos, *Historical Sketch of Religious Painting*, 80–190. And cf. J. Willumsen, *La Jeunesse du Peintre El Greco* (Paris, 1927) 76–100, esp. 93–96.

[45] On the Madonneri (who worked not only in Venice but along both sides of the Adriatic) see S. Bettini, *La pittura di icone cretesi-veneziana e i madonneri* (Padua, 1933) and his *Il Pittore Michele Damasceno e l'inizio del secondo periodo dell' arte cretese-veneziana* (Venice, 1935). Also Chatzidakes, *Les icones*. For Bettini almost all the Cretan artists in Italy were *Madonneri*.

[46] This is also the opinion of Mme A. Bank, curator of the Likhachev icon collection, who kindly showed me the collection in 1964. Prof. V. Lazarev, who was also of great help to me in Russia, believes the theory of the influence of the so-called Cretan school on Russian icons of the fifteenth-sixteenth centuries is wrong.

In addition to the *Madonneri* there was also a number of artists of genuine talent living in Venice's Greek community. To name a few: John of Cyprus and the Cretan Michael Damaskinos (often called, erroneously, the teacher of El Greco), both of whom have left beautiful examples of their work at San Giorgio in Venice or in Crete, as have the Cretans Emmanuel Zanfurnaris and the miniaturist George Klontzas, and later in the seventeenth century Emmanuel Tzanes.[47] All or most of these men could paint *alla greca* or *all' italiana*, that is in both the old traditional Byzantine (Cretan) or the new Renaissance Italian style.

The celebrated El Greco, born the Cretan Domenikos Theotokopoulos, was himself also probably strongly influenced as a young man by the Cretan tradition of his native island (we are not here, of course, referring to the hacks called *Madonneri*.) A remarkable notarial document in fact has been recently discovered referring to a 'Maestro Menegos Theotokopoulos' as a painter (*Zgourafos*, it calls him) living in Candia, Crete in 1566.[48] If this refers to El Greco, as it certainly seems to ('Menegos' is a diminutive Cretan form of the name 'Domenico'), it indicates that El Greco, at that time probably twenty-five and already a guildsman with the title of Maestro, was old enough to have been strongly affected by the artistic *milieu* of his birthplace, that is by the Byzantine-Cretan style then prevalent there.[49] In any event, if we accept this as correct El Greco seems to have spent some four years in Venice, and it is impossible to believe that as a proud Cretan who usually signed his pictures 'Domenikos

---

[47] Chatzidakes, *op. cit;* Xyngopoulos, *Sketch, passim;* Willumsen, *Greco*, 134–36. Padre Catepan has found in Venetian archives names of over 100 Cretan painters in Venice c. 1300–1500 (Mertzios, cf. next note, found 42 new painters).

[48] C. Mertzios, 'Gleanings from the records of the Notary Michael Mara', (in Greek) *Kretika Chronika*, I (Herakleion, 1961–62) 302ff.

[49] Mertzios, *loc. cit.*, 302. Also the important article of M. Chatzidakes, 'The Youth of Theotokopoulos' (in Greek), *Epohes* (Aug. 1963) 32–37, who indicates which works (or kinds of works) El Greco painted in his youth in Crete and Venice. Willumsen, *Jeunesse*, 136 ff.; P. Kelemen, *El Greco Revisited: Candia, Venice, Toledo,* 96 and *passim.*, and a recent Spanish view emphasizing the influence on El Greco of Byzantine-Cretan art: S. Cirac, 'L' hellénisme de D. Theotokopoulos', *Kretika Chronika*, II (1961) 224 ff. Prof. Cirac believes, as he told me in Barcelona in the summer of 1964, that the schematic, pallid, elongated figures of the great Greek artist Manuel Panselinos (whom he, unlike M. Chatzidakes, considers one of the Cretan School) can be seen also in El Greco's work. A recent work strongly opposing the Byzantine influence on El Greco is H. Wethey, *El Greco and his School* (Princeton, 1962) *passim*. Now also K. Kalokyres, *Theotokopoulos the Greek* (Athens, 1964), saying Greco left for Venice in 1566 at 25 years of age, and a new ed. of Kelemen (1964), Addenda.

Venice in 1492. From *Supplementum Chronicarum*, Venice, 1492.

Interior of St. Mark's, Venice.

Plate 9

Interior of St. Sophia, Constantinople. Lithograph by Fossati.

Greek church of San Giorgio. An engraving of the late 18th or. early 19th century, from Venice. (See p. 120.)

Plate 10

Theotokopoulos *Kres*' (the Cretan) and *always* in Greek letters, he was not drawn into the life of the Venetian Greek community, the population of which was then in fact largely Cretan.[50] Thus, even had he left Crete at the age of eighteen, as was formerly believed, he would still probably have been influenced by the Greek painters of Venice's Greek colony, thereby reinforcing the Byzantine influence.

To be sure El Greco may have become a Uniate early in life, but by this time in Venice this would have posed no problem to close association with his fellow countrymen. Other documents found in the Venetian archives refer to a certain Manoussos Theotokopoulos, evidently El Greco's brother, who twice failed to win election to the Council of the Greek community and collected ships' dues from Cretan seamen for their 'Mutual Benefit Association', of which he was treasurer.[50a]

To conclude: in our discussion we have had to omit the names of many other Greeks connected with the Greek colony who made a contribution to the intellectual and artistic history of Venice in the fifteenth and sixteenth centuries. We should emphasize here, however, not so much the importance of individuals as the underlying significance of the total cultural contribution made under the influence of the existence of an entire Greek community situated in the heart of Venice. Constantly reinforced by new arrivals from the East, including many skilled in the Greek language and literature, the colony, for over two centuries, was able to become the focal point of social and intellectual interaction between Venice and the entire Greek world. And at the same time it served as a kind of funnel for emigrés wishing to move still further into the West. This magnet-like attraction of Venice for the Greek exiles, in connection with Venice's favorable location, economic prosperity, and the work of Aldus and other Latin Hellenists, was one of the basic factors which permitted Venice to supersede Florence as the chief center and disseminator of Greek learning to western Europe. This is an important point, the significance of which is not usually appreciated by western scholars of the Renaissance.

Certainly even without a Greek colony the Venetians would

[50] C. Mertzios, *Thomas Flanginis*, 186 ff., and his 'New Information about Cretans' (in Greek), *Kretika Chronica* (1948).
[50a] Mertzios, 'Gleanings', 297.

sooner or later have succumbed to the interest in Greek studies which was attracting practically all of the learned circles of Renaissance Italy. Yet we may be reasonably sure that, had the colony not existed, considerably fewer Greeks from Crete and the rest of the East would have been drawn to Venice. It was no small satisfaction to the exiles that upon arrival in the Serenissima they would be among their own people and could carry on virtually unhindered the practice of their own customs and religion. This sentiment is not infrequently expressed by the Greeks, intellectuals or otherwise, resident in Venice.

It is obvious that the colony could not have existed apart from the city of Venice itself, and one should take care therefore not to exaggerate the community's significance in the sense that it alone was responsible for Venetian primacy in Greek scholarship. Earlier Florence had enjoyed this predominance, owing primarily to the teaching there of one individual, the Byzantine Manuel Chrysoloras. And during his tenure there existed no Greek colony to speak of in Florence.[51] But this was much earlier, during the late fourteenth century, and before the large-scale emigation of Greeks to Italy. Moreover, Chrysoloras' teaching served to draw to Florence only western Hellenists yet unschooled in Greek, not learned Greeks from the East. It would seem to be more than mere coincidence that Venice's displacement of Florence as the leader in Greek studies and her establishment as the main center of Greek printing occurred at the very time that the Greek colony in Venice began to flourish and its population to burgeon.

It is difficult to divorce the reasons for the cultural growth of the colony from the commercial prosperity of Venice and from the latter's strategic position as intermediary between East and West. And we certainly cannot overlook the remarkable achievement of Aldus, whose vision, organizational ability, and publications did so much for the dissemination of Greek learning in Europe. All of these factors interact with and depend upon one another. But the point even more to be emphasized is that the lives and careers of the Greek exiles, many of whom were Aldus' chief associates, and without whose aid his work would have been

---

[51] Which is not to say that no individual Greek exiles then lived in Florence, as some did.

far less effective if not virtually impossible, take on much more meaning when viewed, as they have not been, against the background of the Greek colony of Venice. With the addition of this new dimension to the Venetian scene, a more complete and accurate picture is provided to explain the primacy of Venice in Greek letters during the period of the late fifteenth and early sixteenth centuries when she became the leading intellectual center of all Europe.

It is clear then that the community imbued the Greek emigrés, whether they chose to live within the colony or not, with a feeling of security, a sense of belonging, which permitted them to look upon Venice as a second homeland. We should discard therefore the stock image of the Byzantine or post-Byzantine scholars coming to Italy during the Renaissance as for the most part lone, friendless refugees with no particular place for themselves in the West. To be sure, certain Greeks, especially in more distant northern Europe, remained aloof, isolated, forgotten. But for most of the Greeks of the diaspora, particularly in Italy, there was for several centuries a substitute motherland to be found in the Greek colony. According to the nineteenth century Greek historian Veludo, it was this community in Venice which in the period of the Greek nation's disappearance best preserved the Hellenic tradition. Cardinal Bessarion had put it even more succinctly as he bestowed what was for him the ultimate accolade: 'Venice is truly another Byzantium'.[52]

[52] Veludo, II. Cf. K. Paparegopoulos in his important *History of the Greek Nation* (in Greek) (Athens, 1932 ed.) 164–65. For Bessarion's remark see above, text for note 7.

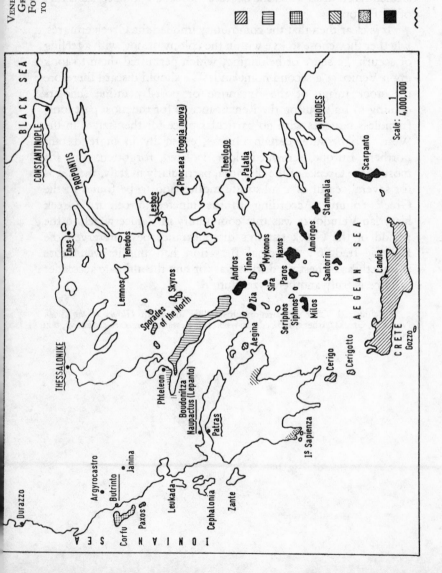

VENETIAN COLONIES IN THE
GREEK EAST FROM THE
FOURTH CRUSADE (1204)
TO THE RENAISSANCE

Map 3

Scale: $\frac{1}{4,000,000}$

	Regno of Candia.
	Regno of Negropont.
	Government of Corfu and dependencies.
	Government of Nauplia.
	Coron and Modon.
	Protectorates of the Aegean.
∿	(Venetian) trading posts.

CHAPTER FIVE

THE CRETAN ROLE IN THE TRANSMISSION OF GRECO-BYZANTINE CULTURE TO WESTERN EUROPE VIA VENICE

In the history of the revival of Greek letters in western Europe during the later Middle Ages and Renaissance the most basic role, at least from the point of view of the actual transmission of these letters to the West, was played by the Greek scholar-exiles from the Byzantine or former Byzantine areas of the East. And of these Greek scholars some of the most important, certainly the most numerous, came from the former Byzantine, subsequently Venetian-held island of Crete. For over two centuries, from about 1400 to well past 1600, Crete exported along with its choice wines and oils scores of intellectuals and artists, who wherever they went in western Europe held high positions of influence. We find Cretans from one end of the Mediterranean to the other, from the monasteries of Sinai and Athos to the peninsula of Spain and, in northern Europe, from England to as far east as Russia. They decorated churches, created masterpieces of painting, served as scribes, teachers, and advisers to western humanists and kings, founded printing presses for the publication of first editions, anticipating in this respect the great Aldus Manutius. In the fifteenth century Crete even produced a pope in the person of Alexander V, and in the sixteenth a Cretan humanist at Geneva, converted to Calvinism, contributed pamphlets for the defence of Protestantism against Catholic attack.

We are not here concerned with all the manifestations of this astonishing Cretan diaspora throughout Europe.[1] Rather we shall limit our presentation to those Cretans who in the fifteenth and sixteenth centuries emigrated to the city of Venice, either to settle there permanently or, using Venice as a stepping stone, to

---

[1] On the Cretan contribution to western culture c. 1204–1600 (aside from the role of ancient Minoan Crete) no book-length synthesis has been written. I am preparing a monograph on this subject, to include also a discussion of the Cretan contribution to the culture of Russia and the rest of Slavic Europe in this period. The focus of the recent, useful work of A. Embiricos, *La Renaissance Crétoise* (Paris, 1960) is essentially the later, seventeenth century Renaissance in Crete itself.

fan out from there to other cultural centers of western Europe. In our discussion we may observe a basic difference between these two centuries: in the fifteenth most of the Cretans who emigrated westward remained in Italy, especially in Venice, while in the sixteenth century, although a good many continued to reside in Venice, we note a movement of Cretans to the more distant territories of northern Europe and the Iberian peninsula. As our investigation proceeds we must try to answer certain fundamental questions, the answers to which will provide us with the background necessary for an understanding of the sudden emergence of so many Cretans to prominence in western European letters and artistic endeavours. Why in the first place did the Cretans find it necessary to emigrate from their homeland? Why did they converge on Venice? And, finally, why in the sixteenth century did they find it advisable to leave Venice for more distant European centers?

I

During the first two and one-half centuries of Venetian rule, from 1204 to *c.* 1453, Crete led what might be called a more or less culturally stagnant existence. Frequent revolts on the part of the freedom-loving populace had led the Venetian rulers to take some rather drastic measures. In order to diminish the influence of the Orthodox episcopate, the Venetians stripped the Cretan church of its hierarchy, appointing instead a series of *protopapades* (first priests), who were to act merely as administrative officers without the power to ordain.[2] In certain areas of the island many Greeks were dispossessed of their lands by newly arrived Venetian colonists. Most detested was the enforced labor called *angaria*, which required all Cretan males of the lower classes to serve for a time as rowers in the Venetian fleet.[3] Such measures rendered

[2] On the question of the Greek hierarchy in Crete see Geanakoplos, *Greek Scholars in Venice*, Chap. 2, esp. pp. 42–47. Also M. Manousakas, 'Venetian Documents on the Church History of Crete of the Fourteenth to Sixteenth Centuries' (in Greek), *Deltion Hist. Ethnol. Hetaireias Hellados*, XV (1960) 149–233; and N. Tomadakes, 'The Orthodox Priests under Venetian Domination and their Ordination' (in Greek), *Kretika Chronika*, XIII (1959) 39–72. Basic documents on Cretan history are published in G. Gerola, *Monumenti dell'isola di Creta*, 4 vols. (Venice, 1905–1932).

[3] Embiricos, *La Renaissance Crétoise*, 27, shows that the detested forced service (corvée) in the Venetian marine did not apply to all classes in Crete, but generally only to the peasants. Probably there was a type of land *angaria* also.

Cretan social and economic conditions repressive, a fact which in turn tended to discourage intellectual activity. These conditions obtained in general until the fall of Constantinople to the Turks in 1453, at which time and shortly thereafter the island was suddenly inundated by a flood of refugees from Constantinople and the Greek mainland.[4] As a result of this influx, plus the fact that the island was the only important Greek area free of Turkish domination, Crete now became the main center of Hellenism in the old Byzantine world.

Among those who entered the island was a large number of highly educated persons whose presence served to raise the hitherto low cultural level of Crete. The intellectual standard of the clergy, in whose hands rested whatever meagre educational facilities still existed, was especially affected.[5] There had been of course exceptions such as the scholar-prelate John Simeonachis, who in the late fourteenth century taught an occasional Italian who came searching for manuscripts, like Rinuccio of Arezzo, or members of the Venetian administrative staff. And in the same century even Leontius Pilatus, the teacher of Petrarch and Boccaccio, may have visited Crete for a time in order to perfect his Greek. Cultured Byzantines from Constantinople at times had also entered Crete, Joseph Bryennios or Maximos Chrysoberges for example in the early fifteenth century.[6] But these were usually involved in the bitter struggle between unionists and non-unionists and seem to have had little effect on the general cultural level of the populace.

Crete before 1453 seems to have possessed no schools in the rural areas and relatively few even in the urban districts. No higher school of learning, Greek or Venetian, existed even as late as the sixteenth century, the only schools of any competence

[4] On this emigration from Byzantium see Geanakoplos, *Greek Scholars in Venice*, 48–49. S. G. Mercati, 'Di Giovanni Simeonachis Protopapa di Candia', *Misc. G. Mercati*, III (Vatican, 1946) 13, refers to it as an 'inundation'.

[5] Certain scholars, esp. N. Tomadakes, argue that the cultural level of Crete in this period, before the Byzantine emigration to the island, was not quite so low as is usually believed. I have recently found several documents in the Venetian archives attesting to the same thing. I hope to publish these in my work on Crete.

[6] On Rinuccio see D. Lockwood, 'De Rinucio Aretino', *Harvard Studies in Classical Philology*, XXIV (1913) 51–109 and S. Mercati, article cited above. On Bryennios and Chrysoberges see N. Tomadakes, *Joseph Bryennios and Crete around* 1400 (in Greek) (Athens, 1947) 85–102. On Pilatus, see A. Pertusi, *Leonzio Pilato fra Petrarca e Boccaccio* (Venice-Rome, 1964) 30 f.

being those attached to monasteries, notably that of St. Catherine of Sinai in Candia, the island's capital. Many famous Greeks, Maximos Margounios and the later patriarch Meletios Pigas among them, were to be trained at St. Catherine's, but its curriculum, largely a combination of ancient Greek and Latin literature together with Christian theology, was not much more than rudimentary.[7] Yet it was sufficient to permit its students to pursue more advanced studies elsewhere, their usual choice being the University of Padua in Venetia.

The virtual invasion of Crete after 1453 by Constantinople and mainland refugees brought to the island some famous exiles: Michael Apostolis, scholar and scribe and father of the even better known Arsenios Apostolis;[8] also the humanist Janus Lascaris, and earlier the parents of George of Trebizond, who, since he was born in Crete, may be considered a Cretan. Usually stripped of their possessions and without means of support, these learned refugees turned naturally to intellectual pursuits, especially teaching or the trade of a copyist. The latter profession, because of the increasing Renaissance demand for Greek manuscripts, now made Crete a prime center for the copying of old texts. The chief center for the dissemination of these Cretan copied manuscripts was, logically, the capital city Venice. And as time went on the reputation of the Cretan scribes, native as well as refugee, spread throughout all of Europe. Nevertheless, the astonishing productivity of the Cretans, invaluable as it was for the preservation of the ancient writings, was too often commercial in nature and did not always result in the most accurate reproduction of a text.[9]

Noble Venetians frequently acted as patrons for the Cretan scribes, thus helping to foster the production of Greek texts. Such patrons included the Barozzi family to whom we owe the famous Barocci collection in the Oxford Bodleian library. Also the Venetian statesmen Francesco Barbaro, Marco Lipomanno, Duke of Candia (the latter had commissioned the Cretan John Simeonachis to copy works of Lucian, Aristotle, and Michael

---

[7] On the schools see Geanakoplos, *Greek Scholars*, 45–47. Also Mercati, *loc. cit.* On St. Catherine see below Chap. 6.

[8] For biographies on Michael and Arsenios Apostolis see Geanakoplos, *Greek Scholars*, Chaps. 4–5.

[9] See J. Irigouin, *Histoire du texte de Pindare* (Paris, 1952) 365–66.

Psellus), Thomas Celso the prefect of Crete, Lauro Quirini, and Girolamo Donato.[10] The most notable of the many Cretan scribes was the Byzantine-born Michael Apostolis. Under a commission from Bessarion to search for manuscripts in out of the way areas of Crete, Apostolis created a kind of school of copyists in Candia. Nevertheless, Michael died almost in penury, bitterly lamenting his failure to secure a lucrative teaching position in Italy. His name lives on, however, through specimens of his calligraphy which are today to be found in every major European library.

Michael is representative of the Greek men of letters who helped to make Crete a kind of mid-point between the old Byzantine world and the rising Italian centers of humanistic scholarship, especially Venice. Among his private students in Crete were two little-known but important figures, Laonikos, later to become the editor of the first Greek book published in Venice,[11] and Emmanuel Adramyttenos, a talented young man who subsequently in Italy taught Greek to Aldus, and at Mirandola influenced his good friend, the great philosopher Pico della Mirandola.[12]

With Crete flooded with newcomers, the old social and economic structure of the island could no longer support its population. For the more restless and ambitious Crete offered virtually no chance for advancement. The ecclesiastics resented the Venetian refusal to permit them to rise to higher status in the church. More intolerable was the plight of the intellectuals. The lack of schools of higher education blocked the more able and ambitious from securing professional positions. Hence they had to content themselves with the private teaching of a few pupils or with the deadening monotony and meagre recompense of long hours of manuscript copying. In the light of this situation of frustration and stagnation many Cretan men of letters chose to emigrate to western Europe where greater opportunities might be found. This meant of course Italy and above all the home city, Venice.

In Venice, as noted in a previous essay, there existed the largest

[10] On these see works cited in Geanakoplos, *Greek Scholars*, 50–51.

[11] Opinion of the authoritative V. Scholderer, *Greek Printing Types*, 1465–1927 (London, 1927) 5.

[12] On Adramyttenos little work has been done. He needs a biography. For his correspondence with Michael Apostolis see H. Noiret, *Les lettres inédites de Michel Apostolis* (Paris, 1889) 155ff. Laonikos, chief priest of Canea in Crete, edited the *Batrachomyomachia*, and Alexander edited the Psalter. References in my book, 58.

concentration of Greeks in the western world. Venice offered many opportunities to the skilled Hellenist, either as a scribe for a wealthy patron, as teacher in the Venetian schools, chancery, or at the nearby University of Padua, or, finally, as editor or typesetter in Venice's newly developing Greek press. Already in 1476 at Milan, Demetrius Damilas, born in Crete of Latin parents, had published the *Erotemata* (Grammar) of the Byzantine Constantine Lascaris. This was the first entirely Greek book to be printed anywhere in Europe. Soon afterwards, in 1486, two Greek Cretans Laonikos and Alexander established a press in Venice and produced what some affirm to be Venice's first Greek book.[13] This was almost a decade before the initial production of the great Aldus Manutius, who is commonly given most of the credit for the foundation of the Greek press in Venice.

But the outstanding example of the Cretan contribution to the Greek press of Venice was provided by the printing establishment of Zacharias Calliergis, whose entire staff consisted of Cretan compatriots. In the first phase of his career in Venice, Calliergis produced several important works including that greatest of the Greek dictionaries, the *Etymologicum Magnum*. Zacharias was also an excellent scribe and first class editor as well as competent technician of printing. It should be noted that in his work, Calliergis, like so many of his compatriots, was motivated by a high degree of ethnic pride. Himself a descendant of an imperial Byzantine family, he took as his printers' mark the Byzantine double-headed eagle with a shield superimposed. Calliergis' works were usually characterized by a fine execution and in many cases were superior even to those of Aldus, whose production methods were often marred by undue haste.

After the unsettled political conditions and economic depression overtaking Venice after the War of the League of Cambrai (1509), Calliergis appeared in Rome in 1515, attracted by the Medici Pope Leo X's promotion of humanistic learning. With the financial support of the wealthy merchant Agostino Chigi, Zacharias opened the first Greek press in the papal capital, producing first editions of such notable Greek authors as Pindar, Theocritus and Thomas Magister, as well as Greek liturgical works. Aldus Manutius, Calliergis' rival in Venice, also employed a large number

[13] Scholderer, 5. Cf. A. Pertusi, 'Erotemata', *It. Med. e. Um.*, *V* (1962) 324.

of Cretans, especially after Calliergis had to close up shop and move to Rome.[14] Among the thirty-six or so members of Aldus' famous Academy more than a dozen were Greeks, over half of whom were Cretans employed usually in the capacity of editors or typographers.[15]

In the later sixteenth century, as is not usually realized, many more Greek presses were to be established in Venice, some owned and operated by Cretans such as the Glykys family. The documents available to us indicate that these Cretans lived for the most part in the constantly expanding Greek colony of the city, close by the docks, their newly constructed church, and others of their compatriots.[16]

Hardly less important for the dissemination of Greek learning was the teaching by Cretans in Venice and at the University of Padua. Padua had followed Florence and Bologna in the establishment of a chair of Greek studies and as its first occupant the Venetian government had appointed in 1463 the Athenian Demetrius Chalcondyles. His successor in this post seems to have been the Uniate Greek priest Alexander Zeno, a Corfiote, and much later, in 1508, the Cretan Marcus Musurus raised the Paduan Greek chair to a prestige unequalled in all Europe. Musurus was also at various times chief editor for the Aldine press (he edited no less than 11 or 12 first editions of the most important Greek authors such as Plato), official censor of Greek books for the Venetian government, and an accomplished poet. His poem addressed to Plato has established his reputation, at least from the philological point of view, as the greatest poet of the Greek language since the ancient world.

No less important than his first editions was the remarkably wide influence Musurus exercised over a large group of humanists drawn from all areas of western Europe who had come to listen to his lectures at Padua and later in Venice. Indeed his six-year period of instruction at Padua constitutes an important landmark in the development of western Greek studies and is comparable

[14] On Calliergis see Geanakoplos, *Greek Scholars*, Chap. 7.
[15] See above Chap. 3. Also D. Geanakoplos, 'Erasmus and the Aldine Academy of Venice: A Neglected Chapter in the Transmission of Greco-Byzantine Learning to the West', *Greek, Roman, and Byzantine Studies*, III (1960), 107–34.
[16] See esp. documents in Legrand, *Bibliographie hellénique* II. Also Veludo, *Greek Colony of Venice* (in Greek), 126–34, who lists the Greek and especially the Cretan printers.

only to the success achieved by Manuel Chrysoloras a century before in Florence, and later by Guarino of Verona in Ferrara. Many of the most eminent Hellenists of the day were Musurus' pupils: Italians such as Lazzaro Bonamico, and the aged Raffael Reggio, who arose very early each morning, he tells us, to reach Musurus' lectures on time, and Girolamo Aleandro, who after study with Musurus helped to inaugurate the teaching of Greek in Paris. Germany was represented by John Conon, who according to one historian is the true founder of Greek studies in Germany. From France came Germain de Brie, later secretary to the French Queen, and the French ambassador to Venice, Jean de Pins. From Hungary came Janus Vertessy, and from Prague the young Gelenius, who after working with Musurus went to Basle, where he produced editions of ancient Greek poets.[17]

But the best known of the northerners who profited from Musurus' instruction was certainly the Dutchman Erasmus. We are told by his pupil Beatus Rhenanus that Erasmus would consult Musurus whenever he encountered a difficult Greek passage. Erasmus credited the Greeks of the Aldine circle, and especially Musurus, with the loan to him of many rare manuscripts, some yet unprinted or inaccessible to him. These included the works of Plato, Plutarch, Athenaeus, Hermogenes and the *Rhetoric* of Aristotle; also the scholia on Hesiod, Theocritus, and the even more valuable scholia of Eustathius of Salonika on Homer; finally, the large collection of ancient Greek and Byzantine sayings compiled by Michael Apostolis which Erasmus secured by way of Michael's son Arsenios, then a member of the Aldine circle. The texts comprised some of the most celebrated works of Greek antiquity in the fields of rhetoric, philosophy, ethics, geography, epic and lyric poetry. And the large majority of these, with the exception of the works of Plato, Aristotle, and Plutarch were virtually unknown to the West before their subsequent publication by the Aldine press. Only in Venice, owing to the peculiar circumstances of its connections with the old Byzantine East could Erasmus have been provided with such a variety of important and unexploited authors. Much of this material Erasmus incorporated into the Aldine edition of his *Adages*,

[17] On Padua, and also Musurus' career there see above, Chap. 4, and Geanakoplos, *Greek Scholars*, Chap. 5.

which, as is well known, established his reputation as Europe's foremost scholar. It was through Erasmus' great reputation and his ability to 'popularize' that the learning of the Greeks was able to reach a wider audience than ever before in north-western Europe.[18]

II

It is often assumed by historians that there was a marked falling-off of interest in Greek studies in Italy after the sack of Rome in 1527.[19] Whether this be true or not, it is little realized that this was certainly not the case with respect to Venice. Although no scholars appear really comparable to Musurus and Janus Lascaris, emigration to Venice from Crete and the East continued throughout the entire sixteenth and even seventeenth centuries. And a long sequence of lesser but competent Greek men of letters established residence there. A major part of these were still Cretans, most prominent among them being the very able Maximos Margounios of the late sixteenth century, whose career (as shown below) encompassed the manifold activities of bishop, theologian, editor of texts for the press, translator, poet, and advocate of union between the Greek and Roman churches.[20]

Venice still remained the great international center of the book manuscript trade, especially of Greek works.[21] But a surplus of scholars of Greek was now developing in Venice so that some Cretans (including many manuscript copyists),[22] feeling the competition not only of fellow-Greeks but of the growing number of able Latin Hellenists as well, decided to emigrate to more distant, culturally undeveloped areas. In the countries of northern and western Europe, especially in France and Spain, Greek printing had not yet made its appearance. Thus from about the

---

[18] Geanakoplos, 'Erasmus and the Aldine Academy of Venice', 107–34.

[19] J. Burckhardt, *The Civilization of the Renaissance in Italy* (Oxford, 1945) 118 and J. Sandys, *A History of Classical Scholarship*, 3 vols. (Cambridge, 1903–08), II, 100 and 103.

[20] On Margounios' career see below Chap. 6.

[21] See L. Cohn, *Verzeichnis der von der Königlichen Bibliothek zu Berlin erworbenen Meermanhandschriften des Sir Thomas Philipps* (Berlin, 1892) p. i.

[22] Zacharias Scordylis, Antonios Episkopoulos and John Nathaniel are a few of the Cretan scribes working in Venice in the later sixteenth century.

early sixteenth century we find Cretan intellectuals, one by one, sometimes in small groups, making their way across the Alps to the north or to the Iberian peninsula in the hope of finding new opportunities for employment. The stream of Greek and Cretan refugees to these areas, however, dwindles in proportion to the distance they travelled from Venice or Crete. And the normally tight cohesion of the Cretan group observed in Venice and other Italian centers becomes looser, although communication with someone, a close friend or relative, was always maintained. It is only haphazardly in some cases that we can trace the careers of these seemingly isolated individuals. Manuscript subscriptions, signatures on paintings, university records, documents in libraries, records of commercial transactions and so on are our sources of of information. One thing we can always be certain of, however, that all or virtually all the Cretans who moved to the north in this period passed first through Venice, that chief point of debarkation for Greeks coming to the western world.[23]

Perhaps the first Cretan to appear in Spain was the humanist-printer Demetrius Ducas. He tells us himself that while working in Venice at the press of Aldus he was summoned to Spain by none other than Cardinal Ximenes in order to teach Greek at the newly established university of Alcalá. And, as I have tried to show elsewhere, he supervised the edition of the Greek New Testament text of the Cardinal's celebrated Complutensian Polyglot Bible.[24] While in Spain and perhaps on his own, Ducas also issued (in 1514) the two very first Greek books to be printed in the Iberian peninsula. Ducas disappears shortly thereafter, not to reappear until a decade or so later (in 1526–27) as 'public' professor of Greek at the papal University of Rome. We have no record of his activities in the meantime but it seems very probable that the Greek scholar 'Rindaceno' or 'Rindacos', who is recorded as coming in 1525 to Barcelona and Toledo in the retinue of Cardinal Salviati, son of Pope Leo X, should (as has not hitherto been realized) be identified with the great post-Byzantine humanist and diplomat in the service of France, Janus Lascaris, called

---

[23] A study of the many Greek scholars and theologians in the West mentioned in Legrand, *Bibliographie hellénique . . . des XVe et XVIe siècles* (Paris, 1885–1906) vols. I–IV, bears out this function of Venice.

[24] Demonstrated (for the first time) in Geanakoplos, *Greek Scholars*, 239–44. Ducas had not previously been the subject of a biography. See *ibid.*, 253.

'Rhindacenos' from the place of his family's origin. It may well have been through Lascaris that Ducas was persuaded to go to Rome, where the following year we find him teaching.[25]

Ducas' considerable contribution to Spanish humanism has been almost entirely ignored by modern scholars, some even confusing his identity with that of two other Greeks called Demetrius. Spanish historians in particular have given him short shrift, patriotically passing him over in favour of the native Spanish Hellenists, some of whom were undoubtedly his pupils or had been inspired by his work.

The activities of Ducas in Spain may have opened the way to the arrival of other Cretans. Pedro de Candia, a Cretan adventurer, accompanied Pizzaro on his famous expedition for the conquest of Peru (c. 1532), and for his services was granted by the Queen of Spain herself the rank of chief gunner and a title of Spanish nobility. We know that Pedro had with him on the expedition many compatriots (termed *Levantini* in the sources), also trained in the manufacture of cannons and firearms. According to certain (perhaps exaggerated) reports they were even responsible for the invention of a new kind of gun-powder which made easier the campaign of conquest against the Incas.[26] It seems that in the later sixteenth century a small community of Greeks existed in Toledo.[27] And it was to that cosmopolitan city that after the battle of Lepanto in 1571 many Greeks from the East, though usually poor and ignorant of the Castilian tongue, came to raise funds for the ransom of relatives or friends captured by the Turks in raids on the Cretan coast or the Greek mainland. A series of royal documents, dated 1602–08 and before, contains the names, distorted in Spanish, of four Greek bishops, two

[25] See Ámada López de Meneses, *Francisco I y otros ilustres extranjeros en Guadalajara en 1525 (Instituto de Historia de España)* (Buenos Aires). Also cf. B. Knös, *Un ambassadeur de l'hellénisme: Janus Lascaris* (Upsala-Paris, 1945) 20, 187 ff. Geanakoplos, *Greek Scholars*, 249.

[26] On Pedro de Candia, who is well known to historians, see W. H. Prescott, *History of the Conquest of Peru*, I (New York, 1921) 201, 210–11.   Prof. Marcel Battaillon, Director of the Collège de France in Paris, writes me that in his opinion Pedro and his Cretans, though important, did not, as some believe, invent a new type of gun-powder.

[27] See G. Marañón, *El Greco y Toledo*, 2nd ed. (Madrid, 1958) 161–62, who also says El Greco's thought and some of his figures were influenced by the Jewish colony in Toledo; also P. Kelemen, *El Greco Revisited* (New York, 1961) 88, and now Wethey, *El Greco and his School* (Princeton, 1962) 14.

monks, and several laymen, who had come to Toledo for this purpose.[28]

When in 1563 King Philip II of Spain began the construction of the great Escorial, he began to collect there a large library, which included one of the finest collections of Greek manuscripts in the world. Some forty calligraphers, we are told, worked at the Escorial making copies of old manuscripts for the Spanish monarch.[29] We know of several Cretans by name, including a Jacobus Episkopopoulos, who also worked in Germany, and Nicholas Turrianos (de la Torre in Spanish), who not only copied but classified and entitled the numerous Greek codices of the Escorial. Nicholas, who had earlier been in Paris and Venice,[30] found such favor with Philip that he became the first calligrapher to hold the official title of copyist to the king. A painter of miniatures in addition, he, like so many other Cretans, took care to sign his name in Greek characters, proudly adding the word *Kres* (the Cretan), as El Greco himself was wont to do. El Greco was in fact painting in the Escorial (he did the Dream of Philip II for instance) when Turrianos was there and it may be assumed that the two compatriots often found themselves in one another's company.[31] Another Cretan, Antonios Kalosynas (who was not, as sometimes believed, employed at the Escorial) achieved a certain reputation in Toledo as a physician, author, and poet as well as copyist of Greek manuscripts. Before this, as is clear from the numerous manuscripts in his rather gross hand now to be found in the National Library at Madrid, he had been present at and worked as a scribe at the famous Council of Trent in northern Italy, where still another Cretan scribe, Michael Makrokephalites, was in the same period also employed.[32]

[28] See documents in F. de B. San Román, 'De la vida del Greco', *Arch. Esp. de Arte y Arqueol.*, VII (1927) 144–47, 165–71; and Marañón, 161–65.

[29] See Ch. Graux, *Essai sur les origines du fonds grec de l'Escurial* (Paris, 1880) 31, 48–50, 110 ff.; and A. Revilla, *Catálogo de los códices griegos de la biblioteca del Escorial*, I (Madrid, 1936).

[30] The Escorial has a ms. dated 1567 and signed by Turrianos who copied a work of Joseph Bryennios. See Graux, *op. cit.*, 151, n. 2. When Turrianos signed his name in Greek he wrote 'Turrianos', when in Spanish, it was 'de la Torre'. He never apparently signed in Latin.

[31] So I was told (in 1964) at the Escorial by Father Gregorio de Andrés, Director of the Escorial library; and see Omont, *Fac-similés de manuscrits grecs*, 14. Also on Turrianos as scribe see Andrés' article, 'La Biblioteca Laurentina', in *El Escorial*, 1593–1963 (Madrid, 1963) 706 ff. and A. Tovar, *Catalogus Codicum Graecorum Universitatis Salamantinae*, *Fil. y Let.*, *XV*, 4 (1963) nos. 557–562 esp.

[32] On these Cretans see Legrand, *Bibl. hell.*, I, 317; also Graux, *loc. cit.*, 31, 48, 50, 110 ff. And now S. Cirac, 'L'hellénisme de D. Theotokopoulos', *Kretika Chronika*, II

Christis in Benediction. Icon from Lavra, Mt. Athos
(14th century). (See p. 50.)

Christ in Benediction. Mural in church at Kritsa, Crete
(14th century?). (See p. 50.)

Plate 11

Christ in Benediction. Icon by Michael Damaskinos (?), 16th century Cretan. (See p. 151.)

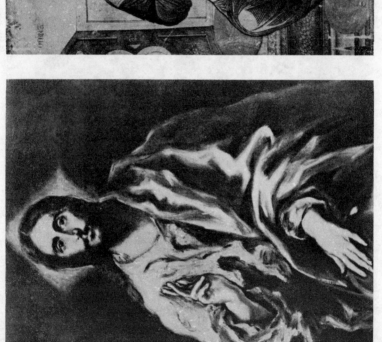

Christ in Benediction. Painting by El Greco in Greco Museum, Toledo, Spain. (See p. 151.)

Plate 12

Certainly the best known Cretan to appear in Spain was the celebrated painter El Greco, born Domenikos Theotokopoulos. Like Ducas he left his birthplace in Crete to share in the opportunities offered by cosmopolitan Venice, where Greeks, Italians, and northerners (including even German Lutherans studying at Padua) mingled in a melting-pot of races. It is inconceivable that El Greco would have failed to associate with the numerous Cretans of Venice's Greek colony. To be sure, the register of the Greek community of San Giorgio does not include his name for the period of his residence there (1566–70) but, as we have shown elsewhere, this is not necessarily significant. Moreover, the name of his older brother Manoussos Theotokopoulos, who joined him later in Toledo, does appear several times.[33] The colony had many Cretan painters working in the more or less traditional Byzantine manner for the Greek church of San Giorgio, then in the process of completion—artists such as Michael Damaskinos of Crete whom some erroneously believe to have been El Greco's teacher. El Greco in any event studied in Venice with Titian and Tintoretto, acquiring there the Venetian quality of colorful pigment, which he fused with his own creative genius, inspired in turn by the dual Cretan-Venetian influences of his native island.[34]

In 1570 El Greco went for a time to Rome but after a relatively short stay returned to Venice. What induced El Greco to leave the sophisticated environment of Venice to emigrate to the more backward one of Spain we are not certain. Probably it was the promise of greater opportunity—especially in connection with the famous project of the Escorial then under construction

(1961) 224–25. Also certain mss. in the Madrid National library copied by Kalosynas: e.g., a Greek ms. no. 4856 containing acts of the Ephesus council of 431, copied in 1563 at Trent for Martin the Archbishop of Segovia. Also ms. 4858. See now J. M. Fernandez Pomar, 'La catalogación del fondo griego de la Biblioteca Nacional', *Helmántica*, XIV (1963) 341–79. I believe that there are no Greek mss. of Turrianos in the Madrid National Library. Also see E. Miller, *Catalogue des Mss. grecs de la bibliothèque del Escurial* (Paris, 1848) e.g., p. XXII, on Kalosynas' Mss. On Makrokephalites and Kalosynas at Trent see Martin, 'Rapport sur une mission en Espagne et en Portugal', *Nouvelles Archives des missions scientifiques et littéraire*, II (1892) 44, 23, 37–38, etc. On Turrianos as a painter see Manuel Cossio, *El Greco* (Madrid, 1908).

[33] See above Chap. 4, after note 50.
[34] For the influences on El Greco's style, a controversial question, see preceding Chap. text and notes 48–50. R. Byron, supporting the emphasis on his Byzantine heritage, says El Greco furnished the 'epilogue and climax to Byzantine culture' (*The Byzantine Achievement* [New York, 1929] 218). Some of Byron's views are exaggerated but this remark. I think has something to be said for it. Cf. now also the opinion of the Spaniard S. Cirac, *op. cit.*, above. Also cf. note 37 below.

—since Spain was now the world's foremost and wealthiest power.[35] It is worthy of note that El Greco was not the first Greek or possibly even Cretan painter to appear in Spain. If we accept the testimony of certain documents, he was preceded by two other Greek artists: a certain Pedro 'el Greco' (according to some scholars to be identified with the noted Pedro Serafín), who is listed in 1563 as both a painter and poet active in Barcelona and Tarragona, and a Nicholas Greco, painter and *pirotécnico* who installed a fireworks display at Segovia and for the same city painted the funerary monument in honor of Philip II.[36] At Toledo El Greco (Theotokopoulos, that is) mingled with the Greek community. He knew Kalosynas and it is recorded that in 1582 he acted as interpreter for a Cretan youth named Michaele Rizo Carcondil (probably Chalcocondyles in Greek), who had been haled before the dreaded Inquisition for suspected Moorish sympathies.[37]

The talent of El Greco and his contribution to Spanish art, though insufficiently appreciated in his own day, is now so universally admired that he may be considered one of the supreme painters of all time. It seems certain, however, that in the unique blend of Byzantine, Venetian, and, finally, Spanish elements from which he was able to fashion his perfected artistic synthesis, there always remained the influence of his Cretan homeland.[38]

The first appearance of Cretan emigrés in France is difficult to establish. It is, however, probably tied to the slowly developing

[35] See now José Camón Aznar, 'El Greco y Filipe II', *El Escorial*, I, 353 ff. Also Wethey, *El Greco*, 10. Cf. Kelemen, *El Greco*, 72.

[36] José L. Rodríguez Escorial, 'El Pintor Nicolás Greco, Pirotécnico', *Instituto D. de Colmenares, Estudios Segovianos* (Segovia, 1949) 585–86, for baptismal record listing his name and profession. Also on Pedro Serafin, see José Madurell Marinón, *Pedro Nunyes y Enrique Fernandes Pintores* (Barcelona, 1944), esp. 271 and documents where he is termed a Greek. D. J. Puiggari, 'Noticias de algunos artistas catalanes', *Memórias de la real Academia de . . . Barcelona*, III (1880) 9, 167 ff., identifies the poet 'Pedro el Greco' ('compatriot of the great El Greco') with Pedro Serafín, who left important paintings at Montserrat. Is it possible that Nicholas Greco is Turrianos, who was a painter of miniatures and married a Segovian woman?

[37] See esp. F. de B. San Román, 'De la vida del Greco', VII (1927) 7–57. Also his *El Greco en Toledo, o nuevas investigaciones* (Madrid), 1910 3–7. Cf. Kelemen, 89–91. Also on the Greek community see Marañón, *El Greco y Toledo*, 161–62 and now the fine work of José Camón Aznar, *Domenico Greco*, I (Madrid, 1950) 21 ff. with long bibl. Prof. V. Lazarev of Moscow told me that the elongation of figures typical of El Greco (and which some critics believe is of Byzantine influence) is rather attributable to the influence of Florentine 'Mannerism'. See also K. Hugo Kehrer, *Greco als Gestalt des Manierismus* (Munich, 1939) 23.

[38] See the recent article of Cirac, *loc. cit.*, 211–227 and Chatzidakes' article (in Greek), 'The Youth of Theotokopoulos', *Epohes* (Aug. 1963) 35–37.

French interest in humanistic studies, partly as a result of influences flowing northward from Italy. To be sure individual Greeks had appeared in France earlier in the medieval period, the Byzantine Emperor Manuel II Palaeologus himself remaining in Paris the better part of two years in 1400–02 in his search for allies against the Turkish peril threatening his Empire.[39] Nor can we overlook the Cretan who achieved the most exalted position of all his countrymen in the West, Petrus Philarges, who in 1409 at the council of Pisa was elected pope. Previously he had taught scholastic theology at the University of Paris. We have of course seen many Greeks serving as professors in Italian universities. This was the first time, however, that a Greek had assumed a professorial chair in the north, and at that in the West's pre-eminent university, Paris. But fate had far greater things in store for Philarges. Born of a humble Cretan family, uprooted as a boy from his native society and installed in a Latin monastery of Candia by a sympathetic Franciscan monk, Philarges entered the Franciscan order. When his bent for letters made itself manifest, he was sent for higher study to the monastery of the order at Padua and thence to Oxford in England, where in 1370 he received his Bachelor of Theology degree. From there he went on to the great University of Paris, where he achieved a considerable reputation lecturing on the *Sentences* of Peter Lombard. Philarges' intellectual orientation seems to have been molded by the western scholastic tradition and to have owed much less to the intellectual influences of his native East. In this respect he was not typical of the Cretan refugees who came to the West after 1453, almost all of whom retained the basic orientation of their native Greco-Byzantine culture. But he had not entirely forgotten his Greek heritage. For after attaining the supreme post of western Christendom, almost at once he directed papal diplomacy to a project close to his heart, the launching of a western Crusade to rescue Byzantium from its impending doom. At the same time he dispatched at least one embassy to Constantinople to negotiate the question of ecclesiastical union.[40] But Alexander V, as he is

[39] B. de Xivrey, *Mémoire sur la vie et les ouvrages de l'Empereur Manuel Paléologue* (Paris, 1853); also G. Schlumberger, 'Un Empereur de Byzance à Paris et à Londres', *Revue des Deux Mondes*, XXX (1915) and others.

[40] On Philarges see the old, unsatisfactory work of M. Renieris, *The Greek Pope Alexander V; Byzantium, and the Synod of Basle* (in Greek) (Athens, 1881). More

known to history, was a unique and preliminary figure among the Cretan emigrés. Isolated and arriving in the West before the movement of the Greek diaspora may be said properly to have begun, he had virtually lost his eastern roots and become almost completely assimilated to the West both from a cultural and religious point of view.

After 1453 the first refugee Greek intellectual in France of whom we seem to have record is the Spartan humanist-teacher George Hermonymus. Hermonymus, who arrived in Paris in 1476, taught Greek to the great French Hellenist Guillaume Budé and the German Johannes Reuchlin. But his pupils did not have a high regard for the worth of his teaching nor even for his knowledge of Greek.[41] That there were other Greeks at this time in France is indicated by records of King Charles VII, which for the years before 1461 include the names of royal pensioners from Byzantium. These were evidently men who provided military service to the King. The most important was a Byzantine of the last imperial family, George Disypatos Palaeologus, who was given command of several fortresses in Normandy and who at his death in 1490 held a patent of nobility from the French king.[42] There is no evidence, however, that they were numerous enough to form a corps, as was the case of the *stradioti* in Venice. Nor can we tell how many were Cretans.

As early as the fifteenth century a Cretan printer made his appearance in Brittany. Wishing to establish the first printing press in that area, Jean de Rohan, a Breton nobleman and man of letters had in 1484 imported (from where is unknown) two printers, Robin Foucquet, evidently French, and his helper known to us simply as Jean Cres (meaning probably 'the Cretan'). Together they set up a small press at Bréhant-Loudéac. After collaboration on at least ten books in French, five of them religious works and another on Aristotle, the two dissolved their partnership. But

important is that of Cardinal F. Ehrle, the one major student of his work, *Der Sentenzen Kommentar Peters von Candia* (Münster, 1925) who calls Philarges' philosophical approach (at the University of Paris where he taught) 'Scotism colored with Nominalism'. See E. Gilson, *History of Christian Philosophy in the Middle Ages* (New York, 1955) 469–70.

[41] See H. Omont, 'Georges Hermonyme de Sparte, Maître de Grec à Paris et copiste de manuscrits, *Mémoires de la Société de l'histoire de Paris et de l'Ile-de-France*, XII (1885) 65–92.

[42] Omont, 'Hermonyme', 67. Also Kelemen, *El Greco Revisited*, 87.

until 1491 Cres continued to publish several works on his own, again in French, not in Greek, though one is the famous travels of Sir John Mandeville through Greek areas to the Holy Land. After this Cres disappears.[43] If we are correct in taking Cres to mean 'Cretan'—there are certainly other cases such as that of El Greco and Turrianos in which Cretans signed themselves thus—it is notable, as has not hitherto been observed, that as early as the late fifteenth century a Cretan made his way even to distant Brittany in order to profit from the rising demand for technicians in the new art of printing.

The study of Greek in Paris was given real impetus by the arrival in 1494 of the aristocratic Byzantine Janus Lascaris. A first-class scholar and teacher much superior to Hermonymus, Lascaris had previously worked in Florence and Rome for the Medici family. Attracted by the opportunities that were beginning to present themselves to scholars of Greek in Paris, he had followed the French King there from Italy after the latter's invasion of that country. In Paris Lascaris achieved a considerable success and finally, as a tribute to his diplomatic as well as his scholarly talents, he was appointed French ambassador to Venice. In that capacity he took such a paternal interest in the welfare of Greek men of letters in Italy that he became known as the 'Patron of the Greeks.'[44]

Meantime the Cretan intellectuals in Venice were feeling more and more the pinch of competition in the overcrowded city and cast their eyes northward toward France. Anthony Eparchos, the Corfiote Greek scribe, had made a grant of thirty Greek manuscripts to the French king which formed the nucleus of the French royal library at Fontainebleau.[45] As this library began to expand, the post of librarian became increasingly prized by the Hellenists of France. In 1535 the position was awarded to the Cretan Angelos Vergikios, and it is with him that we come to the

[43] On Cres and Foucquet see Arthur le Moyne de la Borderie and B. Pocquet, *Histoire de Bretagne*, IV (Rennes, 1906) 626–29 and bibl. on 630. That Cres did not publish in Greek is not surprising; there was as yet little interest in Greek in Brittany. Also F. C. Longchamp, *Manuel du Bibliophile Français*, 1470–1920 (Paris, 1927) II, 362, 496, 502, 537.

[44] B. Knös, *Un Ambassadeur de l'hellénisme*, 85, 93. P. de Nolhac, 'Le Grec à Paris sous Louis XII', *Revue des études grecques*, I (1888) 61. Geanakoplos, *Greek Scholars*, 158.

[45] On Eparchos see Legrand, *Bibl. hell.*, I, p. ccxiv ff. Also L. Dorez, 'Antoine Eparque', *Mélanges d'archéologie et d'histoire*, XIII (1893) 281–364.

most important of the Cretans to appear in France. Vergikios had arrived in Venice around 1530 from Crete and after working there for about five years moved on to France. The reasons for his departure are obscure but may be the result of an invitation from George de Selve, the French King Francis I's ambassador to Venice. Despite occasional poverty, Vergikios did well in his early years at Paris, and was appointed 'écrivain ordinaire' (official scribe) to the King. He copied manuscripts at Fontainebleau and prepared a catalogue of the Greek manuscripts of this library, besides teaching Greek to supplement his income. His calligraphy was so beautiful and so widely admired that the phrase 'écrire comme un Ange' has been often presumed, though probably wrongly, to have referred to him. Vergikios also had close connections with the publication of certain of the first Greek books to appear in France. In fact the original Greek letters cut for the royal Greek press in France by Garamond and then by the celebrated Henry Stephanus, were, some scholars believe, modeled directly after the handwriting of Vergikios.[46] The modern authority H. Omont, however, would give much of the credit in this matter rather to the Spartan, George Hermonymus.[47]

Working with Vergikios as a copyist was another Cretan, Pierre Vergikios, probably a relative who had come from Crete at Angelos' behest. Still another compatriot was Constantine Palaeokapas, likewise engaged as a scribe at Fontainebleau. Palaeokapas had previously been employed in Venice and at Padua, and for his services to the Venetian state was appointed by the government a Cretan bishop, contrary to Venetian regulations for the island. But Palaeokapas is best—or perhaps we should say worst—remembered for his many clever forgeries of ancient manuscripts, for which there was then a lucrative market in Venice and later at Paris.[48]

Angelos Vergikios had a son with him in Paris, Nicholas by

---

[46] On Vergikios see esp. Legrand, *Bibl. hell.*, I, p. clxxv–clxxxvi, esp. clxxxiii and clxxxix (on Georges de Selve); also H. Pernot, 'Les Crétois hors de Crète', *Études de littérature grecque moderne* (Paris, 1916) 176ff. On the Greek letters cut for the press see Legrand, I, p. clxxxiii.

[47] Omont, 'Hermonyme', 69.

[48] On Palaeokapas see Legrand, *Bibl. hell.*, II, 7, 8, etc. Also H. Omont, *Facsimilés de manuscrits grec des XVe et XVIe siècles* (Paris, 1887) 11–12 and 'Catalogue des mss. grecs copiés à Paris, au XVIe siècle par Constantin Palaeocappa', *Annuaire de l'Association des études grecques* (1886) 41–79.

name, who seems also to have been born in Crete. Unlike his father, however, he may have come directly to France without staying in Venice. Moreover, he knew French very well, so well in fact that he could write French poetry and mingle with the leading French *literati* of the mid-sixteenth century. He became a shadowy appendage to that literary group of early Renaissance French literature known as the Pléiade. Nicholas does not seem to have supported himself by his literary work but rather as an artist illustrating and illuminating his father's famous manuscripts. Or he might have copied a few manuscripts himself. After his death in Normandy in 1570, soon after that of his father, a touching tribute was paid him by his good friend, the great poet Ronsard, a member of the Pléiade. Ronsard provided Nicholas with a true epitaph, as he put the following words into the mouth of the dead Cretan:

> 'Crete gave birth to me, France nourished me, Normandy holds me here rotting.
>
> O proud destiny that torments men and makes a Greek perish at Coutance. . . .
>
> One sole road leads us to Rhadamanthes.'[49]

These few but expressive words might have been written about almost any Cretan exile in northern Europe, isolated and nostalgic for his country, at the end to sink into oblivion.

England is the only major country of western Europe in this period for which no specific traces of Cretan intellectuals have yet come to light. Yet during the late fifteenth century we know that a primary incentive to Greek studies in England was provided by several Greek refugees: George Hermonymus, Andronicos Callistos, and later John Serbopoulos and a certain Manuel, all except for the first probably from Constantinople.[50] We have few details on these men; in several cases we do not even know their place of origin. But given the wide range of the Cretan wanderings, it is unlikely that the English Channel would have been a bar to the arrival of Cretans in England. (An unpublished document in my possession refers in fact to the presence in England of a

[49] See Legrand, *Bibl. hell.*, I, clxxxiii–clxxxvi, esp. last page, for Ronsard's verses.
[50] R. Weiss, *Humanism in England during the Fifteenth Century* (Oxford, 1941) 144–48. On Callistos in particular see G. Cammelli, 'Andronico Callisto', *Rinascita*, XXIII–XXIV (1942) 3–64.

family of Cretan merchants.)[51] Perhaps a better explanation is that English interest in Greek studies had not yet progressed to the point that intellectual opportunities were assured to them. Or perhaps it is simply that research in this connection has not yet been sufficiently concentrated on England.

In Germany, on the other hand, several traces of Cretans have been found. For example we are told that in Breslau in 1552 Cretans printed a Greek book entitled *Elements of the Christian Faith*. And there is a record of the Cretan copyist mentioned above, Jakobus Episkopopoulos, who before going to work at the Escorial had copied manuscripts in Germany.[52]

Perhaps the only Cretan to have been converted to Protestantism in this period was Franciscus Portus, born in Rethymno, Crete, but whose forebears had originally come from Vicenza, Italy. A non-conformist with a skeptical and caustic train of mind, he scandalized many of his contemporaries by his conduct and eternal contentiousness, thus bringing down upon his head the wrath of powerful enemies. We have little evidence about the early years of his career, though it is certain that, like so many Cretans, he too gravitated to Venice. The eighteenth century Greco-Venetian writer Niccolo Papadopoli, who is often suspected of forging documents, affirms that Portus, after studying philosophy for five years at the University of Padua, was appointed teacher in the Greek community of Venice. In any event we know that, seeing little future for himself in Venice, Portus decided to go to France, where opportunities for Hellenists were more plentiful. Before he was able to carry out his intention, however, he found employment at the Italian court of Modena, where he was to teach Greek and later to enter the noted humanistic academy of the city. Suspected of sympathies for Protestantism, the beliefs of which had recently penetrated to Modena, he subsequently left Modena to enjoy an illustrious career as Professor at the nearby court of Ferrara. But now succumbing openly to the attractions of Protestantism as well as (if we can believe what are probably the exaggerations of his detractors) to those of his

[51] I hope to publish the document on the Cretan merchants in England in my book on Crete.

[52] See M. Vogel and V. Gardthausen, *Die griechischen Schreiber des Mittelalters und der Renaissance* (Leipzig, 1909) 154, and cf. Ch. Graux, *Essai sur la formation du fonds grec de l'Escurial* (Paris, 1880). Also Kelemen, *op. cit.*, 89.

patron's wife the Duchess of Ferrara—she was the daughter of the King of France and a Protestant sympathizer herself—he fled to Venice and then to Rome. After wandering for a time in Europe he finally settled down, in 1561, in Geneva, Switzerland. There for nineteen years in that theocratic center of the Calvinist religion he taught Greek with much sucess as Professor at the municipal Academy. Among his numerous students was the later celebrated philologist Isaac Casaubon, who succeeded to Portus' chair after his death.

During this period Portus published a number of Greek editions and Latin commentaries of such authors as Pindar, Apollonius, Sophocles, Xenophon, Thucydides, Aristotle, Euripides, and the orator Hermogenes. At the time he found time to enjoy the close friendship of Theodore Beza and to consort with Calvin himself. An admirer of the famous French Huguenot Admiral Coligny, Portus, after the admiral's assassination, composed in his honor (in 1573) eight elegiac Greek poems. Devoting his energies also to the cause of Protestantism Portus wrote several polemical pamphlets in Latin and French, thus contributing as a 'citizen' of Geneva to the defense of the Calvinist reformers against the French king and the papists.

So esteemed was Portus' knowledge of Greek in Geneva that after the printing of his Hermogenes the press there would publish no Greek work without his participation, utilizing his services either as editor, commentator, or contributor of Greek epigrams. It was largely through the work of Portus (and to a lesser extent of his son Emilius, who later was named Professor of Greek at Lausanne and then at the University of Heidelberg) that Geneva, in the latter part of the sixteenth century, became one of the important centers of Greek studies and publication. The extraordinary family of Portus also included a nephew, John Casimatis of Crete, who achieved a certain fame as poet at Ferrara and who signed himself 'Giovanni Greco' or 'Cretense' (the Cretan).[53]

Franciscus Portus died in 1581, to the end contentious and apparently dissatisfied over the course of his life. Whatever may have been his involvements in conflicts over religion (we may be sure that his fellow-Cretans did not look with much favor on his

---

[53] On Casimatis see Legrand, *Bibl. hell.*, II, pp. xxi–xxii.

conversion) and however far the paths of his exile took him, two things never seem to have left his thoughts: the desire to cultivate Greek letters and a nostalgia for his Cretan homeland.[54]

It is amazing that so small an island as Crete, under foreign domination and suffering many misfortunes, was able in the relatively short period of the two centuries under discussion to export such a remarkable number of intellectuals to almost every corner of western Europe. No less remarkable is the emergence of so many of these individuals to prominence in the various countries of their exile. In our discussion we have observed that it was primarily the unfavorable social and cultural conditions in Crete, especially the over-abundance of intellectuals, in turn brought about by the influx of Byzantine emigrés after 1453 and later, that forced the Cretans to emigrate to other shores. Given the Venetian domination of the island and the ease of communication with the home city, it was only natural that emigration took place to Venice, that funnel of Hellenism to the West, which soon came to represent a second homeland for the Cretans.

In the sophisticated, half-Byzantine environment of Venice, the Greeks, and especially the Cretans, the Greek community's largest contingent, found the opportunities enabling them to give full expression to their abilities. Without the favorable conditions provided by Venice with her background of centuries of relations with the East, many of the Cretans probably would not have achieved what they did. Indeed, it is likely that they would not even have remained long in Venice. And in fact, in the second quarter of the sixteenth century, when Venetian primacy in Greek studies had begun to decline along with Venetian economic supremacy, and Venice itself had become congested, as it were, with a plethora of Hellenists, Latin as well as Greek, then we see the Cretans once more beginning to move. Crete had been too small and confining, but now even Venice offered too limited a field of action for the more ambitious Cretans. To be sure, the Greek colony of Venice, as we have seen, continued to

[54] On Portus I have checked the relevant materials in the library of the University of Geneva. For Portus' teaching in Geneva I have used Ch. Borgeaud, *Historie de l'université de Genève, l'académie de Calvin* (Geneva, 1900) 117 ff., 17 ff. On Portus' life see also Legrand, *Bibl. hell.*, II, pp. vii–xx, and for his attitude at the end of his life see Embiricos, *La Renaissance Crétoise*, 59–60. Cf. N. Papadopoli, *Historia gymnasii patavini*, II (Venice, 1762) esp. 238, A. Moustoxydes, *Hellenomnemon*, 364–84, and G. Tiraboschi, *Storia della letteratura italiana*, VII, 66–75, 238–49, 1695–1709.

flourish, and in this later period there are many examples of the contributions made by the colony to Greek scholarship, such as in manuscript copying and the printing of Greek liturgical books[55]— the latter a contribution little known to modern western historians. But the more ambitious and adventurous intellectuals now had their gaze fixed further afield. And so the later history of the colony becomes one largely of the activities of rich merchants, shipowners, clerics, and some intellectuals, but usually of the second rank and drawn largely from among the clergy.

In the north of Europe, meantime, which had lagged behind Italy in humanistic endeavors, new opportunities for Greek scholars were beginning to emerge, partly because of the influences penetrating from Italy and partly on account of the more receptive northern attitude, itself a result of more favorable social and economic conditions. In France and Spain, and somewhat later in Germany and Geneva, Greek presses were being established under royal or ecclesiastical patronage. And to provide the skilled technicians and editors required, Greeks, most often Cretans, were employed. Thus we see Cretans associated with the establishment of most of the earliest Greek presses both within and outside of Italy—in Spain with Ducas, at Paris with Vergikios, at Geneva with Portus, and, of course earlier with Damilas at Florence, Laonikos and Alexander in Venice, and with Calliergis in Rome.

The northern universities were beginning to emulate the Italian example and to appoint professors of Greek either in connection with classical learning or sometimes, as in Spain and Geneva, as a result of special interest in the original Greek versions of the New Testament. Some of the greatest Greek teachers of western Europe were Cretans: to mention only the most influential of all this period, Musurus, whose instruction at Padua and Venice is a landmark in the teaching of Greek during the Renaissance. Scores of leading humanists from every part of Europe came to Venice to hear Musurus, many of whom, like the great Erasmus, returned to their homes to become bearers, in some cases pioneers, of Greek studies in their native countries.[56]

Let us compare the two phases in the process of the Cretan role in the transmission of Greek learning to the West via Venice—

[55] See Veludo, *Greek Colony, passim*, and Legrand,*Bibl. hell.*, vols. I–IV, *passim*.
[56] See Geanakoplos, *Greek Scholars*, Chap. 5.

first the movement from Crete to Venice, and later in the sixteenth century from Venice to the north. The first phase was more direct, intensive, and richer in result, probably because of the presence of the Greek colony within Venice and its continuing connections with the Greek East. It should not be forgotten that these Cretans were not the only Hellenists in Venice. Besides other Greeks there is also the important contribution of such Venetian Hellenists as Aldus. But the Italians themselves, and we may recall here the speech of Bembo,[57] often paid tribute to the primary role of the Greeks in their midst. Then too we should not overlook the commercial prosperity of Venice and its economic and diplomatic connections with most of Europe.

In the north the result of this Cretan diffusion is more obscure. Here the Cretans generally appear as isolated individuals or in small clusters, one emigré perhaps together with a relative or friend summoned from the home town. The fact that few Greek colonies, if any (except perhaps for that of Toledo in Spain), may be found in the more northern areas is due partly to the greater distance from Venice and Crete, and probably also to the fact that the northern reception of the Greeks and Greek studies was less congenial than seems to have been the case in Italy. The contribution of the Cretans in the north was then as a whole less decisive than had been the case in Venice, and the work of each Cretan must be evaluated individually in the context of the developing humanism of each country.

The Cretans who appear in Italy and the north in the fifteenth and sixteenth centuries cannot, for the most part, be said to have made an original contribution to western culture in the creative sense. They were fundamentally transmitters, purveyors one might say, of Greco-Byzantine learning. But it should be noted that what the western Renaissance world primarily desired, perhaps the north even more than Italy, was not the Byzantine element but the ancient classical learning. The Cretans were therefore used as a means of getting at something else, not as a mold for creating anything new. And this fact, together with their being too often associated in the western mind with the 'schismatic' eastern church, was frequently a bar to any complete acceptance of the Cretans on the part of western society. On the other hand, the

[57] See above Chap. 4, text for note 25.

intense patriotism of the exiles would itself not have permitted a real assimilation. Aside from Pope Alexander V and perhaps the Greco-Italian Franciscus Portus, there are virtually no examples to be found of Cretans who were genuinely converted to the Catholic or Protestant faiths. To be sure, once arriving in the West, practically all Cretans professed to be Uniates, but this was necessary were they even to be given a chance to work in their new environment. Can one imagine a Ducas in the employ of the Grand Inquisitor Cardinal Ximenes at Alcalá or an El Greco working for his most Catholic majesty Philip II at the Escorial while remaining an Orthodox Greek?[58] And yet at least one famous Cretan was able to break out of the old traditional molds and to produce creative masterpieces of the highest order. Although we cannot say that Musurus' famous elegiac poem the 'Hymn to Plato' was truly creative (its importance in my view lying rather in its technical perfection, the effective use for the first time in centuries of the difficult ancient Greek versification),[59] the paintings of the great El Greco in Spain are impressive and original in the highest degree. El Greco, in the last and longest phase of his career, was of course deeply influenced by Spanish mysticism in the environment of Toledo, the landscape of which must have reminded him of his birthplace in Crete. But El Greco, as is well known, was unable to instil his creative talent in any of his pupils, not even his own son, and thus left no real successors in Spain.[60]

To conclude then—in the formation of the intellectual and psychological make-up of each Cretan that he carried with him to his place of refuge in the West, there were three basic components: first, the old Byzantine tradition of Hellenism that continued to live on in Crete, second, the deep patriotism of the Cretan for his native island and race, and, finally, the influence of the Venetian culture both on Crete and on the Greek colony in Venice. It was

[58] And yet H. Wethey, *El Greco and his School*, 5 and note 23, whose thesis minimizes the Byzantine heritage of El Greco, calls El Greco a 'sincere Catholic'. The Greek church in Venice was nominally Uniate until the end of the sixteenth century (for western and papal consumption) but in actual fact it was Greek Orthodox and under the jurisdiction of the Constantinople Patriarch. See Geanakoplos, *Greek Scholars*, Chap. 3, pp. 65–68.

[59] Musurus' contemporary, the famous Paolo Giovio, *Le iscrittioni poste sotto le vere imagini degli' huomini famosi* (Florence, 1552) 63 and, more recently, Legrand, *Bibl. hell.*, I, p. cxvi, call his poem the greatest Greek poem since the ancient Greek world. I think this is true philologically but less so creatively.

[60] The paintings of El Greco's pupil, Luis Tristan, do not rank as major art works.

the blending of this Venetian element with the native Byzantine tradition that later in the seventeenth century was to produce on the island of Crete itself a remarkable, if belated, Cretan Renaissance.[61] But that is another chapter. In the last analysis the basic contribution of the Cretan intellectuals of the fifteenth and sixteenth centuries lies in their forging of intellectual links between the Hellenism of the old Byzantine East and the emerging Hellenism of the West. They thus helped to construct one of the most important cultural bridges for the development of the civilization of the modern world.

[61] This Cretan Renaissance, which is little known to the West except to specialists, produced such refined dramatic and poetical works as the 'Erofile' of Chortazes, 'The Sacrifice of Abraham', and the celebrated 'Erotokritos' of Cornaro. In these works the Venetian and Cretan-Byzantine currents were blended.

CHAPTER SIX

AN OVERLOOKED POST-BYZANTINE PLAN
FOR RELIGIOUS UNION WITH ROME:

Maximos Margounios the Cretan
Humanist-Bishop and his Latin Library
Bequeathed to Mt. Athos

Though virtually unknown to western historians, Maximos Margounios was probably the most outstanding figure in the intellectual and theological history of the Greek Orthodox Church during the later sixteenth century. Born in Venetian-dominated Crete, he was one of the flood of intellectuals who left that island to emigrate to western Europe, there to become active as bearers of the Greco-Byzantine cultural tradition. Margounios' rather short but full life (c. 1549–1602) encompassed the activities of a bishop-in-absentia, author of many theological works some still unpublished, editor of texts for the press, translator, writer of religious poetry, and, as a student of both the eastern and western ecclesiastical traditions, avid proponent of union between the Greek and Roman churches.[1] Indeed his views on religious union, though usually overlooked today, created a minor furor in the post-Byzantine East of his time.

Margounios spent the most active and creative phase of his career in the tightly knit, prosperous Greek community of Venice, the chief center of the Greek diaspora in western Europe. Before his death in 1602, in Venice, Margounios provided for the disposition of his rich library, which contained a large number of Greek manuscripts as well as many valuable printed books, both Latin and Greek. The Greek books he bequeathed to the monastery of St. Catherine of Candia in Crete, a dependency of the more famous parent monastery of the same name on Mount Sinai.[2] It is, however, the Latin books of his library, now in the

---

[1] No study on Margounios has, to my knowledge, appeared in English. For bibl. on him see Appendix, Bibliographical Note E. and notes below, esp. 28.

[2] On the Greek colony in Venice in the later sixteenth century see above Chap. 4; and on St. Catherine's monastery in Candia see Chap. 5.

possession of the monastery of Iviron on Mount Athos in accordance with the terms of his will, that will provide a nucleus for this
study. Until now the contents of this collection have not been
known to scholars. We therefore print below a preliminary
draft of a catalogue of these works, drawn up during a visit made
to Mt. Athos in the summer of 1962.[3] An analysis of the significance of the various books in this collection may shed more light
not only on the formation of Margounios' intellectual and religious outlook but, even more important, on a significant though
unappreciated chapter in the history of the question of union
between the Greek and Western churches during the late Renaissance and Reformation periods. In order to place the books in
proper context, however, let us first present a sketch of Margounios' life.

I

Candia (today Heraklion), the largest city of Crete, situated
near the ancient Knossos, was Margounios' birthplace (c. 1549).
His father was Greek but on his mother's side he was descended
from the Italian family of the Colonna. His education was
acquired in various places: early knowledge of Greek and Latin
literature from the recently founded school at St. Catherine's
monastery, under the Greek teacher Joasaph Doryanos, and a
more extensive knowledge of Latin under the learned Roman
Catholic Bishop of Sitia, Gaspar Viviano.[4] Like many of his
compatriots, Margounios completed his studies in Italy at the
celebrated University of Padua, where there was a veritable
colony of Greek students and where in the past famous Greeks,
notably the Athenian Demetrius Chalcondyles and the Cretan
Marcus Musurus, had occupied the chair of Greek studies.[5] There

[3] The American Philosophical Society provided funds to make possible my
research on Mount Athos.

[4] On Doryanos see Margounios' letter to him listed in Astruc, 'Correspondance,'
218 and Doryanos' mss. listed in Ch. Patrinelis, 'Greek Codicographers of the
Renaissance,' (in Greek) Ep. Het. Mesaionikou Archeiou, VIII-IX (1958–59) 80.
Legrand, II, p. xxiii says Viviano, Archbishop of Sitia (on the coast of Crete) and
also Vicar-general of the island, was so esteemed by Pope Gregory XIII that he was
consulted on the papal plan to create a Collegio Greco in Rome.

[5] See above, Chap. 4. Margounios' German friend John Scheurlin wrote in 1577
to his friend Martin Crusius that since there was no longer 'Greece in Greece or
Athens in Athens', a large number of Greeks were wont to gather in Venice and

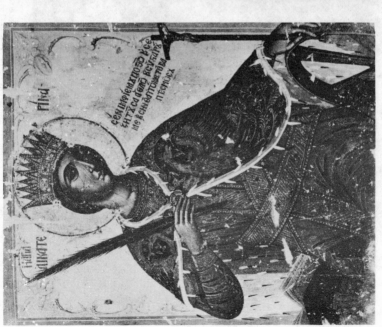

St. Catherine of Alexandria. Icon in Heraklion, Crete. (See p. 50.)   St. Catherine of Alexandria. Painting by El Greco in Metropolitan
Museum of Art, New York. (See p. 150-151.)   Plate 13

John the Baptist. Painting by Titian, Venice E.N.T.E. Plate 14 (See p. 151.)

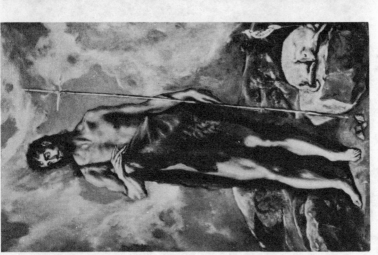

John the Baptist. Painting by El Greco, San Francisco, M. H. de Young Memorial Museum. (See p. 151.)

for some eight years he studied philology, philosophy, theology, and medicine.[6] Among his fellow students was Gabriel Severus, later the Bishop of the Greek colony in Venice, and Emmanuel Pigas, the future Patriarch of Alexandria, Meletios. With the help of letters of recommendation from Gaspar Viviano, Margounios was able to enter the circle of Hellenists in Padua, which included the noted Venetian scholar Thomas Trevisan.

In 1577 an event occurred which was to influence the course of his entire career: the Greek Patriarch Jeremiah II invited the young Margounios (and Severus also) to come to Constantinople. There Margounios was to have received holy orders and to have reorganized the patriarchal school—an institution the chief function of which was to train future prelates for the Orthodox church. In recent years, however, under the Turkish domination, the prestige of the school had fallen off sharply. Margounios was eager to accept this important assignment but because of family obligations, especially toward his father, had to decline. He remained to continue his studies at Padua.

Already in 1572 he had evidenced his competence in Greek and Latin philology by publishing a Latin translation of a Greek manuscript he had discovered, the dialogue of the eighth century Byzantine church father, John of Damascus, 'Against the Manichaeans'.[7] Another testimony to his increasing mastery of classical philology is a remark of the German medical student at Padua, John Scheurlin, who, in a letter to his German humanist

Padua, many of whom were clerics (Legrand, II, p. xxx, n. 5). On Musurus see Geanakoplos, *Greek Scholars in Venice*, Chap. 5. I am planning shortly to publish, with critical commentary, Chalcondyles' inaugural discourse at Padua in 1463 on the occasion of the beginning of Greek studies there.

[6] Legrand, II, p. xxv. The question of the date of Margounios' arrival in Padua and of the subjects he studied there is disputed. I follow Legrand, II, p. xxix-xxxiii and his more secure evidence. His views are based on a letter of Margounios himself. Cf. N. Papadopoli, *Historia gymnasii Patavini* (Venice, 1726) 267 and 264, who gives a much earlier date for his Paduan arrival and says (this particular point may well be correct) that at Padua Margounios studied Latin, philosophy, and Scotist theology. At Padua, affirms Papadopoli, with the inheritance from his wealthy [?] merchant father, Margounios established a printing press near the convent of San Antonio where, before fire destroyed the press, he published a number of Greek works (see also Veludo, *op. cit.*, 128). Legrand disproves all this and also some additional remarks of Papadopoli regarding Margounios' supposed visits to Rome, Pisa, and even Paris. Cf. G. Zaviras, *Nea Hellas Hellenikon Theatron* (in Greek) (Athens, 1872) III, 465, and Fedalto, *op. cit.*, 9–10.

[7] Legrand, II, p. xxiv. See also K. Dyobouniotes, *John of Damascus* (in Greek) (Athens, 1903) which lists the editions.

friend Martin Crusius of the University of Tübingen, describes Margounios as *Cretensis juvenis doctissimus*.[8]

In perhaps 1578 Margounios left Padua to return to Crete where he revealed his true bent by entering holy orders and taking monastic vows. On this occasion, according to Orthodox custom, he changed his first name, from that of Emmanuel (Manuel) to Maximos, the name under which he is generally known. For five years he lived in Candia at the monastery of St. Catherine, teaching and preaching. It is probable that he was named head of the school attached to the monastery where earlier he himself had studied. In 1583 Margounios wrote what appears to be his first original theological work, entitled 'Three Books on the Procession of the Holy Spirit,' dedicated to the Patriarch Jeremiah II. At the end of the same year Maximos went again to Venice. Shortly afterwards Patriarch Jeremiah repeated his invitation to Margounios to reorganize the patriarchal school. This time Margounios accepted. But when, in 1584, he arrived in Constantinople, Margounios found the Patriarch imprisoned by the Turks and ecclesiastical affairs in confusion. Inspired, it seems, with disgust and apprehension at the oppressive Ottoman treatment of the Greek clergy (and perhaps at the venality of the latter as well), he now refused to accept the high position offered him in the patriarchal school. Instead, surprisingly, he requested an appointment to the very modest, then vacant bishopric of the Venetian-held, Aegean island of Cythera. Far removed from the cares of the world, he apparently hoped that on that isolated isle he could devote all his time to study and pastoral duties.

The proposal was accepted and in August of 1584 Margounios returned to Crete, from whence he proceeded to Cythera to take possession of his see.[9] But now the Venetian authorities would not approve his nomination. In vain he addressed several petitions to the Venetian Council of Ten, all of which were refused. The grounds for refusal are not clearly stated but seem more than anything else to have been political in nature. The

---

[8] Letter in I. Lamius, *Deliciae eruditorum seu veterum anekdoton opusculorum colectanea* (Florence, 1739–40), I, 150 and 134.

[9] On all this see Legrand, II, pp. xxxii–xxxvi, and Lamius, *op. cit.*, 154–58. On the Greek venality see Margounios' letter in Lamius, IX, 203. On the difficult question of why Margounios requested the bishopric of Cythera see K. Sathas, *Documents inédits relatifs à l'histoire de la Grèce au Moyen Age*, V, 66–67 and esp. Fedalto, *op. cit.*, 12.

Venetian government was apparently apprehensive that there might be a repetition of what had repeatedly occurred in previous centuries in Crete—the fanning of popular discontent even to the point of revolution by highly educated, patriotic Greek clerics. Such attitudes are expressed at least indirectly in the relevant Venetian documents, one letter citing the 'misuse' of episcopal power by Margounios' clerical predecessor in Cythera. The end result was that Margounios' nomination was rejected. As compensation, however, the Venetian authorities offered him a post as teacher of Greek and Latin to students in Venice (one official Venetian document terms him 'very expert in both Greek and Latin and with few peers in all Greece in erudition') with a subsidy of fifty ducats a year, and the title of Bishop-in-partibus. Under pressure Margounios accepted[10] and he was to spend all his remaining years in Venice.

With unlimited time and sufficient funds at his disposal, Margounios now devoted himself entirely to his philological and theological proclivities. Of particular interest to him was the question of the reunion of the Latin and Greek churches after the abortive attempt at union of the famous Council of Florence in 1439. Well versed (unlike most of the earlier Byzantines) in the writings of *both* the Greek and Latin church fathers, Margounios, through wide reading and reflection, had come to the conclusion that perhaps he could point the way, theologically, to a new agreement on the question of the procession of the Holy Spirit, the chief doctrinal difference separating the two churches. But here he soon came into direct conflict with his old fellow-pupil, the intransigent defender of the Orthodox position Gabriel Severus, now leader of the Greek community in Venice and titular Metropolitan of Philadelphia. From 1583 until 1590 many strongly worded letters were exchanged by the two adversaries over this problem, and the Patriarchs of Constantinople and Alexandria,

[10] See letters in Sathas, *Documents inédits*, V, 70–73 where the Venetian *Proveditore* of the Regno di Candia (Crete) opposes Margounios' appointment. Also Fedalto, 11ff. on the question of this appointment and the Venetian refusal. It is not impossible that the pope as much as the Venetians opposed Margounios' going to Cythera because no bishops were then permitted in Crete, Cythera, or Corfu—only *protopapades* (see Geanakoplos, *Greek Scholars*, Chap. 2). C. Mertzios, *Thomas Flanginis* (Athens, 1939) 257, adduces archival evidence that Margounios' salary in 1587 was 120 ducats a year and in 1589 144 ducats.

Jeremiah and Meletios Pigas, frequently tried to make peace between them.[11]

Severus maintained the traditional Greek view of the question of the *filioque*. Emphasizing the Father as the unique source or principle in the Godhead, Orthodox theology affirms (see above, Chapter 3) that the Holy Spirit cannot also proceed from the Son, since this would imply two first principles (*archai*) in the Godhead. To be sure at the Council of Florence the Greeks had conceded that the Holy Spirit could proceed from the Father *through* the Son, but the emphasis in their view was still on the Father as the unique source. The Latin view, on the other hand, with its emphasis more on the trinity of persons in the Godhead, maintained that what is attributed to the Father ought equally to be attributed to the Son—apart of course from the property of Fatherhood: hence the Spirit must of necessity proceed from the Son as well as the Father.

Margounios' views on this question are scattered throughout the several treaties he wrote on the problem. In effect what he tried to do was straddle both sides of the controversy. While basically seeming to maintain the traditional Greek view—he was undoubtedly always Greek in spirit—he shows himself at the same time sympathetic to the Latin church, especially to the method of the Latins. To bridge the difference he distinguishes, theologically, between two processions—one eternal, the other temporal. He maintains (especially in his letter to the Holy Synod of Constantinople defending his Orthodoxy) that in the beginning the Greeks and Latins had held the same doctrine, but that subsequent theologians had confused the issue, not only because of theological but, he implied, of other factors. According to Margounios when the ancient Fathers said that the Holy Spirit proceeded from the Father they were referring to the eternal procession, that is within the Godhead, and when they spoke of the Spirit's procession from the Son they were referring to the temporal procession, that is from the Son to the world. This basic distinction, affirmed Margounios, had been lost sight of by later theologians

---

[11] See Legrand, II, pp. xli-lv For the Margounios-Severus correspondence see also Lamius, *Deliciae eruditorum*, IX, 186 ff. P. Nicolopoulos, "Maximos Margounios' Homily on Reconciliation' (in Greek), *Epeteris Hetaireias Byzantinon Spoudon* (1951) 283-95, summarizes the conflict. Cf. Ch. Tsiter, *Greek Scholars after the Conquest: Studites, Severus, Kritias* (Athens, 1935) (in Greek).

who did not understand or did not wish to understand, with the result that great confusion had come about. In Margounios' view a general acceptance of this simple but basic distinction would open the way to a *rapprochement* or, more accurately, a *modus vivendi* between the two churches. Each church, however, was to be able to retain its traditional wording of the creed.[12]

In one important sense at least Margounios was right. As he realized, the question of the *filioque* had become encrusted with the prejudices of centuries, psychological and cultural as well as theological. And thus any Orthodox who exhibited, or even suggested, any tolerance of the Latin view was suspect, even though in earlier centuries Maximus the Confessor and Gregory of Cyprus seemed to have suggested a rather similar approach. Now that the Greek homeland was in the hands of the Turks, the Greeks had become so sensitive about their religious and cultural tradition that any deviation from the Orthodox interpretation of the *filioque* was tantamount to a betrayal of their entire heritage. More than ever the *filioque* issue had become not only a symbol of the religious schism but representative of the deep cultural abyss that had now crystallized between East and West.

In order to find theological support for his theories Margounios searched widely in the works of the church fathers, in the Latin (above all in Augustine)[13] as well as the Greek, and also in the long

---

[12] Petit, *Dict. théol. cath.*, IX[2], col. 2041. Legrand, *op. cit.*, p. xli. Also see G. Fedalto's rather brief 'Processione dello Spirito Santo e unione della chiesa greca e latina in Massimo Margounios', *Studia Patavina* (1963) 301–307. But M. Jugie, *De Processione Spiritus Sancti ex fontibus Revelationis et secundum Orientales dissidentes* (Rome, 1936) 66–68, 322, 343–45, affirms that this kind of distinction in the Procession of the Holy Spirit was unknown in the patristic writings. Mss. of Margounios on the Holy Spirit are today in the Synodal library of Moscow (no. 244), in the Metochion of the Holy Sepulcher of Constantinople, and in Bucharest (see Fedalto, 40). Margounios' first work on the Procession of the Holy Spirit was dedicated (in a letter) to Patriarch Jeremiah II on August 16, 1583. His second treatise on the subject was dedicated, in another letter, to the Prince of Vlachia (see Legrand, II, p. xxxiii). Also cf. P. Nicolopoulos, 'Maximos Margounios, Two Unedited Letters,' in *Epeteris Hetaireias Byzantinon Spoudon* (in Greek) (1950) 331 ff. After his troubles with the Venetian government in 1587, Margounios wrote still another, small tract on this question, published by his German friend David Hoeschel in Frankfurt in 1591. Here Margounios summarizes his views on the Holy Spirit's procession (Legrand, p. lxv.)

[13] A ms. of Margounios written in Latin, now at the Patriarchal Library in Jerusalem, analyzes Augustine's views on the Trinity. Also in Legrand, I, 13, a treatise of Margounios is listed, published in 1602 in Venice, and written in Latin, with Greek translation by Margounios in which he shows keen knowledge of the theology of Augustine, Ambrose, and Scotus on the problem of salvation. Cf. also

and wearisome debates over the question at the Council of Florence. It was his interest in this problem that doubtless accounted for much of his zeal in amassing his large Latin library, a catalogue of which is given below. Born and raised in the Orthodox East and doubtless influenced by the close reasoning of western Scholastic theologians at the University of Padua, Margounios, a warm, irenic personality, was the ideal person to attempt to bridge the eastern and western beliefs on the celebrated *filioque* question.

After prolonged altercation and attempts at conciliation, Margounios and Severus were, in 1593, reconciled (actually for the second time). But the final settlement was essentially on Severus' terms and meant defeat for Margounios' notions of a *rapprochement* between Catholicism and Orthodoxy. Nevertheless, despite the failure, Margounios' views have no little historical importance in that they constitute the first and only significant attempt on the part of a Greek theologian to bring about a closer understanding between the two churches after the failure of the famous Council of Florence.

In the years 1590-91 the western church itself took an interest in the controversy between the two Greeks. And despite Margounios' apparent sympathy for the western view of the *filioque* question, Rome found what it considered to be unorthodox anti-Catholic ideas in his writings. (It is possible, according to certain scholars, that Margounios himself visited Rome.) Pope Clement VIII thereupon asked the Venetian government to deliver Margounios to the Inquisition for trial.[14] But the Venetian government refused to hand him over, asserting, according to the report of the Venetian legate at the Vatican Paul Paruta, that the Greeks living under Venetian domination were free to exercise their own religious predilections and that the Venetian Republic would not deprive them of this right for any reason whatever. Nevertheless, Paruta's correspondence also reveals that Margounios' sallies into the question of the Holy Spirit, in particular his arguments with the influential Severus, had aroused

B. Altaner, 'Augustinus und die griechischen Patristik,' *Revue Benedictine*, LXII (1952) 201-13. (Also now G. Fedalto, 'Ancora su Massimo Margounios', *Bolletino dell' istituto di storia . . . veneziano*, V–VI [Venice, 1964] 209-13.)

[14] In the West Margounios (and other Greeks) were generally considered to be Uniates, though their allegiance was almost always to Constantinople.

concern 'among the 400,000 Greek subjects of Venice in the East', and especially among the Greeks under Turkish rule 'who might in some way want to draw closer to the Turks.'[15] This is a very revealing statement which indicates how much the Greeks still distrusted the Latins, to whom it seems many preferred even the Turks.

Whatever happened in Venice—and the sources are not clear —a letter of Margounios indicates that he was at this time impelled to write a long explanation to the Holy Synod itself at Constantinople in defense of his position. The immediate reason for his letter was apparently the publication by the Protestant David Hoeschel in Germany of a treatise of Margounios containing a statement of the latter's views on the *filioque* question. In the letter which he addressed to the Patriarch Jeremiah II, Margounios alludes to his own defense of 'our Orthodox dogma' and cites not only the Greek fathers Dionysius, Athanasius, Basil the Great, Gregory, Cyril, Chrysostom, and John of Damascus but the Latins Cyprian, Hilary, Augustine, Ambrose, and Jerome as well.[16] The eloquence and wording of the epistle produced their effect and the Holy Synod was able to acknowledge Margounios as an Orthodox in good standing while at the same time tacitly rejecting his views on the *filioque*. Though this did not solve the problem, it served effectively to reduce much of the heat which had been generated by the question.

Margounios' voluminous correspondence, especially during his later years in Venice, contains epistles devoted to this issue of the procession of the Holy Spirit as well as to many other theological-intellectual problems. Such letters were addressed to both western and eastern humanists and theologians of the period. A good deal of this correspondence, still in manuscript form, has yet to be read and its study will doubtless throw additional light on certain aspects of the relations between the sixteenth century German Protestant humanists and those of the East.[17]

Some years before Margounios' conflict with Severus, there

[15] P. Paruta, *La legazione di Roma di Paolo Paruta, 1592-95* (Venice, 1887) I, 281. Cf. Fedalto, *op. cit.*, 28.

[16] Legrand, II, pp. xlvii–lix and Fedalto, 24. On Jeremiah see K. Sathas, *Biographical Sketch of Patriarch Jeremiah II* (in Greek) (Athens, 1870) who also publishes some of Margounios' letters.

[17] See Enepekides, *Der Briefwechsel, passim* (cited as 'Correspondence'), and Astruc, 'Correspondance', *passim*.

had been advances made to the Patriarch of Constantinople on the part of leading Lutheran theologians of Tübingen, Germany. And in September of 1574 Jacob Andreä, a Lutheran bishop, and Martin Crusius, the German philhellene and professor of Greek at Tübingen University, had sent, via the Lutheran theologian Stephen Gerlach, Melanchthon's Greek translation of the Augsburg Confession to the Patriarch Jeremiah, requesting an expression of his judgment. The patriarch responded with a long letter in the form of a treatise expounding in turn the Greek theological position. Several epistolatory exchanges ensued. But finally the patriarch, seeing no tangible result in what for him seemed an opportunity to 'correct' the western theological position on the questions of the *filioque* and the sacraments, put an end to the amicable correspondence, obliquely referring to the Lutherans as schismatics or heretics.[18] (The correspondence of this fascinating initial episode in Lutheran-Orthodox relations has recently been published, in German, by the Evangelical Church of Germany). Margounios must have known of this correspondence, but it seems that he played no part in the affair. At any rate, after his settlement in Venice, he began to correspond with Crusius and other German Protestants[19] who may or may not have been involved.

Margounios' most important and frequent correspondence was with the noted German scholar and editor of Augsburg David Hoeschel and extended from 1590 to Margounios' death in 1602. Margounios sent many Byzantine manuscripts to Hoeschel who printed a number of them, for example a work of the eleventh century Byzantine philosopher-historian Michael Psellus. It was

[18] For the episode see Sathas, *Jeremiah II*, 18–46. Fedalto, who mentions it briefly, gives different dates for Gerlach's embassy. But cf. Sathas' note, 24. Also see J. Karmires, *The Dogmatic and Symbolic Monuments of the Orthodox Catholic Church,* (in Greek) (Athens, 1952) 370–72.

[19] The German publication is *Der Briefwechsel über Glauben und Kirche 1573 bis 1581 zwischen den Tübinger Theologen und dem Patriarchen von Konstantinopel* (Luther-Verlag, Witten, 1958) 11 ff. Also cf. the work of the Greek scholar J. Karmires, *Orthodoxy and Protestantism* (in Greek) (Athens, 1937) I, 79 ff. It is worthy of note that Margounios later wrote to Patriarch Jeremiah II that M. Crusius' (now famous) work, *Turcograecia* (Basle, 1584) was secretly anti-Greek (or rather anti-Orthodox). See Fedalto, 21. It was Crusius who introduced Margounios to Hoeschel and, as noted, it was Hoeschel who published Margounios' tract on the Holy Spirit, in Frankfurt in 1591. On Crusius' correspondence with another Greek prelate, Symeon Kabasilas, and with Margounios see N. Tomadakes, 'Maximos Margounios to Symeon Kabasilas' (in Greek), *Epeteris Hetaireias Byzantinon Spoudon* (1949) 292–310 (new ed. in *Metabyzantina Philologika* [Athens, 1965] esp. 60, n. 5).

also the Protestant Hoeschel, who, as pointed out, published in 1591 another treatise of Margounios on the procession of the Holy Spirit. Typical of their correspondence is a letter (dated July 3, 1590) in which Margounios requests Hoeschel to send him the theological works of the Greek father Clement of Alexandria and the Acts of the third Ecumenical Council of Ephesus, which apparently he had not found in Italy. And in another epistle Margounios asks Hoeschel to send him, at his own expense, books (printed) of the Greek Orthodox liturgy. Margounios in exchange sent Hoeschel manuscripts of the works of Symeon Kabasilas, while later seeking a manuscript of the catechism of Cyril, then to be found in the Augsburg library. Other manuscripts exchanged were those of St. Basil, Theodoret, Athanasius, and the historians Appian and Zonaras. In March of 1601, not long before his death, Margounios dispatched to Hoeschel a graceful epigram to be printed in the projected first edition of the famous *Bibliotheca* of the ninth century Greek Patriarch Photius, for which edition Margounios had previously sent manuscript materials copied in his own hand. This *editio princeps* of Photius appeared in Augsburg under Hoeschel's editorship in 1601.[20]

Margounios also carried on a correspondence, though less regular, with many other western humanists. These included the distinguished German philologist Frederic Sylburg (whose relations with Margounios were only of short duration), the Jesuit savant, born in Antwerp, Andreas Schott, the lesser-known Italian Hellenists Philip Siminello and Rinaldo Molinetti, also the Cretan-born Venetian, Aloysio Lollino. Lollino, a boyhood friend to Margounios, later named to the important Italian bishopric of Belluno, carried on an active and lengthy epistolatory exchange with Margounios. The latter, as we know from his extant letters, also collaborated with a professor of the University of Bologna, Ascanio Persio, in the publication of a collection of poems written in Greek, Latin, and Italian. These concerned a miraculous icon of the Virgin preserved on Mount Guardia near

[20] On all this see Enepekides, 'Correspondence,' VI, 35–58 and esp. his 'Margounios an deutsche und italienische humanisten,' 101–31. Also on the Photius see B. Laourdas, 'Maximos Margounios and Photios' (in Greek), *Orthodoxia*, XXVI (1951) 311–18. On Hoeschel see also Jöcher, *Gelehrten Lexicon*, pt. 2, p. 164 f. Still unpublished letters of Margounios to Hoeschel are contained in an Athos ms. 6257 (=Panteleimon 750), which, I am told, the Russian scholar B. Fonkich plans to publish.

Bologna, the painting of which was attributed to St. Luke. Besides this collaboration Margounios also revised a Homeric index made by Persio. Still another scholar-friend of Margounios, the Venetian Dardi Bembo, undertook the formidable task of translating into Italian the works of Plato, and an extant letter of his to Margounios requests that the latter check the original Greek text against the Italian version made by Bembo. That Margounios carried out the request we know from Bembo's foreword to the published work, in which the latter bestows high praise on Margounios' scholarship. One more correspondent of Margounios, the German scholar Conrad Rittershusius, translated and published in Latin some religious anacreontic poems written by Margounios.

Only two months before his death Margounios, in a letter to David Hoeschel, mentions that he was in the midst of preparations to collaborate with the English Hellenist Henry Savile, on a great edition of the works of John Chrysostom.[21] This work, the *editio princeps* of Chrysostom's *Opera omnia*, appeared in 1612 in England but after Margounios' death. Savile's commentary to the work notes the collaboration of the Greeks Gabriel Severus and Andrew Scotus as well as of Margounios, but it gives no indication of the actual extent of Margounios' assistance.[22]

The information that may be gleaned from this wide correspondence of Margounios with the various scholars and theologians mentioned above is important in broader perspective because it sheds a little more light on the complex question of the transmission of Byzantine ecclesiastical texts to western Europe. This is a phase of cultural and religious history not nearly so well-known as the dissemination of the ancient classical writings from the East.

[21] On Sylburg see Enepekides, 'Margounios.' 131–35 and *ibid.*, 141–45 on Persio. Also see Legrand, II, pp. lix–lx and MPG, vol. 55, cols. 563 ff.. Fedalto, *op. cit.*, 30. On Lollino esp. see L. Alpago Novello, 'La vita e le opere di Luigi Lollino, vescovo di Belluno,' *Arch. ven.*, XIV (1933) 15–116 and XV (1934) 199–304. Also note 30 below. And see Legrand II, lix–lx and MPG, vol. 55, cols. 563 ff. Fedalto, *op. cit.*, 30. I am told by M. Theochari that the Byzantine icon of the Virgin on Mount Guardia was painted probably in the twelfth century and covered with silver in the sixteenth.

[22] See in the English ed. (Eton, 1612) Savile's introduction to the Epistles, vol. 7, Codex 51, Bodleian Miscel. containing Savile's plans for the edition (see H. Coxe, *Catalogi codicum manuscriptorum bibliothecae Bodleianae* [Oxford, 1853] I, 650).

Margounios died in Venice at the age of 53, having long suffered from the stone. On June 26, 1602, after his malady had become aggravated by a high fever, Margounios, sensing his end approaching, called to his home, in the Greek colony of Venice,[23] the Venetian notary John-Paul Dario. To Dario he dictated his last wishes. The exact time of Margounios' death may be fixed in the night between June 30 and July 1, as attested by both the register of the Greek church of San Giorgio and the Venetian obituary catalogue of San Martin.[24]

II

In the will which Margounios dictated from his bedside to the Venetian notary John-Paul Dario he took particular care to dispose of his rich library of manuscripts and printed books. The will informs us that he bequeathed to 'Messer Manusso Moschioti', a Greek of Candia, the manuscripts he had copied in his own hand. (From an unpublished Greek ms., no. 238, in the Historial Museum of Moscow, we know that Manusso was a copyist and writer of letters).[25] To the monastery of San Antonio de Savatiana of Candia he left other remaining manuscripts (*'libri vecchi de bergamino'*) except for *'un libro'* (doubtless here meaning a manu-script) containing *Nomocanones* (legal regulations) which he directed to be sent to the monastery of St. Catherine at Mount Sinai.

Other books (perhaps both manuscript and printed), in

[23] In Margounios' testament he wrote: 'Lying in my bed, in the house of my residence, situated in the area of S. Antonin ('jacendo in letto, in casa dell'habit-atione mia posta nella contrà de S. Antonin,' Legrand, *Bibl. hell.*, II, 391). S. Antonin was the section of Venice where the Greek community was located. See above Chap. 4, text for note 17.

[24] The date and place of Margounios' death have been heatedly debated. Papadopoli, *op. cit.*, 265 (who was apparently not averse to falsifying documents) says he died in Crete, even citing verses inscribed as an epitaph on his supposed tombstone. But I could find no trace of this when I searched in Crete in the summer of 1963. Legrand, whose views I follow, bases his data on the records of the Greek church of San Giorgio and of the parish of St. Martin, which read that Maximos died 'nelle case de chà Bragadin' [property of the Bragadin]. See also C. Mertzios, *Thomas Flanginis kai ho Mikros Hellenomnemon* (in Greek,) (Athens, 1939) 258. (Flanginis, the Greek philanthropist, had probably heard Margounios lecture in Venice.) Kyrou, *Hellenes . . . Anagenneseos* (1938) 262 says Greco knew Margounios.

[25] Boris Fonkich writes me from Moscow that ms. 441 indicates that through Moschiotes, Margounios' companion in Venice, three of Margounios' autographs came to Crete.

addition to the 'approximately fifteen' ('*quindese incirca*') in the hands of his friend 'Signor Rafael Sosomeno', presumably a Greek, he ordered to be delivered to the monastery of St. Catherine at Candia 'for the benefit', as he puts it, reflecting his Cretan patriotism, 'of the students of the monastery and universally of all the Greek nation'. He further specified that the books never be removed but remain there permanently for the use of the students. If a student wished to borrow a volume for private study, he had to put up a pledge for its security with the *Oikonomos* (administrator) of the monastery.[26] This monastery, in which he himself had studied as a youth and was later probably to teach for some five years, was the chief educational center on the island. For over a century many Cretan intellectuals had studied or were to study and instruct in that school. We may believe, since we have no evidence to the contrary, that the provisions of Margounios' will were duly carried out and that students of his monastery were able to derive the profit he intended from the perusal of his books. Yet today on Crete there seems to be no trace of the books left there by Margounios. The monastery itself was destroyed or perhaps turned into a mosque after the Turkish conquest of the island in 1669, and on what is believed to be its site only a small Orthodox church now stands. The few monks that today remain belong to the monastery of St. Matthew situated in the same general area and which, like St. Catherine's before it, still maintains close relations with Mt. Sinai.[27]

The question of the disposition of the many valuable Greek codices possessed by Margounios, either autographs or those copied by other hands, is a difficult one. Legrand makes no attempt to calculate the total but on the basis of a consideration of printed catalogues such as those of the Vatican, Mt. Sinai, Mt. Athos, the Patriarchal Library of Jerusalem, Oxford, and of

[26] As some scholars have not realized, there are evidently three wills of Margounios, though the one whose terms are cited here seems to be the one made last (the first will seems yet to be missing). This version, which is printed in Legrand, II, 391–93, was drawn up in Italian. There is a Greek version of this will, ed. by K. Amantos, *Unpublished Sinaitic Monuments* (in Greek), *Hellenika*, Appendix 1 (Athens, 1928) pp. 23–27. Cf. the brief superseded will of Nov. 25, 1584, ed. A. Papadopoulos-Kerameus, *Viz. Vrem.* I (1894) 219 (refers also to first will).

[27] Rumor has it that old mss., perhaps of Margounios, are hidden at St. Matthew's, but I was unable to persuade the old caretaker-monk to show me anything. On St. Catherine's see also M. Paranikas, *Schediasma* (in Greek) (Constantinople, 1867) 153 ff.

libraries in Belgium and elsewhere, it may be estimated that Margounios' library contained some 100 Greek manuscripts, 40 of these copied in his own hand and 25 of which we know are now in the Historical Museum (the former Patriarchal Library) of Moscow. How manuscripts of Margounios ended up in Russian libraries makes an interesting story. Of the manuscripts Margounios bequeathed to the monks of Crete, five to seven, according to Beneševic's catalogue, got to the parent monastery of Mt. Sinai after Margounios' death. With the Turkish conquest of Crete and probably incapacitation of St. Catherine's monastery at Candia some of the manuscripts in the monastery's possession, especially the autographs of Margounios, were evidently transferred to the patriarchate at Constantinople by the Greek Grand Interpreter of the Turks, Panagiotes Nicousios. These codices were deposited in the Constantinopolitan monastery (*metochion*) of the Holy Sepulchre, eighteen of these in turn being in 1692 presented to Moscow. Of the Greek manuscripts of Margounios in the libraries on Mt. Athos, a number were in 1655–56 taken to Russia by a famous visitor to Athos, the Russian monk Arsenii Sukhanov.[28]

[28] For all this see esp. V. N. Beneševic, *Catalogus codium manuscriptorum graecorum ... in monasterio Sanctae Caterinae*, vols. I and III (Petropolis, 1911–17); S. Lampros, *Catalogue of Greek Manuscripts on Mt. Athos*, 2 vols. (Cambridge, Eng., 1895–1900) for ca. 10 mss. of Margounios with a very important one (containing his letters) at Pantaleimon (no. 750; Athos ms. 6257). On Panagiotes see H. Omont, *Les missions archéologiques françaises en Orient aux XVIIe et XVIIIe siècles* (Paris, 1902), 2 vols., pp. 177, 242, 245, etc. On Arsenii Sukhanov see S. Bielokurov, *Arsenii Sukhanov, I Biografiya Arseniya Sukhanova* (Moscow, 1891) = *Chteniya v Imperatorskom Obschestve Istorii i Drevnostei Rossiiskikh pri Moskovskom Universitete* (1891. Bks. 1 and 2.) For a list of Sukhanov's mss. see Iakovos Vatopedinou, *The Moscow Synodical Library of Mss.* (in Greek) (Moscow, 1896) and esp. the much more complete work of Archimandrite Vladimir, *Systematic Catalogue of Mss of the Synodal Library* (in Russian) I, *Greek Mss* (Moscow, 1894). On Margounios' mss see also above, n. 1, 12, 19a, and Ch. Patrinelis, 'Greek Codicographers of the Renaissance,' 95–96. I am indebted to my friend Boris Fonkich of Moscow for his assistance on the question of these manuscripts. While this book was in press Fonkich wrote me, corroborating in general what is written above, that on what is now Moscow ms. 441, Patriarch Dositheos of Jerusalem wrote that Nicousios, after Crete's fall in 1669, brought that ms. and others to Constantinople, and that in 1674 Dositheos received several mss. (evidently Moscow nos. 244, 245, 252, those apparently willed to Moschiotes) from Nicousios' wife, who had given them to the *Metochion* of the Holy Sepulcher in Constantinople. Fonkich believes that ms. 238 was also taken by Nicousios from Crete. See Fonkich's forthcoming article 'Patriarch Dositheos of Jerusalem and his Mss. in Moscow', *Viz. Vrem.*, xxviii. Also for Margounios' autograph mss. in the Bodleian Library see R. Barbour, 'Summary Description of the Greek Mss. from the Library at Holkham Hall', *Bodleian Library Record*, VI, no. 5 (1960) 591–613.

Besides his bequests to Crete mentioned above, Margounios left a legacy of many *printed* books to one of the most famous of all Greek monasteries, that of Iviron on Mt. Athos (see catalogue below, part III). His will informs us that he had previously sent to Athos 'nine cases of books of various kinds' ('*nove casse de libri di diverse sorte*'.)[29] This statement is corroborated by a letter of Margounios himself to his good friend, the German humanist and publisher David Hoeschel, dated May 8, 1602, almost two months before Margounios' death (which occurred less than a week after the drawing up of the will referred to above). In his letter to Hoeschel, Margounios tells of the Englishman Henry of Savile's plan to edit the works of Chrysostom and requests a list of these works:

'About two years ago I sent to the Holy Mountain of Athos the commentary of the Gospel according to Matthew and the commentary on the Gospel according to John and the essays on the birth of that holy man Chrysostom along with some other books of mine. I have kept only the notes on the *Acts of the Apostles* and the commentary of the Psalter, which is according to the Anglican catalogue, except for the twelfth and fiftieth psalms. These are the books of Chrysostom which I have. There are some other books of Chrysostom owned by the very reverend and most wise Bishop Lollino. These I have not seen. Even when he was in Venice, he did not permit me to see his treasures. He who was entrusted with the care of his flocks [Lollino] is in prison, which makes our search difficult.'[30]

One other reference to Margounios' library is provided by his contemporary the German Mark Velser, consul of the republic of Augsburg. Thanks to his relations with David Hoeschel, Velser was presumably in a position to be well informed about Margounios. From Augsburg on July 31, 1602, Velser wrote to the scholar Joseph Scaliger:

[29] Legrand, II, 39.

[30] My translation. Letter printed in vol. 8, pp. 114–15 of Henry Savile's ed. Cf. Legrand, II, p. lxi–lxii. The Bishop Lollino [of Belluno] mentioned was the famous Venetian humanist Aloysio Lollino who had been born in Gortyna, Crete. On Lollino's library see P. Battifol, *Les Mss. grecs de Lollino évêque de Belluno*, in *Mélanges d'arch. et d'hist.*, *école française de Rome*, IX (1889), 28–48. Also see L. Alpago-Novello, *loc. cit.*

'Margounios died in Venice at the end of last month. He left his Greek library to the Cretan monks, for Crete was his homeland and, foreseeing his expected end, a little before his death, he sent there nine chests filled with books.'[31]

Legrand, who cites this passage *in extenso*, seems to overlook a possible contradiction between Velser's statement and the testament of Margounios himself. According to Margounios' will, nine cases of books are specifically mentioned as having been sent to Iviron on Mount Athos. In any event, regardless of the number of cases, Velser's passage, with its reference to *Greek* books, may well imply that it was his *Latin* library that Margounios sent to Iviron. Indeed, the catalogue printed below seems to substantiate this, since all of Margounios' books listed there are in Latin.

Iviron today possesses one of the most important collections of Latin and Greek first editions to be found in the Balkan peninsula. There is a remarkable number of Aldine first editions of various authors, including certain rare Greek editions that can be found elsewhere only with difficulty—perhaps in the Vatican library or in Venice itself. How many Aldine publications were in the possession of Iviron at the time of Margounios' donation, possibly to serve as a stimulus to his own bequest, is hard to say. In any case, from the marginal notations on the printed pages of the various first editions of Athos that I was able to examine in the summer of 1962, it is clear that certain Greek scholar-emigrés in Italy, and Venice in particular, were in the habit of sending books to Athos for the use of the monks. We know that the monks themselves on occasion would order books from abroad, especially Greek first editions, and that at the time of their acceptance into the monastic community of Athos they were permitted to bring with them whatever books they had in their possession. It is therefore likely that Margounios, a sincere pro-unionist at heart, believed that by sending his Latin library consisting primarily of Catholic theological works to the very citadel of Orthodoxy, some inspiration might be provided for the beginnings of a better understanding between the churches. It is also possible, in view of Margounios' voluminous and far-flung

---

[31] 'Bibliothecam graecam monachis Cretensibus Creta enim illi patria, legavit novem cistas libris oppletas eo misit' (Legrand, II, p. lxiv).

correspondence with eastern ecclesiastics and monks as well as western humanists (he wrote, for example, at least one letter to the Athonite monk Theonas of the monastery of Dionysiou),[32] that he had personal friends at Iviron, perhaps even a former fellow-student or pupil from his earlier days in Crete or Venice.

This collection of Margounios, today housed at Iviron, is not in very good condition even though it is kept in a special library building attended by a librarian-monk. The bindings of many of the books are cracked, certain pages are torn or worm-eaten, and some volumes appear to be missing. Margounios' books occupy six or seven open shelves in the center of the library, the folio volumes being kept separate from the quartos. The distinguishing mark of Margounios' possession is his ownership entry *ek ton Maximou*, which is usually inserted in Greek at the bottom of the title page of each volume, presumably in Margounios' own hand. Scattered throughout the collection I found several volumes that could not possibly have been in his possession, dated as they are subsequent to his death and lacking his typical ownership entry (e.g., the *Opera* of Cicero, published in 1783). These have probably been mistakenly shelved there by the monks. Since the collection as a whole is not kept entirely separate from the rest of the library, and since I was required to copy the data from each volume in more haste than I would ideally have wanted, it is very possible that a few errors may have crept into the catalogue printed below.

For the sake of convenience, the catalogue has been broken down into the following classifications:

1. Greek classical authors (transl. into Latin or Italian).
2. Latin classical authors.
3. Greek Fathers of the church (transl. into Latin).
4. Latin Fathers of the church.
5. Twelfth and thirteenth century Latin authors.
6. Lesser known and post-scholastic Latin authors.
7. Secular author.
8. Books whose authorship is unknown to us.

[32] See Astruc, 'Correspondance,' 229.

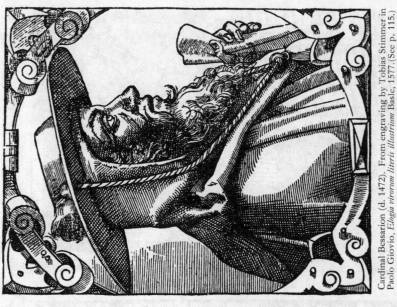

The Cretan Pope Alexander V (d. 1410). Sketch from mosaic in church of St. Paul, Rome, published in *Chronologia Romanorum Pontificum superstes in pariete australi Basilicae Sancti Pauli Apostoli*, Rome, 1751, p. 105. (See p. 153.)

Cardinal Bessarion (d. 1472). From engraving by Tobias Stimmer in Paolo Giovio, *Elogia virorum literis illustrium* Basle, 1577. (See p. 115.)

Plate 15

Metropolitan Gabriel Severus (d. 1616). After oil painting conserved in Greek Colony in Venice. (See p. 168.)

Plate 16

Marcus Musurus (d. 1517). From engraving by Tobias Stimmer in Paolo Giovio, *Elogia virorum literis illustrium*, Basle, 1577. (See pp. 145-46.)

III

LIST OF LATIN BOOKS CONTAINED IN
MARGOUNIOS' LIBRARY AT IVIRON ON MOUNT ATHOS

1. *Greek Classical Authors* (transl. into Latin or Italian).
    Dioscoridis Pedanii *Ex Sudae Collectionibus* (Venice, no date)
    [I cannot find this very curious title listed in the British
    Museum, Paris Bib. Nat., or Graesse catalogues.]
    Euclidis Megarensis philosophi solo introduttore delle
    Scientie Matematiche.
    (Venice, 1565; publ. by Curtius Troianus 316 pp., in 4°,
    Books I–XV transl. into Italian by Nicolo Tartalea,
    with an extensive exposition by him) [lacks Margounios'
    ownership entry.]
    Hermetis Mercurii Trismegisti *Pymandres cum commento
    Fratris Hannibalis Rosseli* (Cracow, 1586; publ. by Lazari)
    [A 6 vol. set in 3 tomes was publ. between 1585–1590.]

2. *Classical Authors* (original Latin works).
    C. Plinii Secundi *Historia Mundi Libri XXXVII*.
    (Lyons, 1561; publ. at press of Io. Frellonius) [Only 1
    volume found here. The British Museum Catalogue
    lists a 4 volume work of the same title and date publ. by
    'haeredibus Jacopi Junti', and ed. by A. Marguaesius].
    Sallustii *Haec omnia continentur* . . . (Venice, 1539; publ. by
    press of Ioannes Tacuinus Tridinus, fol., cum comment.
    Laur. Vallae, Leoniceni, Ascensii, et Chrys. Soldi Brixiani).
    [Not listed in British Museum Catalogue, Paris Bibl.
    Nat., Graesse, or Brunet. Cf. Mittaire, III, 301.]
    Senecae *Opera et ad dicendi facultatem adiecta sunt scholia* (Basle,
    1529; Froben Press, ed. by Erasmus, in fol.)
    Tibullus Catullus et Propertius cum Commento [Date and
    publisher lacking. Graesse, supplement, lists such a work
    publ. in Venice, 1516.]
    Virgilii Maronis *Opera* (Venice, 1555; publisher Scotus [?])
    [The British Mus. Cat. lists two similar works publ. in
    Venice in the same year, one by Paul Manutius, the other,
    in 2 vols., containing the *Bucolica*, *Georgica*, and *Aeneis*,
    with scholia of Nic. Erythraeus.]

3.   *Greek Fathers* (translated into Latin).

Athanasii Episcopi Alexandrini *Contra idola oratio* (Basle, 1564; publ. by Nicolaus and Eusebius) [Title page lacking here, but note that at Basle in 1564 Nicolas Episcopius publ. a 4 volume opera omnia of Athanasius in Latin. This vol. may be part of Episcopius' set.]

Divi Ioannis Chrysostomi *Opera . . . per sacrae theologiae magistros explicata* (Venice, 1583; in 4°, publ. by Fr. Zilettus) [Only one volume publ.]

Divi Ioannis Chrysostomi *Operum, tomus secundus quae ad elucidationem Matthaei Marci Lucae pertinet* (Venice, 1583; publ. by Dominicus Nicolinus, in 4°). [On May 8, 1602, Margounios wrote to David Hoeschel that he had sent 'two years before to the Holy Mountain of Athos' the commentaries of John Chrysostom on Matthew and John, and a few other books of his own, and he had kept Chrysostom's commentary on the Acts of the Apostles and his explanation of the Psalter. This volume may have been the one in question. Margounios' letter is found in vol. 8, pp. 114–15, of the works of Chrysostom, ed. by Henry Savile. Cf. Legrand, *Bibl. hell.*, II, pp. lxi–lxii.]

Divi Ioannis Chrysostomi *Operum tomus quartus omnium epistolarum Beati Pauli Apostoli commentarium complectens* (Venice, 1583; publ. by Dom. Nicolinus).

Divi Ioannis Chrysostomi *Operum tomus quintus* (Venice, 1583; publ. by Dom. Nicolinus). [The above 3 vols. are part of a 5 vol. set, of which vols. 1 and 3 are missing from Margounios' library. Either they were never sent to Athos or are lost.]

Luciani Samosatensis *Opera quae quidem extant omnia e graeco sermone in Latinum, partim iam olim diversis authoribus, partim nunc per Iacobum Micyllum translata* (Lyons, 1549; publ. by Ioannes Frellonius, fol.) [Erasmus, Melancthon and others contributed to this volume.]

Theodoreti Cyrensis episcopi *Opera omnia latine* (Cologne, 1573, publ. by Jo. Birckmann) 2 vols., fol., transl. by Jo Picus and Gentianus Herretus.

Theophylactus archiepiscopus [title page missing, but title is doubtless *Explicationes in Acta Apostolorum concise et*

breviter ex Patribus collectae, transl. by Laur. Sifanus Pruns-
feldius. 'His accesserunt orationes quinque . . . Gregorii
Nysseni, Amphilochii Iconii, Joa. Chrysostomi, Cyrili et
Timothei Hierosolymorum. Item Gregorii Nysseni oratio
de Deitate filii et Spiritus Sancti eodem Sifano interprete;'
two editions were published in 1567 and 1568, both in
Cologne by Am. Birckmann, fol.]

4. *Latin Fathers* (in the original Latin text).

Divi Ambrosii *Milleloquium summam totius doctrinae illius
Ambrosii sub mille titulis . . . complectens*, authore fratre
Bartholomaeo Urbinate episcopo (publ. by M. Bonhomme,
Lyons, 1556, fol.)

Divi Ambrosii Mediolanensis episcopi *Omnia . . . opera
primum per D. Erasmum . . . mox per Sig. Gelenium, deinde per
alios . . . castigata, nunc per Ioannem Costerium . . . emendata*,
5 vols., fol. (Basle, 1555; publ. by H. Froben and N.
Episcopius). [Of the 5 vol. set Margounios' library
contains vols. 4, 5, and another of which the title page
lacks.]

Divi Augustini Hipponensis episcopi *Opera omnia ex emend.
Des. Erasmi*, 10 vols., fol. (Venice, publ. by Junta, 1570).
[Margounios' library today contains vols. 1, 5, 7; Vol. 5
with 22 books of the *De Civitate Dei*, Vol. 1 bound with
index.]

Divi Hilarii Pictavorum episcopi *Quotquot extant opera*
(Paris, 1572; printed by Michael Sonnicus).

Divi Hieronymi Stridonensis *Tertius Tomus Epistolarum, una
cum argumentis et scholiis Des. Erasmi Roterodami* (Basle,
1516; publ. by Io. Froben, fol.) [part of a 9 vol. fol. set of
Jerome's *Opera omnia*; only this volume remains at Athos.]

5. *Twelfth and Thirteenth Century Latin Authors.*

Alexandri de Ales Angli *Summa theologiae* (Venice, 1575;
printed by Franciscus Franciscius) [part of a 4 vol. set.]

Alexandri de Ales Angli *Summa theologiae*, cum quintuplici
indice, Joannis Bolainii Andrii . . . (Venice, 1575–76), 4
vols. in fol. [Margounios' library now has only 2 vols. of
the set, one of 1575, the other of 1576].

Divi Bernardi *Operum divi Bernardi Clarevallensis Abbati,* ed. by A. Marcellinus (Basle, 1552; publ. by Io. Hervagius, fol., vol. 1–2). [Title page lacking for vol. 2.]

Bonaventurae Seraphici Doctoris Ordinis Minorum *Opuscula theologica* (Venice, 1584; publ. by heirs of H. Scottus, in fol.).

Hugonis de Sancto Victore *Opera, tribus tomis digesta, nunc a donno* [sic] *Thoma Garzonio de Bagnacaballo postillis . . . ac vita auctoris expolita* (Venice, 1588; publ. by Io. B. Somaschus, 3 vols. in fol.)

Divi Thomae Aquinatis *Opera Omnia . . . ad exemplar Romanae impressionis restituta,* 17 fol. vols. (Venice, 1593–1594; publ. by D. Nicolinus and associates).

[Margounios' library on Athos contains 13 vols.: 6, 9, 10, 12, 13, and 15. The other extant volumes are not numbered. Vol. 6=*Scripta in primum et secundum.*]

Sententiarum Magistri Petri Lombardi (1593). Title pages missing of Vols. 9, 10, and 12.

Vol. 13=*Complectens expositionem in Iob . . . Davidis, etc.* (1593).

Vol. 15=*Complectens catenam auream in Matthaeum, Marcum, Lucam et Ioannem* (1593).

6. *Lesser Known and Post-Scholastic, Latin Ecclesiastical Authors.*

Alvari Pelagii *De planctu ecclesiae* (Venice, 1560, publ. by F. Sansovinus, fol.) [Alvaro Pelayo, Bishop of Silves in Portugal, was a famous 14th century Franciscan theologian and writer on papal power].

Bernardini de Novaria *Tabula Scoti.*

[Part of *Primus (secundus) Sententiarum doctoris subtilis Scoti tomus* (Venice, 1490; fol.) This is Margounios' oldest book at Athos, evidently his sole fifteenth century incunabulum remaining].

Durandi a sancto Porciano *In Petri Lombardi Sententias theologicas commentariorum libri quatuor* (Venice, 1586; publ. by Gasparus Bindonus, in fol.) [The author of the commentaries was Dominican Bishop of Limoux.]

Decani et eiusdem florentissimae academiae cancelarii *Omnia quae haberi potuerunt opera quorum Iudicem benevole lector vide pagina sequentem* (Cologne, 1582) [Author's name missing; I cannot find it in Bibl. Nat., Br. Museum, Brunet, or Graesse catalogues].

Dionysii Carthusiani *Eruditae ac piae enarrationes* (Cologne, 1572). [No other data available.]

Georgii Bulloci *Oeconomia Concordantiarum scripturae* (Venice, 1585; publ. by Melchior Sessa, 2 vols.) [Margounios' library contains only vol. 2].

Gregorii de Valentia *Commentariorum theologicorum . . . in quibus omnes materiae quae continentur in Summa Theologica D. Thomae Aquinatis ordine explicantur* (Ingolstadt, 1597). [Part of a 4 volume set; the others are missing. Gregory was a Spanish Jesuit who, at Ingolstadt, defended the Counter-Reformation].

Fratris Hieronymi ab Oleastro Lusitani *Commentaria in Moysi Pentateuchum, etc.* (Antwerp, 1569; fol., publ. by J. Stelsius).

Ioannis Arborei *Commentarii . . . cum veteris tum novi testamenti expositionem, etc.* (Paris, 1553; publ. by Ioannes de Roigny) [evidently the last vol. of a 3 vol. work.]

Josephi Zontii Clodii Angeli (Cologne, 1530). [I can find no mention of this author in the standard reference works].

Martini ab Azpilcueta doctoris Navarri *Enchiridion sive Manuale Confessariorum et Paenitentium* (Venice, 1584; publ. by Franciscus Ziletius) ([book included in Margounios' collection at Iviron, but lacking his ownership entry; hence it may not be his.]

Petri de Bergamo *Tabula aurea . . . in omnia opera divi Thomae Aquinatis* (Venice, 1593; publ. by Dom. Nicolinus).

Ruardi Taddei *Abenchusia* [?] *ecclesiae Collegiatae S. Petri* (Louvain, no date). [Not listed in the standard catalogues, nor certain it belonged to Margounios].

Ruperti abbatis monasterii Tuitiensis *De Victoria verbi Dei libri tredecim* (Coloniae Agrippinae, 1577). [Rupert was Abbot of the Benedictine monastery at Deutz and wrote treatises mentioning the αζυμα (unleavened bread), a liturgical difference between Greek and Latin churches.]

Sedulii Scoti Hyberniensis *In omnes Epistolas Pauli Collectaneum* (Basle, 1528; in fol., publ. by H. Petrus).

Theodori Zuingeri *Theatrum Vitae Humanae, omnium fere quae in hominem cadere possunt bonorum et malorum exempla historica, ethicae, philosophiae* (Basle, 1565; publ. by Io. Oporinus) [Included is another vol., with title page missing, probably belonging to this set. The words *De Iusticia in genera* are added to the title. Cf. British Museum Catalogue under Thomas Zwinger, for similar vols. publ. in Basle in 1571.]

Thomae Vavaldensis, Anglici Carmelitae, theologi praestantissimi [Title missing but according to British museum catalogue it is probably this: *Doctrinale antiquitatum fidei Ecclesiae Catholicae cum . . . J. B. Rubei . . . Scholiis* (Venice, 1571; 3 vols., printed by V. Valgrisius). [Only 2 vols. seem to have remained in Margounios' library. Thomas was an opponent of the Lollards].

Vincentii Burgundii *Speculum Maius* (Venice, 1590–91; 4 vols., fol., publ. by D. Nicolinus.)

Margounios' library still possesses no less than 25 volumes of Alphonsus Tostatus (or Tostado), the great fifteenth century Castilian bishop of Avila (called by his contemporaries *stupor mundi*), who appeared at the Council of Basle and who wrote many penetrating commentaries on the Scriptures, especially on the Trinity (hence, probably the interest of Margounios).

Margounios' library seems to contain the complete set of 23 volumes of the third edition of Tostatus, published in Venice in 1596 by D. Nicolinus. (See the British Museum Catalogue listing under Tostatus. Cf. *Dict. Theol. Cath.*, Vol. I, 921, which lists 17 vols. for this ed.) The title for the set reads: Alfonsi Tostati *Opera omnia, quotquot in Scripturae Sacrae Expositionem et alia, adhuc extare inventa sunt* (Venice, 1596; printed by Io. Baptista., 23 vols., fol.) [This set contains Old Testament commentaries on Exodus, Leviticus, Numbers, Deuteronomy, Paralipomena, Joshua, Ruth and Judges, Kings; also Matthew from the New Testament].

7. *Secular Author.*

Pamphilii Saxi Mutinensis. [Title page missing, but according to the British Mus. Cat. title is doubtless:]

Opera del praeclarissimo poeta misser P. Sasso . . . Sonetti CCCCVII. . . . (Venice, 1501; in quarto). [This is apparently the second oldest work in Margounios' collection as it exists today. It is also the sole purely Medieval or Renaissance secular Latin author, exclusive of the ancient classics, possessed by Margounios.]

8. *Books for which we have the title but no author.*

Parainetica videlicet ea que ad vitam recte instituendam pertinent complectens una cum scholiis Des. Erasmi Rotterodami, Tomus primus (Basle, no date, publ. by Froben). (Is analogous to *Catonis Disticha moralia, Latine et Graece, cum scholiis D. Erasmi* (Basle, 1534) (publ. by Froben); but this latter is in *one* volume.]

Bibliotheca homiliarum et sermonum priscorum ecclesiae patrum . . . in qua evangeliorum . . . (Lyons, 1508 or 1588) [date unclear and no publisher listed.]

Castigationum in Nonium Marcellum Finis (Venice, 1527).

De compunctione et Complanctu Christianae perfectionis et animae reformatione ad perfectionem (Venice, 1504) [No publisher listed; this is Margounios' third oldest book.]

Orthodoxographia Theologiae sacrosanctae ac syncerioris fidei doctores auctores partim Graeci partim Latini (Basle, 1555; ed. by J. Heroldt, fol.)

[The above work may contain another work, evidently included in the library] *Evangeliorum Harmonia et Petri Epistolae* (Basle, 1555).

Vita Christi Domini Salvatoris (Venice, 1581; publ. by Curevalos fratres and Franciscus Zilettus) [Not clear if this belongs to Margounios' library, though it seems so.]

Oeconomia Bibliorum sive Partitionum Theologicarum Libri Quinque (Cologne, 1582; publ. by Georgius Ederus).

Expositio in omnes libros Veteris et Novi Testamenti (Rome, 1553) [No author listed.] (publ. by Valerius and Aloisius Porici fratres Brixienses).

Three volumes so mutilated that it was difficult accurately to make out any distinguishing data. The first is a book in Latin, possibly commentaries on the Bible. The second, evidently a religious work, contains only part of a title: *In Vigilia S. Andreae.*

Above the first extant page are the words: *S. Bernardi*, *Augustini*. The third work contains on its mutilated opening pages the word *Ambrosianum*; the work was possibly published by M. Bonhomme. Of the last group of 12 volumes, under section 8, numbers 2, 5, and 6 definitely constituted part of Margounios' library. The remainder probably did so but it is not certain.

IV

If the books in this catalogue are a reasonably accurate reflection of Margounios' literary and theological interests, it would appear that he was profoundly interested in scriptural exegesis. Of the total number of c. 114 books to be found in this Latin library as it is preserved today, no less than 33 are separately bound volumes of Biblical exegesis (note even the works of such relatively obscure writers as Georgius Bullocus, Ioannes Arboreus, etc.). Moreover, in the multi-volume *opera omnia* of many authors, there are also included Biblical commentaries (e.g., in the works of John Chrysostom, Aquinas, Ambrose). Of particular interest in this respect is the enormous number of Biblical commentaries in Margounios' possession written by the amazingly prolific Castilian theologian Alphonsus Tostatus of Avila (c. 1400–1455) whose very learned but turgid works are seldom read today. Margounios evidently possessed the complete set of his works published in Venice in 1596. At the Council of Basle (convened in 1431, it preceded by seven years the unionist Council of Florence) Tostatus may have come into contact with the few Greeks who appeared as representatives of the Byzantine emperor. In Tostatus' Biblical commentaries there are incorporated long discussions on the Trinity which specifically express the traditional western view on the question of the procession of the Holy Spirit, and as suggested above, this may be a primary reason that Margounios sent these Latin works to the monks of Athos.

Regarding the Latin fathers we may note that a total of nine volumes is listed in Margounios' collection. Four are the works of Ambrose, three of Augustine, and one of Hilary; also included is a volume of Jerome's *Letters*. There are also 13 of the 17 volumes constituting the *opera omnia* of Thomas Aquinas, published by D. Nicolinus in 1593–94 in Venice. Besides these, works of other scholastics are represented—Bonaventura with one volume, Alexander of Hales with four volumes, and Hugo of St. Victor with three. It is reasonable to assume that these Scholastic works reflect an interest of Margounios in medieval Latin philosophy and theology acquired during his student days at Padua University. (We might note that Margounios also possessed two volumes of the mystical writings of Bernard of Clairvaux.) And all this despite the fact that at Padua medieval Scholasticism had by this time been in considerable part displaced by the study of the original Greek texts of Aristotle, an important development largely brought about by the activities and emphases of the post-Byzantine exiles in Venice.[34]

It is of some interest with respect to Margounios' theological orientation that in this collection of some 114 books only eight bear classical Greek or Latin authorship. In this period the western world was still in the throes of a veritable mania for collecting classical authors. What then was the attitude of Margounios toward the classics? His library contains certain classical Greek authors translated into Latin or Italian—Dioscorides, Hermes Trismegistus, and Euclid. None of the three may be termed literary, all belonging rather to the scientific or pseudo-scientific sphere. In the classical Latin field he had in his possession a work of Sallust and the *Historia Naturalis* of Pliny, in addition to writings of the philosopher Seneca and the poets Virgil and Catullus. Nevertheless, despite the apparent paucity of classical works in his library, if one is to judge from his own writings, Margounios' command of Greek and Latin was impeccable and reflects an interest in style which could have resulted only from a wide reading of the classical authors. We know that Margounios himself translated into Latin at least one work of Aristotle (*Liber de coloribus, multis in locis emendatus* [Pavia, 1575]) and also the commentary on Aristotle by the Byzantine Michael Psellus (*Metaphrasis Libri Secundi Posteriorum Analyticorum Aristotelis* [Venice, 1574]).[35] But Margounios translated these in 1574–75, that is a few years before becoming a monk (1578). Subsequently, he seems to have devoted less time to working on classical

[34] See Geanakoplos, *Greek Scholars*, 228–29.
[35] Legrand, II, 206 and 198.

authors, a reflection evidently of his increasing absorption in religious matters.

We may observe, finally, that Margounios had a considerable interest in poetry. Besides the usual dedicatory verses he attached to publications addressed to important European personages, he published two volumes of his own poetry: the *Hymni Anacreontici* with a Latin translation by Conrad Rittershusius printed in Augsburg in 1601, and a collection of Greek religious poems published by his good friend David Hoeschel in 1592 also in Augsburg.[36] The latter included an apostrophe addressed to his monastery of St. Catherine in Crete, a dogmatic poem directed to the later famous Cretan Patriarch Cyril Loukaris, and a third poem written for the philosopher, doctor, and poet John Battista Ponan of Verona. From these various poems it is clear that while Margounios was skillful enough in writing Greek verse— more than any other author he seems to have imitated the fourth century father Gregory Nazianzenus—Margounios cannot be termed a truly creative poet.

It might be noted that none of the works of Margounios himself or of his friends such as Hoeschel are to be found among his books in the Iviron library—a fact which certainly suggests that his library was larger than what is today preserved on Athos.

To conclude, we see in Margounios an attractive and very erudite figure interested in classical scholarship and above all in theology. As such he is a worthy successor to the great Byzantine theologian-humanists such as Nicephorus Blemmydes, Demetrios Cydones, and Bessarion. In the Greek East this correlation of interest in both humanism and theology, in fact the subordination of classical learning to over-all religious ends, had been typical of the mainstream of Byzantine thought throughout the whole course of its history, and not least during the last two centuries of the Palaeologan period. In this respect Margounios may be compared to certain Northern humanists of his own sixteenth century, especially Erasmus. Indeed, for Erasmus classical learning, however important, was primarily an instrument to be used for a better understanding of the Bible and ecclesiastical writers. The parallel can be carried further: Erasmus, despite the

---

[36] Legrand, *Bibl. hell. du XVIIe siècle* (1894), I, 4, and *Bibl. hell. des XVe et XVIe siècles*, II, 81–83.

pressures exerted upon him, could not be induced to join the rising Lutheran movement, in large part because of his unwillingness to relinquish his ideal of Christian unity. Imbued with something of the same spirit for religious unity and in the face of strong pressures from the Orthodox Severus on the one hand and the Catholic Inquisition on the other, Margounios, though at the end his efforts bore no fruit, never ceased striving for an accord between the two branches of the church.

Any serious student of the doctrinal or other questions involved in the problem of Greco-Latin religious union in the present day would do well to ponder not only the acts of the famous Council of Florence, but also the career and writings of the neglected Cretan theologian-humanist Maximos Margounios. For as he knew well (but is too little realized today), when Byzantium fell at last to the Turks in 1453, Eastern and Western Christendom were cut off from each other almost as effectively by mutual distrust as by the Turkish conquest itself. And so in his time when the bitterness over Florence had not yet subsided and the two churches had drawn completely apart, Margounios aspired to a religious entente on the basis of a scholarly knowledge of the ecclesiastical literature of both East and West and, above all, on a tolerant approach to their differences.

It is only this dual kind of approach—an understanding of all the factors, political, theological, cultural and psychological, making for the separation of East and West in the Middle Ages and a toleration based on such an understanding—that will ultimately succeed, if anything can, in bridging the religious chasm that after a thousand years still separates the Greek and Roman ecclesiiastcal worlds of Christendom.

APPENDIX

BIBLIOGRAPHICAL NOTE

The following bibliographical notes (which are not of course intended to be exhaustive) may be useful to those who wish to pursue further study in the principal topics of these essays.

A. Byzantine Cultural Influences on the West

For a subject as important as the Byzantine cultural influence on the West there is not much written as synthesis. Some relevant material may be found in sections of D. Hesseling, *Essai sur la civilization byzantine* (Paris, 1907); S. Runciman, *Byzantine Civilization* (London, 1933) pp. 236–42; Ch. Diehl, 'Byzantine Civilization', in *Cambridge Medieval History*, IV (New York, 1927) 745ff.; Diehl, *Byzantium, Greatness and Decline* (New Brunswick, 1956) 211–27; N. Turchi, *La civiltà bizantina* (Turin, 1915); D. T. Rice, *The Art of Byzantium* (London, 1962); and his earlier *Byzantine Art* (Oxford, new ed., 1954) 222–38; J. Beckwith, *The Art of Constantinople* (London, 1961); A. Grabar, *Byzantine Painting* (Geneva, 1953); J. Ebersolt, *Orient et Occident, Recherches sur les influences byzantines et orientales en France pendant les croisades* (Paris, 1954); P. Courcelle, *Les lettres grecques en Occident* (Paris, 1943); A. Siegmund, *Die Ueberlieferung der griechischen christlichen Literatur in der lateinische Kirche* (Munich-Pasing, 1949); P. Lamma, *Comneni e Staufer, Ricerche sui rapporti fra Bisanzio e l'Occidente nel secolo XII*, 2 vols. (Rome, 1957); F. Brightman, *Liturgies Eastern and Western*, I (Oxford, 1896); F. Dölger, 'Byzanz und das Abendland vor den Kreuzzugen', *Relazioni del X Congresso Internazionale di Scienze Storiche*, III (Florence, 1955) 67–112; W. Miller, *The Latins in the Levant* (London, 1908) and his *Essays on the Latin Orient* (Cambridge, 1921); W. Ohnsorge, *Abendland und Byzanz* (Darmstadt, 1958); R. Weiss, 'The Greek Culture of south Italy in the Later Middle Ages', *Proc. British Academy* (London, 1953); J. Gay, *L'Italie meridionale et l'empire byzantin* (Paris, 1904); Hans-Wilhelm Haussig, *Kulturgeschichte von Byzanz* (Stuttgart, 1959) (a work lacking footnotes); E. Legrand, *Bibliographie hellénique . . . au XVe et XVIe*

siècles, 4 Vols. (Paris, 1885–1906); R. Bolgar, *The Classical Heritage and its Beneficiaries* (Cambridge, Eng., 1954); and K. Setton, 'The Byzantine Background to the Italian Renaissance', *Proceedings of the American Philosophical Society*, C (1956) 1–76. More recently D. Geanakoplos, *Greek Scholars in Venice: Studies in the Dissemination of Greek Learning from Byzantium to Western Europe* (Cambridge, Mass. 1962); M. Anastos, 'Some Aspects of Byzantine Influence on Western Thought', *Twelfth Century Europe* (Madison, 1961) 131–87; and the collected essays of P. Lamma, *Oriente e Occidente nell' alto Medioevo* (Padua, 1965). We mention last an important work in Russian, Th. Uspensky, *Essays on the History of Byzantine Civilization* (St. Petersburg, 1896). For works on specific aspects of culture see above, notes to Chap. 1. On the Renaissance see below, Appendix D.

B. 'CAESAROPAPISM' IN BYZANTIUM

The literature on the relationship of Byzantine emperor and church, especially on the specific question of the term Caesaropapism, as is well-known, is not very satisfactory. A few authorities who support the thesis of a more limited imperial control over the church are: G. Ostrogorsky, 'Relations between Church and State in Byzantium', (in Russian), *Annales de l'institut Kondakov*, IV (1931) 121ff.; F. Dvornik, 'Emperors, Popes, and General Councils, *Dumbarton Oaks Papers*, no. 6 (1951) 1–23; N. Baynes, 'The Byzantine State', *Byzantine Studies and Other Essays* (London, 1955) esp. 51ff.; E. Barker, *Social and Political Thought in Byzantium* (Oxford, 1957) 92; W. Ensslin, 'The Emperor and the Imperial Administration', *Byzantium: An Introduction to East Roman Civilization* (Oxford, 1948) ed. Baynes and Moss., esp. 275ff.; J. Hussey, *The Byzantine World* (London, 1957) 21 etc.; Ph. Sherrard, *The Greek East and the Latin West: A Study in the Christian Tradition* (London, 1959) 26, 91; D. Obolensky, 'Russia's Byz. Heritage', *Oxford Slav. Prs.*, I (1950) 37 ff.; Runciman, 'Byzantium, Russia and Caesaropapism', *Canadian Slav. Prs.*, II (1957) 1 ff. Examples of scholars supporting the view of absolute imperial control over the church are: M. Jugie, *Le Schisme byzantin* (Paris, 1941) 10 ('Caesaropapism incontestably should bear the chief responsibility for the preparation of the schism.'); Ch. Diehl, *Byzantium: Greatness and Decline* (New Brunswick, 1957)

29 ('The emperor was as absolute and infallible in the spiritual as in the temporal sphere.'); A. Diomedes, 'Source and Extent of Imperial Power in Byzantium' (in Greek), *Byzantina-Metabyzantina*, I (1949) 39–69. ('He ruled the church as he ruled the state . . . consecrating bishops.'); M. Anastos, 'Political Theory in the Lives of the Slavonic Saints Constantine and Methodius', *Harvard Slavic Studies*, II (Cambridge, 1954) 13 ('The emperor was supreme on earth . . . and prevailed even in the formulation of dogma'); Anastos, 'Church and State during the First Iconoclast Controversy', *Richerche di storia religiosa*, I (Rome, 1957), *Studi in onore di G. La Piana* (1957) 279ff. Cf. also F. Dölger, *Byz. Zeit.*, 43 (1950) 146f., 38 (1938) 240; 36 (1936) 145–57. A. Vasiliev, *History of the Byzantine Empire* (Madison, 1952) 258 writes: 'Leo III's view was the accepted Caesaropapistic view of the Byzantine Emperors.' And now G. Pilati, *Chiesa e stato nei primi quindici secoli* (Rome, 1961) uses the term Caesaropapism, 60, etc. Also see A. Alivizatos, 'Caesaropapismus in den byzantinischen kirchlichen Gesetzen und den Canones', *Acts of XI International Byzantine Congress* 1958 (Munich, 1960), 15–20.

C. The Problem of Greco-Latin Ecclesiastical Union

Some works on the problem of union and unionist negotiations in the period from 1054 to 1453 are: for a convenient summary in English L. Bréhier, 'Attempts at Reunion of the Greek and Latin Churches', *Cambridge Medieval History*, IV (1927) Ch. 19; in French, the excellent articles of M. Viller, 'La Question de l'Union des Églises entre Grecs et Latins depuis le concile de Lyon jusqu'à celui de Florence (1274–1438),' *Revue d'Histoire Ecclésiastique*, XVI (1921) 260–305, 515–532; and XVIII (1922) 20–60. Recent works are S. Runciman, *The Eastern Schism* (Oxford, 1955); J. Gill, *The Council of Florence* (Cambridge, Eng., 1959); and Y. Congar, *After Nine Hundred Years* (New York, 1959). Other important or representative works dealing with this period in general are W. Norden, *Das Papsttum und Byzanz* (Berlin, 1903); M. Jugie, *Le Schisme Byzantin* (Paris, 1941) esp. 187–270; G. Every, *The Byzantine Patriarchate*, new ed. (London, 1947) 153–203; G. Ostrogorsky, *History of the Byzantine State*, tr. J. Hussey, (New Brunswick, 1957) *passim;* A. Vasiliev, *History of the Byzantine Empire* (Madison, 1952) 469–478, 540–546, 656–676;

T. Beck, *Kirche und theologische Literatur im byzantinischen Reich* (Munich, 1959); C. Diehl, R. Guilland, etc., *L'Europe Oriental de 1081 à 1453* (Paris, 1945) passim; S. Runciman, *Byzantine Civilization* (London, 1936) 108–136; B. Stephanides, *Ecclesiastical History* (in Greek) (Athens, 1948) 315–364; J. Karmires, 'The Schism of the Roman Church', (Eng. tr.) *Theologia*, XXI (1950) 37–67; A. Demetrakopoulos, *Historia schismatis quod intercedit inter ecclesiam occidentalem et orientalem* (in Greek) (Leipzig, 1867); A. Pichler, *Geschichte der kirchlichen Trennung zwischen dem Orient und Occident* (Munich, 1864–1865); A. Fortescue, *The Orthodox Eastern Church* (London, 1916) 201–220; the essay of H. Grégoire on the Byzantine church in *Byzantium, An Introduction to East Roman Civilization*, ed. Baynes and Moss (Oxford, 1948) esp. 119–127; F. Heiler, *Urkirche und Ostkirche* (Munich, 1937) 135–148; Hefele-Leclercq, *Histoire des Conciles*, esp. VI pt. 1, 153–218 and VII pt. 2, 916–1951; A. Fliche and V. Martin, *Histoire de l'Eglise*, X, 76–85, 446–460, 487–497; and, S. Neill, 'Division and the Search for Unity Prior to the Reformation', *A History of the Ecumenical Movement* (Philadelphia, 1954), 14–19. For other works see above, Ch. 3.

In addition to the general works cited, the following deal with specific unions or aspects thereof. Regarding 1204 and after see J. Longnon, *L'Empire Latin de Constantinople* (Paris, 1945) 135–144; and R. L. Wolff, 'The Organization of the Latin Patriarchate of Constantinople, 1204–1261. Social and Administrative Consequences of the Latin Conquest', *Traditio* (1948) 33ff. On Lyons see the articles of F. Vernet and V. Grumel in *Dictionnaire de Théologie Catholique*, IX pt. 1, cols. 1374–1409; C. Chapman, *Michel Paléologue Restaurateur de l'Empire Byzantin* (Paris, 1926) 99–124; H. Evert-Kapessova, 'La Société Byzantine et l'union de Lyon', *Byzantinoslavica*, X (1949) 28ff., and by the same author, 'Une page de l'histoire des relations Byzantino-Latines. Le clergé byzantin et l'Union de Lyon (1274–1282),' *Byzantinoslavica*, XIII (1952–1953) 68–92; and also my articles, 'Michael VIII Palaeologus and the Union of Lyons'; and 'On the Schism of the Greek and Roman Churches: A Confidential Papal Directive for the Implementation of Union (1276)', *Greek Orthodox Theological Review* (1954) 16–24. Also my *Emperor Michael Palaeologus and the West*, *passim*. For works concerning the union of Florence see notes above, Ch. 3, *passim*. The religious ceremony of 1369 in Rome is not to be considered an ecclesiastical union as the Emperor John V Palaeologus there alone made his submission to the pope. See O. Halecki, *Un Empereur de Byzance à Rome* (Warsaw, 1930) 204; and A. Vasiliev, 'Il Viaggio dell' Imperatore Bizantino Giovanni V Palaeologo in Italia (1369–1371) e l'Unione di Roma del 1369', *Studi bizantini e neoellenici*, III (1931) 151–193. Nor can the Council of Bari in 1098 be termed a union of the two churches, since only the Latin church and the Greek clergy of southern Italy were involved. See B. Leib, *Rome, Kiev et Byzanz à la fin du XIe siècle* (Paris, 1924) 287–297. On the issue of papal primacy and its relation to all the schisms see the recent work of F. Dvornik, *Byzance et la primauté romaine* (Paris, 1964), and earlier J. Meyendorff, 'St. Peter in Byzantine Theology', *St. Vladimir Seminary Quarterly*, IV (New York, 1960) 26–48. Finally, B. Roberg, *Die Union. . . auf den II Konzil von Lyon* (Bonn, 1964); W. de Vries, *Rom und die Patriarchate des Ostens* (Munich, 1963); T. Ware, *The Orthodox Church* (Baltimore, 1963) 51–81; and D. Geanakoplos, 'Edward Gibbon and Byzantine Ecclesiastical History', *Church History* (June, 1966).

D.   BYZANTIUM AND THE RENAISSANCE

On the movement of the dissemination of Greek learning from Byzantium to the West in the period of the Renaissance surprisingly few works of synthesis have been written. The most recent is D. Geanakoplos, *Greek Scholars in Venice: Studies in the Dissemination of Greek Learning from Byzantium to Western Europe* (Cambridge, Mass., 1962). See also K. Setton, 'The Byzantine Background to the Italian Renaissance', *Proceedings of the American Philosophical Society*, C, no. 1 (1956) 1–76; and R. Bolgar, *The Classical Heritage and its Beneficiaries* (Cambridge, Eng., 1958). Also F. Babinger, *Johannes Darius* (1414–94) (Munich, 1961). For biographies of many Byzantines or post-Byzantines, still fundamental is E. Legrand, *Bibliographie hellénique ou description raisonnée des ouvrages publiés en grec par des grecs au XVᵉ et XVIᵉ siècles*, 4 vols. (Paris, 1885–1906), which includes sketches of the more important Greeks and an analytical catalogue of Greek publications during the period. Also the sketches in H. Pernot, 'Les Crétois hors de Crète', *Etudes de littérature grecque* (Paris, 1916)

129–94. Biographies of individual Byzantines have been written by G. Cammelli, *Manuele Crisolora* (Florence, 1941), *Giovanni Argiropulo* (Florence, 1941), *Demetrio Calcondila* (Florence, 1954), and his 'Andronico Callistos', *Rinascita*, XXIII–XXIV (1942) 3–64. Also by L. Mohler, *Kardinal Bessarion als Theologe, Humanist und Staatsmann*, 3 vols. (Paderborn, 1923–42), H. Vast, *Le Cardinal Bessarion* (Paris, 1878), F. Masai, *Pléthon et le Platonisme de Mistra* (Paris, 1956), B. Knös, *Un ambassadeur de l'hellénisme: Janus Lascaris et la tradition greco-byzantine dans l'humanisme français* (Upsala-Paris, 1945), A. de Rosalia, 'La vita di Costantino Lascaris', *Archivio storico siciliano*, III (1957–58) no. 9, 21–70 and E. Denisoff, *Maxime le Grec et l'Occident* (Paris-Louvain, 1943). On this general subject see also R. Sabbadini, *Le Scoperte dei codici latini e greci nei secoli XIV e XV*, 2 vols. (Florence, 1905–14) and A. Firmin-Didot, *Alde Manuce et l'hellénisme à Venise* (Paris, 1875) now fairly outdated. On transmission of Byzantine Mss. to the West see esp. the works of A. Turyn on Ms. traditions of Aeschylus, Sophocles, Euripides, Pindar, etc. Also A. Pertusi, *Leonzio Pilato fra Petrarca e Boccaccio* (Venice-Rome, 1964); P. Kristeller, 'Umanesimo italiano e Bisanzio', *Lettere italiane*, XVI (1964), 1–14. For more bibl. see above Chapter 4 and 5, notes.

E. Maximos Margounios

This is the first study in English on Margounios. But no definitive biography can be written on him until his extremely voluminous works, including the greater part still in manuscript, are published. A useful account, though now old and rather faulty, is E. Legrand, *Bibliographie hellénique des XVe et XVIe siècles*, II (Paris, 1885 ff). pp. xxiii ff., which does not examine Margounios' thought or influence. Cf. the brief account in L. Petit, *Dictionnaire de théologie catholique*, IX² (Paris, 1926) cols. 2039–44, which is based on previous studies as is also, evidently, Ph. Meyer, *Die theologische Litteratur der griechischen Kirche* (Leipzig, 1899) 69–78. See now also G. Fedalto, 'Excursus storico sulla vita e sulla attività di Massimo Margounios', *Studia Patavina*, VIII (1961) 213–44, also (1963) 301–307, and his 'Massimo Margounios e la sua opera per conciliare la sentenza degli orientali e dei Latini sulla Processione dello Spirito Santo', *Pontificia Universitas Gregoriana* (Padua, 1961) which reprints

some of the other work. (Fedalto had access to the Archivio
Secreto in the Vatican.) Modern Greek studies are that of K.
Dyobouniotes, in various fascicules of *Gregorios Palamas* (in Greek)
(1920–21); B. Mystakides, 'The Holy Clergy in the Sixteenth
Century (Maximos Margounios)' (Athens, 1892); and the work (or
rather series of short articles) apparently not known to the western
authors, of Ag. Xerouchakis, 'Maximos Margounios Bishop of
Cythera' (in Greek), *Anagennesis*, 2163ff. The most complete list of
Margounios' writings is printed in A. Demetrakopoulos, *Additions
and Corrections to the Neohellenic Philology of K. Sathas* (in Greek),
(Leipzig, 1871) (also see Legrand, *Bibl. hell.*, II, pp. lxv–
lxxvii). On Margounios' extremely voluminous correspondence see esp. P. Enepekides, 'Der Briefwechsel des Maximos
Margunios, Bischof von Kythera', *Jahrbuch der oesterreichischen
byzantinischen Gesellschaft* (Vienna, 1951) 13ff., also Enepekides,
'Maximos Margunios an deutsche und italienische humanisten',
Jahrbuch der oesterreichischen byz. Gesellschaft, X (1961) 93–145
(which prints 42 of Margounios' letters, most previously unpublished. Legrand had printed some 10 of his letters). And, finally,
Ch. Astruc, 'Maxime Margounios et les recueils Parisiens de sa
correspondance', *Kretika Chronika* (1949) 211–61. For additional
or new comments on Margounios' Mss. which are scattered
throughout Europe (information gleaned during my researches in
Moscow, Mt. Athos, etc.) see notes above to Ch. 6, esp. 28, and
references to Fedalto and Fonkich, who plan to publish Mss. of
Margounios as does N. Foropoulos. Some of Margounios' Mss.
may have gone to G. Severus, whose Mss. are now in the Turin
National Library. Prof. G. Schirò, I understand, will publish, in
the Acts of the Second Cretological Congress, an article on
Margounios and the *filioque* question in the time of Barlaam
(whose works Margounios copied and studied: Moscow Ms. 441)
and of Barlaam's contemporaries.

INDEX

Items mentioned once in the book are usually omitted here.

Aachen, 19, 32 n., 47

d'Adam, Guillaume, 103 n.

Administration, 33–34

Adramyttenos, Emmanuel, 143

Aeschylus, 28

Albanians, 118, 122

Alcalá, 126, 148, 163

Aldus Manutius, Aldine Press, 23, 113, 126–30, 135–36, 143–44, 181

Alexander V, Pope, 139, 153, 163

Alexander (Cretan), 27, 143 n., 144, 161

Alexander of Tralles, 30

Almagest, 15

Amalfi, 16, 32, 35

Anastasius, 27

Andrea of Rhodes, 100

Anointment, 71–73

Antagonism, Greco-Latin, growth of, 1–6, 17, 18, 49, 52, 87, 88, 94 n., 105, 173, 193 and *passim*

Anthemius of Tralles, 26

Apostolis, Arsenios, 121, 129, 142, 146

Apostolis, Michael, 142, 143, 146

Aquinas, Thomas, 22, 190

Arabs, 13, 15, 20, 21, 23, 29–31, 37, 40, 43 n., 44, 53

Arboreus, Ioannes, 190

Archimedes, 26

Arethas, 23

Arianism, 102, 162

Aristippus, 15

Aristophanes, 28

Aristotle, Aristotelianism, 17, 20, 21, 23, 25, 53, 146, 154, 191

Art, 8, 32, 46–51, 132–35, 150–52, 175–76

Athanasius, 42

Athos, Mt., 8, 10, 50, 139, 166, 178–193

Attitudes, Greco-Latin. *See* Antagonism

Augsburg, 174, 180, 192

Augustine, 24, 171 n., 173, 190

Avignon, 91–93

Azyma, 106 n., 187. *See* Rite

Balsamon, Theodore, 58, 59, 67 n., 71, 72 n., 78, 99 n.

Barcelona, 35, 148, 152

Barlaam, 3, 68, 90, 91, 92, 97 n., 110, 200

Basilian monks, 44–45

Basle, 92, 93, 146, 190

Bekkos, John, 85

Bembo, Dardi, 176

Bembo, Pietro, Cardinal, 123, 162

Bessarion, 10, 100, 106 n., 108, 112, 115, 116, 126, 129, 137, 192

Blastares, Matthew, 58, 59

Boccaccio, 28, 141

Boethius, 24

Bologna, 145, 175

Brocardus, 2 n., 103 n.

Bronze doors, 16, 32 and n.

Bryennios, Joseph, 106, 141, 150 n.

Budé, Guillaume, 129, 154

Bullocus, Georgius, 190

Burgundio of Pisa, 16

Burgundy, 42, 46

Caesaropapism, 6, 7, Ch. 2 *passim*, 94

Calabria, 13, 15

Calliergis, Zacharias, 126, 127, 128, 130, 144, 161

Callistos, Andronikos, 157

Calvinism, 139, 159

Candia, 134, 143, 153, 166, 168, 178

Casaubon, Isaac, 159

Casimatis, John, 159

Catalans, 35

Catherine's of Candia, St., 132,

141, 165, 168, 178, 179, 192
Cavallini, 47
Cerularius, Michael, Patriarch, 1, 5, 57, 66, 78, 84
Chalcidius, 16
Chalcondyles, Demetrios, 130, 145, 166
Charlemagne, 1, 12 n., 19, 30 n., 32, 42, 43
Charles the Bald, 24
Chivalry, 51
Chomatianos, Demetrios, 58
Chora (church), 48
Chrysoberges, Maximos, 141
Chrysoloras, Manuel, 28, 112, 124, 136, 146
Cimabue, 49
Comnenus, Alexius I, 5 n.
Comnenus, Manuel I, 5, 26
Complutensian Polyglot, 126, 148
Cluny, 45, 48
Conon, John, 146
Constantine VII Porphyrogenitus, 36, 66 n.
Copernicus, 25, 26
Cosimo de 'Medici, 25
Cres, John, 154, 155
Crete, 8, 9, 10, 18, 50–51, Ch. 5 passim, 114
'Cretan' style, 49–50, 132, 133, 134
Crusade, 1, 5, 17, 39, 84, 110, 115, Fourth Crusade, 1, 2, 4, 17, 18, 22, 31, 45, 85, 103, 114, 116
Crusius, Martin, 132, 168, 174
Cydones, Demetrios, 5 n., 10, 192
Cyprus, 114

Damaskinos, Michael, 134, 151
Damiani, Peter, 39, 45
Damilas, Demetrius, 144, 161
Dante, 24, 27
Dario, John-Paul, 177
Darmarios, Andreas, 122, 130
Denis, St., monastery, 24 n., 47
Dentistry, 30
Desiderius, Abbot, 48
Digenes Akritas, 27

Dionysius the Areopagite, 24
Dioscorides, 29
Diplomacy, 36–37
Donation of Constantine, 98–99
Dorotheos of Mytilene, 88
Drama, Greek, 23, 53 and n.
Dubois, Pierre, 2 n.
Ducas, Demetrios, 126, 128, 148, 149, 161
Duccio, 49

Echoi, 43
Eckhart, Meister, 24
Eleanor of Aquitaine, 38–39
El Greco, 8, 9, 10, 38–39, 49, 134, 151–52, 163
England, 20, 42, 52, 157, 158 n.
Epanagoge, 56, 63
Eparchos, Anthony, 130, 155
Episkopopoulos, Jacobus, 150, 158
Erasmus, 128, 129, 146, 147, 161, 192
Erigena, John Scotus, 23, 24
Escorial, 150, 151
Euchelaion, 73
Eucharist, 99
Eugene the Emir, 15
Eugenius IV, Pope, 92, 93, 95, 107, 108, 109
Euripides, 28
Eusebius of Caesarea, 60, 61, 62

Ferrara, 125, 158
Feudalism, feudal practices, 5 and n., 51
Filioque, 10, 63, 76, 77, 87, 96, 99–106, 169–174
Flanginis, Thomas, 124
Florence, 25, 113, 124, 125–26, 135, 136, 145, 146
Council of, 4, 7, 10, 21, 24, 68, 76, 79, 80, 115, 169, 170, 172, 190, 193, Ch. 3 passim
France, 20, 29, 52, 147, 152–57, 161

Galen, 29, 31
Galileo, 27
Gasmules, 5 n., 104
Geneva, 139, 159, 161
Genoa, Genoese, 16, 18, 35, 104
George of Trebizond, 142
Gerlach, Stephen, 174
Germany, 13, 158, 161, 174
Giotto, 48–49
Glass making, 32–33
Glykys, 130, 145
Great Schism (Western), 92–94
Greek fire, 26
Gregorian chant, 41–42
Gregoropoulos, John, 127, 128
Gregory the Great, Pope, 43
Gregory X, Pope, 3, 85
Gregory of Cyprus, 171
Gregory Nazianzenus, 192
Grottaferrata, 41 n., 42
Guardia, Mt., 175–76
Guarino of Verona, 125, 146
Guilds, 37–38
Gunpowder, 26

Hermogenes, 146
Hermonymus, George, 154, 155, 157
Hincmar, Archbishop, 4 n.
Hippocrates, 29
History, 23
Hoeschel, David, 173–76, 180, 192
Hohenstaufen, 34
Holy Apostles', church, 47
Holy Roman Empire, 1, 2 n., 55
Holy Sepulchre, *Metochion* of, 179
Holy Spirit, 169–173, 175, 190.
    See Filioque, Trinity
Homer, 28, 111
Hostility, Greco-Latin. *See* Antagonism
Humbert of Romans, 3, 85
Hymnology, 27, 41–42

Iconoclasm, 15, 62, 63, 75
Icons, 39, 124, 133, 175–76
Industry, 31–33

Investiture Conflict, 55
Isaurians, 34
Isidore of Kiev, 117
Islam, 4, 5
Italy, 46–51 and *passim*
Iviron, monastery, 10, 166, 180–181 ff., 192

James of Venice, 17
Jeremiah II, Patriarch, 167, 168, 170–74
Jerusalem, 17, 178
John of Cyprus, 134
John of Damascus, 22, 23 n., 41, 63, 167
John of Ragusa, 92, 93 n.
Joseph, Patriarch, 94–95, 107, 108
Justinian, 13, 19, 34, 47, 57 n., 75, 81

Kabasilas, Symeon, 175
Kallinikos, 26
Kalosynas, Antonios, 150, 152
Klontzas, George, 134

Language, difference of, 12–13, 42, 87 n.
Laonikos, 127, 143, 144, 161
Lascaris, Constantine, 144
Lascaris, Janus, 23, 128, 129, 142, 147, 148, 149, 155
Latin Empire, 18, 71
Latinization of Greeks, 2, 3, 18, 18 n., 103 and n., 104 and n., 105, 106
Lavra, monastery, 133
Law, canon and civil, 13, 34–35, 58–60, 65, 69
Leningrad, Hermitage Museum, 133
Leo IX, Pope, 84
Leo X, Pope, 120, 144, 148
Literature, 27–29
Liturgy, 40–44, 175
'Liturgical' privileges, 69–73, 81
Liudprand, Bishop, 4 n., 27
Lollino, Aloysio, 175, 180

Louis the Pious, 24
Lutherans, 151, 174, 193
Lyons, Council of, 2, 3, 8, 68, 75 n., 79, 85, 91, 197

'Macedonian' school, 49–50, 132
Madonneri, 133, 134
Makrokephalites, Michael, 150
Manuscripts, 39, 102, 115, 124, 126, 129, 142, 150, 156, 174, 175, 179
Margounios, Maximos, 9, 10, 131–32, 142, 147, Ch. 6 *passim*
Mariology, 45–46
Mark of Ephesus, 100, 106
Mark's, St., 47, 94 n., 113, 122
Martin of Tours, 42
Martorana, church, 33
Mathematics, 25, 26
Mathematike Syntaxis, 26
Matthew's St., monastery, 178
Maximos the Confessor, 24, 63, 171
Melancthon, Philipp, 174
Medicine, 29–31, 40
Mistra, 24, 49
Modena, 158
Molinetti, Rinaldo, 175
Modino di Luzzi, 31
Monks, 41, 44, 45, 81
Monophysitism, 20, 62, 75
Monothelitism, 63, 75
Monte-Cassino, 32, 44, 48
Mosaics, 46–48
Moschiotes, Manusso, 177
Moscow, 179
Music, 40–44
Muslims, 42, 43 n.
Musurus, Marcus, 9, 23, 25, 31, 127–30, 145, 146, 161, 166
Myrepsos, Nicholas, 31

Narbonne, 20
Navigation, 35, 36, 53
Nicaea, Council of, 68, 71
Nicholas I, Pope, 7, 96
Nicholas of Cusa, 98–99

Nicholas Greco, 152
Nicholas, Orfanos, St. (church), 49
Nicousios, Panagiotes, 179
Nilos Doxopatres, 33
Nilus, St., 44
Nomocanones, 68–69, 177
Normans, 15, 33, 38
Notaras, Anna, 117, 118, 124
Notaras, Lucas, 117

Odo of Deuil, 5 n.
Oikonomia, 74
Ordination, 73 n.
Organ, 43
Otto II, III, Emperors, 19

Padua, 9, 25 n., 123, 125, 126, 130, 131,144, 145, 151, 158, 166, 167, 172, 191
Painting, 46–51, 120, 132–35, 150–52
Palaeokapas, Constantine, 130, 156
Palaeologan Renaissance, 9, 18, 23–25, 28, 48–51
Palaeologus, Constantine XI, Emperor, 8, 67, 73, 77
Palaeologus, George Disypatos, 154
Palaeologus, John VIII, Emperor, 94, 97, 107
Palaeologus, Manuel II, Emperor, 77, 78, 87 n., 153
Palaeologus, Michael VIII, Emperor, 18 n., 34 n., 66, 68, 75 n., 76, 77, 79, 85
Palaeologus, Theodore, 120, 123
Pantaleone, 16
Pantocrator, 47
Parastron, 3, 85
Paris, 17, 22, 150, 153, 155
Paruta, Paul, 172
Paul of Aegina, 30, 31
Pedro de Candia, 149
Pedro 'el Greco' (Serafín, Pedro), 152

Pepagomenos, Demetrios, 31
Pepin, King, 43
Pentarchy, 34, 86, 93, 96
Persio, Ascanio, 175
Peter the Venerable, 5 n.
Petrarch, 3, 5 n., 28, 141
Pharmacology, 30
Philarges, Petrus. *See* Alexander V, Pope
Philoponus, John, 27
Philosophy, 21–26
Photius, Patriarch, 1, 7, 27, 56, 66, 96, 175
Pico della Mirandola, 143
Pigas, Meletios, 142, 167, 170
Pilatus, Leontius, 28, 141
Pisa, 16, 32, 36
Pius II, Pope, 93, 111 n.
Pletho, Gemistos, 26, 112
Plato, Platonism, Neo-Platonism, 15, 22–25, 111, 145–46
Plutarch, 146
Poetics of Aristotle, 23 and n.
Poetry, 27–29
Politics of Aristotle, 23
Political theory, 33–34
Polychronion, 43
Ponan, John, 192
Portus, Franciscus, 158–60, 161, 163
   Emilius, 159
Primacy, papal, 1, 24, 34, 76, 79, Ch. 3 *passim*
Protestantism, 158, 163, 173–75
Psellus, Michael, 142, 174, 191
Ptolemy, 15, 26
Purgatory, 107 n.
Pythagoreanism, 25

Ravenna, 12 n., 13, 19, 47
Reuchlin, John, 129, 154
Reformation, 10, 159, 174–75
Renaissance, Carolingian, 23
   Cretan, 164
   Italian, *passim*
Rhodian Sea Law, 35
Rinuzzio of Arezzo, 141

Rite, ritual, 41, 42, 106 n., 116, 120, 187
Rittershusius, Conrad, 176, 192
Roger II, King, 15, 26, 32, 33
'Romance,' Franco-Byzantine, 29
Romanos the Melodist, 41
Rome, 13, 19, 20, 44, 144, 148, 161
Ronsard, 157
Russia, 9

Sacraments, 70–75, 81
Salerno, 29–30
San Antonio de Savatiana, 177
San Giorgio dei Greci, 120–23, 129, 131, 151, 177
San Vitale, 47
Savile, Henry, 176, 180
Scheurlin, John, 166 n., 167
Schism, 1, 2, 5, 7, 44, Chs. 3, 6 *passim*
Scholarios, Gennadios, 77, 100 n., 107 n.
Scholasticism, 51
Schott, Andreas, 175
Scotus, Andrew, 176
Science, 21, 26–27
Shipbuilding, Greek influence on Venice, 36 n.
Sicily, 13, 31, 33, 44
Siena, 118
Silk, 32, 37–39, 40
Slavs, 8, 12 n.
Sophia, St., 1, 26, 43, 94 n.
Sophocles, 28
Soranus, 29
Severus, Gabriel, 121, 132–32, 167, 169–72, 176, 193, 200
Sigismund, Emperor, 98
Simeonachis, John, 141, 142
Siminello, Philip, 175
Sinai, 139, 165, 178
Sosomeno, Rafael, 178
Spain, 9, 20–22, 31, 42, 147, 151, 161, 163
Steam power, 27
Strabo, 26
Stephanus, Henry, 156

Stradioti, 117, 119–23, 154
Sukhanov, Arsenii, 179
Summa Theologiae, 22
Surgery, 31
Sylburg, Frederic, 175
Synodos Endemousa, 65–66
Syropoulos, Silvester, 88–90, 92, 94 n., 95, 98 n., 106–109, 110 n.

Textiles, 32
Theodore Studites, 63
Theodore of Tarsus, 48
Theonas, monk, 182
Theophanes, chronicler, 27
Theophano, 19, 39
Theophilus, 31
Theophilus, German priest, 32
Theotokopoulos, Domenikos. *See* El Greco
Theotokopoulos, Manoussos, 135, 151
Thessalonika, 49
Thomism, 5 and n.
Timaeus, 15
Titian, 151
Toledo, 51, 102, 148–50, 152, 162, 163
Tostatus, Alphonsus, 188, 190
Tournament, in Byzantium, 5 and n.
Tragedies, Greek, 23, 53 and n.
Transubstantiation, 70–71
Trent, Council of, 150, 151 n.
Trevisan, Thomas, 167
Trinity, 74, 99–103, 169–71, 190. *See Filioque* and Holy Spirit
Trivizios, George, 129
Tübingen, 132, 168, 174–75

Turks, 3, 5, 8, 10, 18, 24, 76, 79, 84, 92, 102, 105, 106, 109, 114, 115, 118, 120, 123, 124, 141, 149, 153, 167, 168, 171, 173, 179
Turrianos, Nicholas (de la Torre), 150, 155
Tuscus, Leo, 16
Tzanes, Emmanuel, 134

Uniates, 116, 117, 120, 121, 130, 135, 163
Union, ecclesiastical, Ch. 3 *passim*, 147, 165, 166, 169, 181. *See* Schism, *Filioque*

Vasilakes, Antonios (Aliense), 8 n.
Velser, Mark, 180, 181
Venetian, 17, 35, 47, 94, 104, 169
Venice, 16, 18, 23, 31, 32, 36 ff.
Greek colony in, 9, 18, 37, 50, 112, Ch. 4, *passim*, 151, 158, 160, 165, 169, 177
colony of, in Constantinople, 16, 17, 37
Vergikios, Angelos, 130, 155–57, 161
Pierre, 156
Viking ships, 35
Viviano, Gaspar, 166–67
Vlastos, Nicolas, 124, 127

Watermill, waterwheel, 26
William of Moerbeke, 22, 23 n., 26

Ximenes, Cardinal, 126, 148, 163

Zanfurnaris, Emmanual, 134
Zeno, Alexander, 130, 145
Zonaras, 58, 67

Selected titles: Revised December, 1966

harper ✦ torchbooks

HUMANITIES AND SOCIAL SCIENCES

American Studies: General

CARL N. DEGLER, Ed.: Pivotal Interpretations of American History   TB/1240, TB/1241
A. S. EISENSTADT, Ed.: The Craft of American History: Recent Essays in American Historical Writing
          Vol. I   TB/1255;   Vol. II   TB/1256
CHARLOTTE P. GILMAN: Women and Economics. ‡ Ed. by Carl N. Degler with an Introduction   TB/3073
MARCUS LEE HANSEN: The Atlantic Migration: 1607-1860. Edited by Arthur M. Schlesinger. Introduction by Oscar Handlin   TB/1052
JOHN HIGHAM, Ed.: The Reconstruction of American History△   TB/1068
ROBERT H. JACKSON: The Supreme Court in the American System of Government   TB/1106
LEONARD W. LEVY, Ed.: American Constitutional Law   TB/1285
RALPH BARTON PERRY: Puritanism and Democracy   TB/1138
ARNOLD ROSE: The Negro in America   TB/3048

American Studies: Colonial

BERNARD BAILYN, Ed.: The Apologia of Robert Keayne: Self-Portrait of a Puritan Merchant   TB/1201
BERNARD BAILYN: The New England Merchants in the Seventeenth Century   TB/1149
JOSEPH CHARLES: The Origins of the American Party System   TB/1049
LAWRENCE HENRY GIPSON: The Coming of the Revolution: 1763-1775. † Illus.   TB/3007
PERRY MILLER & T. H. JOHNSON, Eds.: The Puritans: A Sourcebook   Vol. I TB/1093; Vol. II TB/1094
EDMUND S. MORGAN, Ed.: The Diary of Michael Wigglesworth, 1653-1657   TB/1228
EDMUND S. MORGAN: The Puritan Family   TB/1227
RICHARD B. MORRIS: Government and Labor in Early America   TB/1244
WALLACE NOTESTEIN: The English People on the Eve of Colonization: 1603-1630. † Illus.   TB/3006

American Studies: From the Revolution to 1860

MAX BELOFF: The Debate on the American Revolution: 1761-1783   TB/1225
RAY A. BILLINGTON: The Far Western Frontier: 1830-1860. † Illus.   TB/3012
W. R. BROCK: An American Crisis: Congress and Reconstruction, 1865-67 ° △   TB/1283
GEORGE DANGERFIELD: The Awakening of American Nationalism: 1815-1828. † Illus.   TB/3061
JOHN C. MILLER: Alexander Hamilton and the Growth of the New Nation   TB/3057

RICHARD B. MORRIS, Ed.: The Era of the American Revolution   TB/1180
R. B. NYE: The Cultural Life of the New Nation: 1776-1801. † Illus.   TB/3026
A. F. TYLER: Freedom's Ferment   TB/1074
LOUIS B. WRIGHT: Culture on the Moving Frontier   TB/1053

American Studies: Since the Civil War

MAX BELOFF, Ed.: The Debate on the American Revolution, 1761-1783: A Sourcebook   TB/1225
A. RUSSELL BUCHANAN: The United States and World War II. † Illus.   Vol. I TB/3044; Vol. II TB/3045
EDMUND BURKE: On the American Revolution. † Edited by Elliot Robert Barkan   TB/3068
THOMAS C. COCHRAN & WILLIAM MILLER: The Age of Enterprise: A Social History of Industrial America TB/1054
WHITNEY R. CROSS: The Burned-Over District: The Social and Intellectual History of Enthusiastic Religion in Western New York, 1800-1850   TB/1242
FOSTER RHEA DULLES: America's Rise to World Power: 1898-1954. † Illus.   TB/3021
W. A. DUNNING: Reconstruction, Political and Economic: 1865-1877   TB/1073
HAROLD U. FAULKNER: Politics, Reform and Expansion: 1890-1900. † Illus.   TB/3020
FRANCIS GRIERSON: The Valley of Shadows   TB/1246
SIDNEY HOOK: Reason, Social Myths, and Democracy   TB/1237
WILLIAM E. LEUCHTENBURG: Franklin D. Roosevelt and the New Deal: 1932-1940. † Illus.   TB/3025
JAMES MADISON: The Forging of American Federalism. Edited by Saul K. Padover   TB/1226
ROBERT GREEN MCCLOSKEY: American Conservatism in the Age of Enterprise: 1865-1910   TB/1137
ARTHUR MANN: Yankee Reformers in the Urban Age   TB/1247
GEORGE E. MOWRY: The Era of Theodore Roosevelt and the Birth of Modern America: 1900-1912 † TB/3022
R. B. NYE: Midwestern Progressive Politics   TB/1202
FRANCIS S. PHILBRICK: The Rise of the West, 1754-1830. † Illus.   TB/3067
WILLIAM PRESTON, JR.: Aliens and Dissenters: Federal Suppression of Radicals, 1903-1933   TB/1287
JACOB RIIS: The Making of an American. ‡ Edited by Roy Lubove   TB/3070
PHILIP SELZNICK: TVA and the Grass Roots: A Study in the Sociology of Formal Organization   TB/1230
TIMOTHY L. SMITH: Revivalism and Social Reform: American Protestantism on the Eve of the Civil War   TB/1229
IDA M. TARBELL: The History of the Standard Oil Company. Briefer Version. ‡ Edited by David M. Chalmers   TB/3071

---

† The New American Nation Series, edited by Henry Steele Commager and Richard B. Morris.
‡ American Perspectives series, edited by Bernard Wishy and William E. Leuchtenburg.
* The Rise of Modern Europe series, edited by William L. Langer.
¶ Researches in the Social, Cultural, and Behavioral Sciences, edited by Benjamin Nelson.
§ The Library of Religion and Culture, edited by Benjamin Nelson.
Σ Harper Modern Science Series, edited by James R. Newman.
° Not for sale in Canada.
△ Not for sale in the U. K.

1

ALBION W. TOURGÉE: A Fool's Errand. ‡ Ed. by George
Fredrickson   TB/3074
GEORGE B. TINDALL, Ed.: A Populist Reader ‡   TB/3069
VERNON LANE WHARTON: The Negro in Mississippi: 1865-
1890   TB/1178

Anthropology

JACQUES BARZUN: Race: A Study in Superstition. Re-
vised Edition   TB/1172
JOSEPH B. CASAGRANDE, Ed.: In the Company of Man:
Portraits of Anthropological Informants   TB/3047
W. E. LE GROS CLARK: The Antecedents of Man: Intro.
to Evolution of the Primates. °^ Illus.   TB/559
CORA DU BOIS: The People of Alor. New Preface by the
author. Illus.   Vol. I TB/1042; Vol. II TB/1043
DAVID LANDY: Tropical Childhood: Cultural Transmis-
sion and Learning in a Puerto Rican Village ¶ TB/1235
EDWARD BURNETT TYLOR: The Origins of Culture. Part I
of "Primitive Culture." § Intro. by Paul Radin TB/33
EDWARD BURNETT TYLOR: Religion in Primitive Culture.
Part II of "Primitive Culture." § Intro. by Paul Radin
                                                      TB/34
W. LLOYD WARNER: A Black Civilization: A Study of an
Australian Tribe. ¶ Illus.   TB/3056

Art and Art History

EMILE MÂLE: The Gothic Image: Religious Art in France
of the Thirteenth Century. § ^ 190 illus.   TB/44
MILLARD MEISS: Painting in Florence and Siena after the
Black Death: The Arts, Religion and Society in the
Mid-Fourteenth Century. 169 illus.   TB/1148
ERICH NEUMANN: The Archetypal World of Henry
Moore. ^ 107 illus.   TB/2020
DORA & ERWIN PANOFSKY: Pandora's Box: The Changing
Aspects of a Mythical Symbol   TB/2021
ERWIN PANOFSKY: Studies in Iconology: Humanistic
Themes in the Art of the Renaissance ^   TB/1077
ALEXANDRE PIANKOFF: The Shrines of Tut-Ankh-Amon.
Edited by N. Rambova. 117 illus.   TB/2011
OTTO VON SIMSON: The Gothic Cathdral ^   TB/2018
HEINRICH ZIMMER: Myths and Symbols in Indian Art and
Civilization. 70 illustrations   TB/2005

Business, Economics & Economic History

REINHARD BENDIX: Work and Authority in Industry
                                                     TB/3035
GILBERT BURCK & EDITORS OF FORTUNE: The Computer
Age: And Its Potential for Management   TB/1179
THOMAS C. COCHRAN: The American Business System: A
Historical Perspective, 1900-1955   TB/1080
ROBERT DAHL & CHARLES E. LINDBLOM: Politics, Eco-
nomics, and Welfare   TB/3037
PETER F. DRUCKER: The New Society: The Anatomy of
Industrial Order ^   TB/1082
FRANK H. KNIGHT: The Economic Organization   TB/1214
FRANK H. KNIGHT: Risk, Uncertainty and Profit TB/1215
ABBA P. LERNER: Everybody's Business   TB/3051
PAUL MANTOUX: The Industrial Revolution in the Eight-
eenth Century ° ^   TB/1079
HERBERT SIMON: The Shape of Automation: For Men and
Management   TB/1245
PERRIN STRYKER: The Character of the Executive: Eleven
Studies in Managerial Qualities   TB/1041
PIERRE URI: Partnership for Progress: A Program for
Transatlantic Action   TB/3036

Contemporary Culture

JACQUES BARZUN: The House of Intellect ^   TB/1051
CLARK KERR: The Uses of the University   TB/1264
JOHN U. NEF: Cultural Foundations of Industrial Civi-
lization ^   TB/1024
PAUL VALÉRY: The Outlook for Intelligence ^   TB/2016

Historiography & Philosophy of History

JACOB BURCKHARDT: On History and Historians. ^ Intro.
by H. R. Trevor-Roper   TB/1216
J. H. HEXTER: Reappraisals in History: New Views on
History & Society in Early Modern Europe   TB/1100
H. STUART HUGHES: History as Art and as Science: Twin
Vistas on the Past   TB/1207
ARNOLDO MOMIGLIANO: Studies in Historiography ° ^
                                                     TB/1288
GEORGE H. NADEL, Ed.: Studies in the Philosophy of His-
tory: Essays from History and Theory   TB/1208
KARL R. POPPER: The Open Society and Its Enemies ^
            Vol. I TB/1101; Vol. II TB/1102
KARL R. POPPER: The Poverty of Historicism °^ TB/1126
G. J. RENIER: History: Its Purpose and Method ^ TB/1209
W. H. WALSH: Philosophy of History ^   TB/1020

History: General

L. CARRINGTON GOODRICH: A Short History of the Chi-
nese People. ^ Illus.   TB/3015
DAN N. JACOBS & HANS H. BAERWALD: Chinese Commu-
nism: Selected Documents   TB/3031
BERNARD LEWIS: The Arabs in History ^   TB/1029
BERNARD LEWIS: The Middle East and the West ° ^
                                                     TB/1274

History: Ancient and Medieval

A. ANDREWES: The Greek Tyrants ^   TB/1103
P. BOISSONNADE: Life and Work in Medieval Europe ° ^
                                                     TB/1141
HELEN CAM: England before Elizabeth ^   TB/1026
NORMAN COHN: The Pursuit of the Millennium ^ TB/1037
CHRISTOPHER DAWSON, Ed.: Mission to Asia ^   TB/315
ADOLF ERMAN, Ed.: The Ancient Egyptians   TB/1233
HEINRICH FICHTENAU: The Carolingian Empire: The Age
of Charlemagne ^   TB/1142
F. L. GANSHOF: Feudalism ^   TB/1058
DENO GEANAKOPLOS: Byzantine East and Latin West ^
                                                     TB/1265
MICHAEL GRANT: Ancient History ° ^   TB/1190
W. O. HASSALL, Ed.: Medieval England: As Viewed by
Contemporaries ^   TB/1205
DENYS HAY: Europe: The Emergence of an Idea TB/1275
DENYS HAY: The Medieval Centuries ° ^   TB/1192
J. M. HUSSEY: The Byzantine World ^   TB/1057
SAMUEL NOAH KRAMER: Sumerian Mythology   TB/1055
ROBERT LATOUCHE: The Birth of Western Economy: Eco-
nomic Aspects of the Dark Ages. ° ^   TB/1290
NAPHTALI LEWIS & MEYER REINHOLD, Eds.: Roman Civili-
zation. Sourcebook I: The Republic   TB/1231
NAPHTALI LEWIS & MEYER REINHOLD, Eds.: Roman Civili-
zation. Sourcebook II: The Empire   TB/1232
FERDINAND LOT: The End of the Ancient World and the
Beginnings of the Middle Ages   TB/1044
G. MOLLAT: The Popes at Avignon: 1305-1378 ^ TB/308
CHARLES PETIT-DUTAILLIS: The Feudal Monarchy in
France and England ° ^   TB/1165
HENRI PIRENNE: Early Democracies in the Low Coun-
tries   TB/1110
STEVEN RUNCIMAN: A History of the Crusades ^
            Vol. I TB/1143; Vol. II TB/1243
F. VAN DER MEER: Augustine the Bishop ^   TB/304
J. M. WALLACE-HADRILL: The Barbarian West ^   TB/1061

History: Renaissance & Reformation

JACOB BURCKHARDT: The Civilization of the Renaissance
in Italy ^   Vol. I TB/40; Vol. II TB/41
JOHN CALVIN & JACOPO SADOLETO: A Reformation Debate.
Edited by John C. Olin   TB/1239
G. CONSTANT: The Reformation in England ^   TB/314
G. R. ELTON: Reformation Europe, 1517-1559 ° ^ TB/1270
WALLACE K. FERGUSON et al.: The Renaissance: Six Es-
says. Illus.   TB/1084
JOHN NEVILLE FIGGIS: Divine Right of Kings   TB/1191

2

FRANCESCO GUICCIARDINI: Maxims and Reflections of a Renaissance Statesman (Ricordi) TB/1160
J. H. HEXTER: More's Utopia: The Biography of an Idea. New Epilogue by the Author TB/1195
HAJO HOLBORN: Ulrich von Hutten and the German Reformation TB/1238
JOHAN HUIZINGA: Erasmus and the Age of Reformation.△ Illus. TB/19
JOEL HURSTFIELD, Ed.; The Reformation Crisis △ TB/1267
ULRICH VON HUTTEN et al.: On the Eve of the Reformation: "Letters of Obscure Men" TB/1124
PAUL O. KRISTELLER: Renaissance Thought: The Classic, Scholastic, and Humanist Strains TB/1048
ROBERT LATOUCHE: The Birth of Western Economy. ° △ Trans. by Philip Grierson TB/1290
NICCOLÒ MACHIAVELLI: History of Florence and of the Affairs of Italy TB/1027
GARRETT MATTINGLY et al.: Renaissance Profiles. △ Edited by J. H. Plumb TB/1162
J E. NEALE: The Age of Catherine de Medici ° △ TB/1085
ERWIN PANOFSKY: Studies in Iconology △ TB/1077
J. H. PARRY: The Establishment of the European Hegemony: 1415-1715 △ TB/1045
J. H. PLUMB: The Italian Renaissance △ TB/1161
A. F. POLLARD: Henry VIII △ TB/1249
A. F. POLLARD: Wolsey: Church and State in 16th Century England ° △ TB/1248
CECIL ROTH: The Jews in the Renaissance. Illus. TB/834
A. L. ROWSE: The Expansion of Elizabethan England. Illus. TB/1220
GORDON RUPP: Luther's Progress to the Diet of Worms °△ TB/120
FERDINAND SCHEVILL: Medieval and Renaissance Florence. Illus. Vol. I TB/1090; Vol. II TB/1091
G. M. TREVELYAN: England in the Age of Wycliffe, 1368-1520 °△ TB/1112
VESPASIANO: Renaissance Princes, Popes, and Prelates: The Vespasiano Memoirs TB/1111

History: Modern European

MAX BELOFF: The Age of Absolutism, 1660-1815 △ TB/1062
ASA BRIGGS: The Making of Modern England, 1784-1867: The Age of Improvement °△ TB/1203
CRANE BRINTON: A Decade of Revolution, 1789-1799. * Illus. TB/3018
D. W. BROGAN: The Development of Modern France. °△ Vol. I TB/1184; Vol. II TB/1185
J. BRONOWSKI & BRUCE MAZLISH: The Western Intellectual Tradition: From Leonardo to Hegel △ TB/3001
ALAN BULLOCK: Hitler, A Study in Tyranny ° △ TB/1123
E. H. CARR: German-Soviet Relations Between the Two World Wars, 1919-1939 TB/1278
E. H. CARR· International Relations Between the Two World Wars, 1919-1939 ° △ TB/1279
E. H. CARR: The Twenty Years' Crisis, 1919-1939 °△ TB/1122
GORDON A. CRAIG: From Bismarck to Adenauer: Aspects of German Statecraft. Revised Edition TB/1171
FRANKLIN L. FORD: Robe and Sword: The Regrouping of the French Aristocracy after Louis XIV TB/1217
RENÉ FUELOEP-MILLER: The Mind and Face of Bolshevism TB/1188
ALBERT GUÉRARD: France in the Classical Age △ TB/1183
CARLTON J. H. HAYES: A Generation of Materialism, 1871-1900. * Illus. TB/3039
J. H. HEXTER: Reappraisals in History: New Views on History & Society in Early Modern Europe △ TB/1100
STANLEY HOFFMANN et al.: In Search of France TB/1219
HANS KOHN: The Mind of Germany △ TB/1204
HANS KOHN, Ed.: The Mind of Modern Russia TB/1065
WALTER LAQUEUR & GEORGE L. MOSSE, Eds.: International Fascism, 1920-1945 ° △ TB/1276
WALTER LAQUEUR & GEORGE L. MOSSE, Eds.: The Left-Wing Intelligentsia Between the Two World Wars TB/1286

FRANK E. MANUEL: The Prophets of Paris: Turgot, Condorcet, Saint-Simon, Fourier, and Comte TB/1218
KINGSLEY MARTIN: French Liberal Thought in the Eighteenth Century TB/1114
L. B. NAMIER: Facing East: Essays on Germany, the Balkans, and Russia in the 20th Century △ TB/1280
L. B. NAMIER: Personalities and Powers △ TB/1186
JOHN U. NEF: Western Civilization Since the Renaissance: Peace, War, Industry, and the Arts TB/1113
FRANZ NEUMANN: Behemoth: The Structure and Practice of National Socialism, 1933-1944 TB/1289
DAVID OGG: Europe of the Ancien Régime, 1715-1783 °△ TB/1271
JOHN PLAMENATZ: German Marxism and Russian Communism. °△ New Preface by the Author TB/1189
PENFIELD ROBERTS: The Quest for Security, 1715-1740. * Illus. TB/3016
GEORGE RUDÉ: Revolutionary Europe, 1783-1815 ° △ TB/1272
LOUIS, DUC DE SAINT-SIMON: Versailles, The Court, and Louis XIV △ TB/1250
A. J. P. TAYLOR: From Napoleon to Lenin: Historical Essays ° △ TB/1268
A. J. P. TAYLOR: The Habsburg Monarchy, 1809-1918 °△ TB/1187
G. M. TREVELYAN: British History in the Nineteenth Century and After: 1782-1919 △ TB/1251
H. R. TREVOR-ROPER: Historical Essays °△ TB/1269
ELIZABETH WISKEMANN: Europe of the Dictators, 1919-1945 ° △ TB/1273
JOHN B. WOLF: France: 1814-1919 TB/3019

Intellectual History & History of Ideas

HERSCHEL BAKER: The Image of Man TB/1047
R. R. BOLGAR: The Classical Heritage and Its Beneficiaries △ TB/1125
J. BRONOWSKI & BRUCE MAZLISH: The Western Intellectual Tradition: From Leonardo to Hegel TB/3001
ERNST CASSIRER: The Individual and the Cosmos in Renaissance Philosophy. △ Translated with an Introduction by Mario Domandi TB/1097
NORMAN COHN: Pursuit of the Millennium △ TB/1037
C. C. GILLISPIE: Genesis and Geology: The Decades before Darwin § TB/51
ARTHUR O. LOVEJOY: The Great Chain of Being: A Study of the History of an Idea TB/1009
FRANK E. MANUEL: The Prophets of Paris: Turgot, Condorcet, Saint-Simon, Fourier, and Comte TB/1218
RALPH BARTON PERRY: The Thought and Character of William James: Briefer Version TB/1156
BRUNO SNELL: The Discovery of the Mind: The Greek Origins of European Thought △ TB/1018
PAUL VALÉRY: The Outlook for Intelligence △ TB/2016
PHILIP P. WIENER: Evolution and the Founders of Pragmatism. ° Foreword by John Dewey TB/1212

Literature, Poetry, The Novel & Criticism

JACQUES BARZUN: The House of Intellect △ TB/1051
JAMES BOSWELL: The Life of Dr. Johnson & The Journal of a Tour to the Hebrides with Samuel Johnson LL.D. ° △ TB/1254
ABRAHAM CAHAN: The Rise cf David Levinsky TB/1028
ERNST R. CURTIUS: European Literature and the Latin Middle Ages △ TB/2015
A. R. HUMPHREYS: The Augustan World: Society in 18th Century England °△ TB/1105
ALDOUS HUXLEY: Brave New World & Brave New World Revisited. °△ Introduction by Martin Green TB/3501
ARNOLD KETTLE: An Introduction to the English Novel. △ Volume I: Defoe to George Eliot TB/1011
Volume II: Henry James to the Present TB/1012
RICHMOND LATTIMORE: The Poetry of Greek Tragedy △ TB/1257
J. B. LEISHMAN: The Monarch of Wit: An Analytical and Comparative Study of the Poetry of John Donne ° △ TB/1258

J. B. LEISHMAN: Themes and Variations in Shakespeare's Sonnets °△ TB/1259

SAMUEL PEPYS: The Diary of Samuel Pepys. ° Edited by O. F. Morshead. Illus. by Ernest Shepard TB/1007

V. DE S. PINTO: Crisis in English Poetry, 1880-1940 °△ TB/1260

C. K. STEAD: The New Poetic: Yeats to Eliot ° △ TB/1263

HEINRICH STRAUMANN: American Literature in the Twentieth Century. △ Third Edition, Revised TB/1168

PAGET TOYNBEE: Dante Alighieri: His Life and Works. Edited with Intro. by Charles S. Singleton TB/1206

DOROTHY VAN GHENT: The English Novel TB/1050

E. B. WHITE: One Man's Meat TB/3505

BASIL WILLEY: Nineteenth Century Studies: Coleridge to Matthew Arnold △ TB/1261

BASIL WILLEY: More Nineteenth Century Studies: A Group of Honest Doubters △ TB/1262

RAYMOND WILLIAMS: Culture and Society, 1780-1950 ° △ TB/1252

RAYMOND WILLIAMS: The Long Revolution °△ TB/1253

Myth, Symbol & Folklore

JOSEPH CAMPBELL, Editor: Pagan and Christian Mysteries. Illus. TB/2013

MIRCEA ELIADE: Cosmos and History § △ TB/2050

MIRCEA ELIADE: Rites and Symbols of Initiation: The Mysteries of Birth and Rebirth § △ TB/1236

THEODOR H. GASTER: Thespis: Ritual, Myth and Drama in the Ancient Near East △ TB/1281

DORA & ERWIN PANOFSKY: Pandora's Box △ TB/2021

HELLMUT WILHELM: Change: Eight Lectures on the I Ching △ TB/2019

Philosophy

G. E. M. ANSCOMBE: An Introduction to Wittgenstein's Tractatus. ° △ Second edition, Revised TB/1210

HENRI BERGSON: Time and Free Will °△ TB/1021

H. J. BLACKHAM: Six Existentialist Thinkers ° △ TB/1002

CRANE BRINTON: Nietzsche TB/1197

ERNST CASSIRER: The Individual and the Cosmos in Renaissance Philosophy°△ TB/1097

FREDERICK COPLESTON: Medieval Philosophy ° △ TB/376

F. M. CORNFORD: Principium Sapientiae: A Study of the Origins of Greek Philosophical Thought TB/1213

F. M. CORNFORD: From Religion to Philosophy § TB/20

WILFRID DESAN: The Tragic Finale: An Essay on the Philosophy of Jean-Paul Sartre TB/1030

A. P. D'ENTRÈVES: Natural Law △ TB/1223

MARVIN FARBER: The Aims of Phenomenology TB/1291

PAUL FRIEDLÄNDER: Plato: An Introduction △ TB/2017

W. K. C. GUTHRIE: The Greek Philosophers: From Thales to Aristotle ° △ TB/1008

F. H. HEINEMANN: Existentialism and the Modern Predicament △ TB/28

EDMUND HUSSERL: Phenomenology and the Crisis of Philosophy TB/1170

IMMANUEL KANT: The Doctrine of Virtue, being Part II of the Metaphysic of Morals TB/110

IMMANUEL KANT: Groundwork of the Metaphysic of Morals. Trans. & analyzed by H. J. Paton TB/1159

IMMANUEL KANT: Lectures on Ethics §△ TB/105

IMMANUEL KANT: Religion Within the Limits of Reason Alone. § Intro. by T. M. Greene & J. Silber TS/67

QUENTIN LAUER: Phenomenology TB/1169

GABRIEL MARCEL: Being and Having △ TB/310

GEORGE A. MORGAN: What Nietzsche Means TB/1198

MICHAEL POLANYI: Personal Knowledge △ TB/1158

WILLARD VAN ORMAN QUINE: Elementary Logic. Revised Edition TB/577

WILLARD VAN ORMAN QUINE: from a Logical Point of View: Logico-Philosophical Essays TB/566

BERTRAND RUSSELL et al.: The Philosophy of Bertrand Russell   Vol. I TB/1095; Vol. II TB/1096

L. S. STEBBING: A Modern Introduction to Logic △ TB/538

ALFRED NORTH WHITEHEAD: Process and Reality: An Essay in Cosmology △ TB/1033

PHILIP P. WIENER: Evolution and the Founders of Pragmatism. Foreword by John Dewey TB/1212

WILHELM WINDELBAND: A History of Philosophy
Vol. I: Greek, Roman, Medieval TB/38
Vol. II: Renaissance, Enlightenment, Modern TB/39

LUDWIG WITTGENSTEIN: The Blue and Brown Books ° TB/1211

Political Science & Government

JEREMY BENTHAM: The Handbook of Political Fallacies. Introduction by Crane Brinton TB/1069

KENNETH E. BOULDING: Conflict and Defense TB/3024

CRANE BRINTON: English Political Thought in the Nineteenth Century TB/1071

ROBERT DAHL & CHARLES E. LINDBLOM: Politics, Economics, and Welfare TB/3037

F. L. GANSHOF: Feudalism △ TB/1058

G. P. GOOCH: English Democratic Ideas in Seventeenth Century TB/1006

SIDNEY HOOK: Reason, Social Myths and Democracy △ TB/1237

DAN N. JACOBS, Ed.: The New Communist Manifesto & Related Documents. Third edition, Revised TB/1078

DAN N. JACOBS & HANS BAERWALD, Eds.: Chinese Communism: Selected Documents TB/3031

HANS KOHN: Political Ideologies of the 20th Century TB/1277

KINGSLEY MARTIN: French Liberal Thought in the Eighteenth Century △ TB/1114

ROBERTO MICHELS: First Lectures in Political Sociology. Edited by Alfred De Grazia ¶ ° TB/1224

BARRINGTON MOORE, Jr.: Political Power and Social Theory: Seven Studies ¶ TB/1221

BARRINGTON MOORE, JR.: Soviet Politics—The Dilemma of Power ¶ TB/1222

JOHN B. MORRALL: Political Thought in Medieval Times △ TB/1076

KARL R. POPPER: The Open Society and Its Enemies △
Vol. I TB/1101; Vol. II TB/1102

JOSEPH A. SCHUMPETER: Capitalism, Socialism and Democracy △ TB/3008

PETER WOLL, Ed.: Public Administration and Policy TB/1284

Psychology

ALFRED ADLER: The Individual Psychology of Alfred Adler △ TB/1154

ARTHUR BURTON & ROBERT E. HARRIS, Editors: Clinical Studies of Personality
Vol. I TB/3075; Vol. II TB/3076

HADLEY CANTRIL: The Invasion from Mars: A Study in the Psychology of Panic TB/1282

HERBERT FINGARETTE: The Self in Transformation ¶ TB/1177

SIGMUND FREUD: On Creativity and the Unconscious § △ TB/45

WILLIAM JAMES: Psychology: Briefer Course TB/1034

C. G. JUNG: Psychological Reflections △ TB/2001

C. G. JUNG: Symbols of Transformation △
Vol. I TB/2009; Vol. II TB/2010

JOHN T. MC NEILL: A History of the Cure of Souls TB/126

KARL MENNINGER: Theory of Psychoanalytic Technique TB/1144

ERICH NEUMANN: Amor and Psyche △ TB/2012

MUZAFER SHERIF: The Psychology of Social Norms TB/3072

Sociology

JACQUES BARZUN: Race: A Study in Superstition. Revised Edition TB/1172

BERNARD BERELSON, Ed.: The Behavioral Sciences Today TB/1127

ALLISON DAVIS & JOHN DOLLARD: Children of Bondage ¶ TB/3049

ST. CLAIR DRAKE & HORACE R. CAYTON: Black Metropolis
Vol. I TB/1086; Vol. II TB/1087

ALVIN W. GOULDNER: Wildcat Strike ¶ TB/1176

4

R. M. MACIVER: Social Causation   TB/1153
ROBERT K. MERTON, LEONARD BROOM, LEONARD S. COTTRELL, JR., Editors: Sociology Today: *Problems and Prospects* ¶   Vol. I   TB/1173;   Vol. II   TB/1174
TALCOTT PARSONS & EDWARD A. SHILS, Editors: Toward a General Theory of Action   TB/1083
ARNOLD ROSE: The Negro in America   TB/3048
PHILIP SELZNICK: TVA and the Grass Roots   TB/1230
HERBERT SIMON: The Shape of Automation △   TB/1245
PITIRIM A. SOROKIN: Contemporary Sociological Theories: *Through the first quarter of the 20th Century*   TB/3046
MAURICE R. STEIN: The Eclipse of Community: *An Interpretation of American Studies*   TB/1128
W. LLOYD WARNER & Associates: Democracy in Jonesville: *A Study in Quality and Inequality*   TB/1129
W. LLOYD WARNER: Social Class in America   TB/1013

RELIGION

Ancient & Classical

J. H. BREASTED: Development of Religion and Thought in Ancient Egypt   TB/57
HENRI FRANKFORT: Ancient Egyptian Religion △   TB/77
G. RACHEL LEVY: Religious Conceptions of the Stone Age *and their Influence on European Thought* △   TB/106
MARTIN P. NILSSON: Greek Folk Religion △   TB/78
ERWIN ROHDE: Psyche △ §   Vol. I   TB/140;   Vol. II   TB/141
H. J. ROSE: Religion in Greece and Rome △   TB/55

Biblical Thought & Literature

W. F. ALBRIGHT: The Biblical Period from Abraham to Ezra   TB/102
C. K. BARRETT, Ed.: The New Testament Background: *Selected Documents* △   TB/86
C. H. DODD: The Authority of the Bible △   TB/43
M. S. ENSLIN: Christian Beginnings △   TB/5
JOHN GRAY: Archaeology and the Old Testament World. △ *Ilius.*   TB/127
JAMES MUILENBURG: The Way of Israel △   TB/133
H. H. ROWLEY: Growth of the Old Testament △   TB/107
GEORGE ADAM SMITH: Historical Geography of Holy Land. ○ △ *Revised and reset*   TB/138
D. WINTON THOMAS, Ed.: Documents from Old Testament Times △   TB/85

The Judaic Tradition

MARTIN BUBER: Eclipse of God △   TB/12
MARTIN BUBER: For the Sake of Heaven   TB/801
MARTIN BUBER: Hasidism and Modern Man. △ *Ed. and Trans. by Maurice Friedman*   TB/839
MARTIN BUBER: The Knowledge of Man △   TB/135
MARTIN BUBER: Moses △   TB/837
MARTIN BUBER: The Origin and Meaning of Hasidism △   TB/835
MARTIN BUBER: Pointing the Way △   TB/103
MARTIN BUBER: The Prophetic Faith   TB/73
GENESIS: *The NJV Translation*   TB/836
FLAVIUS JOSEPHUS: The Great Roman-Jewish War, *with The Life of Josephus*   TB/74

Christianity: General

ROLAND H. BAINTON: Christendom: *A Short History of Christianity and its Impact on Western Civilization.* △ *Illus.*   Vol. I   TB/131;   Vol. II   TB/132

Christianity: Origins & Early Development

AUGUSTINE: An Augustine Synthesis. △ *Edited by Erich Przywara*   TB/335
ADOLF DEISSMANN: Paul: *A Study in Social and Religious History*   TB/15
EDWARD GIBBON: The Triumph of Christendom in the Roman Empire. § △ *Illus.*   TB/46
MAURICE GOGUEL: Jesus and the Origins of Christianity ○ △   Vol. I   TB/65;   Vol. II   TB/66
EDGAR J. GOODSPEED: A Life of Jesus   TB/1

ROBERT M. GRANT: Gnosticism and Early Christianity △   TB/136
ADOLF HARNACK: The Mission and Expansion of Christianity in the First Three Centuries   TB/92
R. K. HARRISON: The Dead Sea Scrolls ○ △   TB/84
EDWIN HATCH: The Influence of Greek Ideas on Christianity § △   TB/18
ARTHUR DARBY NOCK: St. Paul ○ △   TB/104
ORIGEN: On First Principles △   TB/311
SULPICIUS SEVERUS et al.: The Western Fathers: *Being the Lives of Martin of Tours, Ambrose, Augustine of Hippo, Honoratus of Arles and Germanus of Auxerre.* △ *Edited and translated by F. R. Hoare*   TB/309
JOHANNES WEISS: Earliest Christianity   Vol. I   TB/53;   Vol. II   TB/54

Christianity: The Middle Ages and The Reformation

JOHN CALVIN & JACOPO SADOLETO: A Reformation Debate. *Edited by John C. Olin*   TB/1239
G. CONSTANT: The Reformation in England △   TB/314
JOHANNES ECKHART: Meister Eckhart: *A Modern Translation by R. B. Blakney*   TB/8
DESIDERIUS ERASMUS: Christian Humanism and the Reformation   TB/1166

Christianity: The Protestant Tradition

KARL BARTH: Church Dogmatics: *A Selection* △   TB/95
KARL BARTH: Dogmatics in Outline △   TB/56
KARL BARTH: The Word of God and the Word of Man   TB/13
RUDOLF BULTMANN et al.: Translating Theology into the Modern Age: *Volume 2 of Journal for Theology and the Church, edited by Robert W. Funk in association with Gerhard Ebeling*   TB/252
WINTHROP HUDSON: The Great Tradition of the American Churches   TB/98
SOREN KIERKEGAARD: On Authority and Revelation   TB/139
SOREN KIERKEGAARD: Edifying Discourses △   TB/32
SOREN KIERKEGAARD: The Journals of Kierkegaard ○   TB/52
SOREN KIERKEGAARD: The Point of View for My Work as an Author §   TB/88
SOREN KIERKEGAARD: The Present Age § △   TB/94
SOREN KIERKEGAARD: Purity of Heart △   TB/4
SOREN KIERKEGAARD: Repetition △   TB/117
SOREN KIERKEGAARD: Works of Love △   TB/122
WALTER LOWRIE: Kierkegaard: *A Life*   Vol. I   TB/89   Vol. II   TB/90
JOHN MACQUARRIE: The Scope of Demythologizing: *Bultmann and his Critics* △   TB/134
JAMES M. ROBINSON et al.: The Bultmann School of Biblical Interpretation: New Directions? *Volume 1 of Journal for Theology and the Church*   TB/251
F. SCHLEIERMACHER: The Christian Faith. △ *Introduction by Richard R. Niebuhr*   Vol. I   TB/108;   Vol. II   TB/109
F. SCHLEIERMACHER: On Religion: *Speeches to Its Cultured Despisers. Intro. by Rudolf Otto*   TB/36
PAUL TILLICH: Dynamics of Faith △   TB/42
EVELYN UNDERHILL: Worship △   TB/10

Christianity: The Roman and Eastern Traditions

DOM CUTHBERT BUTLER: Western Mysticism § ○ △   TB/312
A. ROBERT CAPONIGRI, Ed.: Modern Catholic Thinkers △   Vol. I   TB/306;   Vol. II   TB/307
THOMAS CORBISHLEY, S. J.: Roman Catholicism △   TB/112
G. P. FEDOTOV: The Russian Religious Mind: *Kievan Christianity, the 10th to the 13th Centuries*   TB/370
G. P. FEDOTOV, Ed.: A Treasury of Russian Spirituality   TB/303
ÉTIENNE GILSON: The Spirit of Thomism   TB/313
DAVID KNOWLES: The English Mystical Tradition   TB/302

GABRIEL MARCEL: Being and Having TB/310
GABRIEL MARCEL: Homo Viator TB/397
FRANCIS DE SALES: Introduction to the Devout Life TB/316
GUSTAVE WEIGEL, S. J.: Catholic Theology in Dialogue TB/301

Oriental Religions: Far Eastern, Near Eastern

TOR ANDRAE: Mohammed § △ TB/62
EDWARD CONZE: Buddhism ○ △ TB/58
ANANDA COOMARASWAMY: Buddha and the Gospel of Buddhism. △ Illus. TB/119
H. G. CREEL: Confucius and the Chinese Way TB/63
FRANKLIN EDGERTON, Trans. & Ed.: The Bhagavad Gita TB/115
SWAMI NIKHILANANDA, Trans. & Ed.: The Upanishads: A One-Volume Abridgment △ TB/114

Philosophy of Religion

NICOLAS BERDYAEV: The Beginning and the End § △ TB/14
NICOLAS BERDYAEV: Christian Existentialism △ TB/130
NICOLAS BERDYAEV: The Destiny of Man △ TB/61
RUDOLF BULTMANN: History and Eschatology ○ TB/91
RUDOLF BULTMANN AND FIVE CRITICS: Kerygma and Myth: A Theological Debate △ TB/80
RUDOLF BULTMANN AND KARL KUNDSIN: Form Criticism: Two Essays on New Testament Research △ TB/96
MIRCEA ELIADE: The Sacred and the Profane TB/81
LUDWIG FEUERBACH: The Essence of Christianity § TB/11
ÉTIENNE GILSON: The Spirit of Thomism TB/313
ADOLF HARNACK: What is Christianity? § △ TB/17
FRIEDRICH HEGEL: On Christianity TB/79
KARL HEIM: Christian Faith and Natural Science △ TB/16
IMMANUEL KANT: Religion Within the Limits of Reason Alone. § Intro. by T. M. Greene & J. Silber TB/67
K. E. KIRK: The Vision of God △ TB/137
JOHN MACQUARRIE: An Existentialist Theology: A Comparison of Heidegger and Bultmann ○ △ TB/125
PIERRE TEILHARD DE CHARDIN: The Divine Milieu ○ △ TB/384
PIERRE TEILHARD DE CHARDIN: The Phenomenon of Man ○ △ TB/383
PAUL TILLICH: Morality and Beyond TB/142

Religion, Culture & Society

C. C. GILLISPIE: Genesis and Geology: The Decades before Darwin § TB/51
KYLE HASELDEN: The Racial Problem in Christian Perspective TB/116
WALTER KAUFMANN, Ed.: Religion from Tolstoy to Camus TB/123
JOHN T. MC NEILL: A History of the Cure of Souls TB/126
H. RICHARD NIEBUHR: Christ and Culture △ TB/3
H. RICHARD NIEBUHR: The Kingdom of God in America TB/49
TIMOTHY L. SMITH: Revivalism and Social Reform: American Protestantism on the Eve of the Civil War △ TB/1229
ERNST TROELTSCH: The Social Teaching of the Christian Churches ○ △ Vol. I TB/71; Vol. II TB/72

NATURAL SCIENCES AND MATHEMATICS

Biological Sciences

CHARLOTTE AUERBACH: The Science of Genetics Σ △ TB/568
LUDWIG VON BERTALANFFY: Problems of Life △ TB/521
HAROLD F. BLUM: Time's Arrow and Evolution TB/555
JOHN TYLER BONNER: The Ideas of Biology Σ △ TB/570
WALTER B. CANNON: Bodily Changes in Pain, Hunger, Fear and Rage. Illus. TB/562
W. E. LE GROS CLARK: The Antecedents of Man ○ △ TB/559
W. H. DOWDESWELL: Animal Ecology. △ Illus. TB/543
R. W. GERARD: Unresting Cells. Illus. TB/541
ADOLF PORTMANN: Animals as Social Beings ○ △ TB/572

O. W. RICHARDS: The Social Insects. △ Illus. TB/542
P. M. SHEPPARD: Natural Selection and Heredity △ TB/528
EDMUND W. SINNOTT: Cell and Psyche: The Biology of Purpose TB/546
C. H. WADDINGTON: How Animals Develop △ Illus. TB/553
C. H. WADDINGTON: The Nature of Life △ TB/580

Chemistry

J. R. PARTINGTON: A Short History of Chemistry △ TB/522

History of Science

MARIE BOAS: The Scientific Renaissance, 1450-1630 ○ △ TB/583
W. DAMPIER, Ed.: Readings in the Literature of Science. Illus. TB/512
A. HUNTER DUPREE: Science in the Federal Government: A History of Policies and Activities to 1940 △ TB/573
ALEXANDRE KOYRÉ: From the Closed World to the Infinite Universe △ TB/31
A. G. VAN MELSEN: From Atomos to Atom: A History of the Concept Atom TB/517
O. NEUGEBAUER: The Exact Sciences in Antiquity △ TB/552
HANS THIRRING: Energy for Man △ TB/556
STEPHEN TOULMIN & JUNE GOODFIELD: The Architecture of Matter ○ △ TB/584
STEPHEN TOULMIN & JUNE GOODFIELD: The Discovery of Time ○ △ TB/585
LANCELOT LAW WHYTE: Essay on Atomism △ TB/565

Mathematics

E. W. BETH: The Foundations of Mathematics △ TB/581
H. DAVENPORT: The Higher Arithmetic △ TB/526
H. G. FORDER: Geometry: An Introduction △ TB/548
S. KÖRNER: The Philosophy of Mathematics △ TB/547
D. E. LITTLEWOOD: Skeleton Key of Mathematics: A Simple Account of Complex Algebraic Problems △ TB/525
WILLARD VAN ORMAN QUINE: Mathematical Logic TB/558
O. G. SUTTON: Mathematics in Action ○ △ TB/518
FREDERICK WAISMANN: Introduction to Mathematical Thinking. Foreword by Karl Menger △ TB/511

Philosophy of Science

R. B. BRAITHWAITE: Scientific Explanation TB/515
J. BRONOWSKI: Science and Human Values △ TB/505
ALBERT EINSTEIN et al.: Albert Einstein: Philosopher-Scientist Vol. I TB/502; Vol. II TB/503
WERNER HEISENBERG: Physics and Philosophy △ TB/549
JOHN MAYNARD KEYNES: A Treatise on Probability. ○ △ Introduction by N. R. Hanson TB/557
KARL R. POPPER: Logic of Scientific Discovery △ TB/576
STEPHEN TOULMIN: Foresight and Understanding △ TB/564
STEPHEN TOULMIN: The Philosophy of Science △ TB/513
G. J. WHITROW: Natural Philosophy of Time ○ △ TB/563

Physics and Cosmology

JOHN E. ALLEN: Aerodynamics △ TB/582
STEPHEN TOULMIN & JUNE GOODFIELD: The Fabric of the Heavens: The Development of Astronomy and Dynamics. △ Illus. TB/579
DAVID BOHM: Causality and Chance in Modern Physics. △ Foreword by Louis de Broglie TB/536
P. W. BRIDGMAN: Nature of Thermodynamics TB/537
P. W. BRIDGMAN: A Sophisticate's Primer of Relativity △ TB/575
A. C. CROMBIE, Ed.: Turning Point in Physics TB/535
C. V. DURELL: Readable Relativity △ TB/530
ARTHUR EDDINGTON: Space, Time and Gravitation: An Outline of the General Relativity Theory TB/510
GEORGE GAMOW: Biography of Physics Σ △ TB/567
MAX JAMMER: Concepts of Force TB/550
MAX JAMMER: Concepts of Mass △ TB/571
MAX JAMMER: Concepts of Space TB/533
G. J. WHITROW: The Structure and Evolution of the Universe: An Introduction to Cosmology. △ Illus. TB/504

6